RESUMES AND COVER LETTERS THAT HAVE WORKED FOR MILITARY PROFESSIONALS

Also by PREP Publishing

SECOND TIME AROUND: Patty Sleem, Author

BACK IN TIME: Patty Sleem, author

RESUMES AND COVER LETTERS THAT HAVE WORKED: Anne McKinney, Editor

Resumes and Cover Letters That Have Worked for Military Professionals

Resumes and Cover Letters written by the professional writing team of PREP Inc., specializing since 1981 in military translation

PREP Publishing
Fayetteville, NC

PREP Publishing
1110½ Hay Street
Fayetteville, NC 28305
(910) 483-6611

Library of Congress Cataloging-in-Publication Data
Resumes and Cover Letters that have worked for military
professionals
      / edited by Anne McKinney. — 1st ed.
        p. cm.
     ISBN 1-885288-06-9
     1. Resumes (Employment). 2. Cover Letters. 3.
     Recruiting and enlistment. I. McKinney, Anne,
     1948-   . II. PREP Publishing.
     HF5383.R425 1996
     808'.06665—dc20   96-33822
                              CIP

Printed in the United States of America
First Edition

To all the men and women
who serve their country in military service

CONTENTS

Preface

(Tips from the editor on how to make the best use of this book)

In this preface, I would like to give you some advice on how to make maximum advantage of this book full of exciting resumes and cover letters that have actually worked for military professionals. I have decided to illustrate my advice to you by using a resume and three cover letters designed to focus the same resume on different fields. Following this preface, you will see a resume prepared for Mr. Rick Rowe II which has a "general management" focus. To be frank, Mr. Rowe really had no idea exactly what he wanted to do when he asked PREP to prepare his resume. You will see that, beginning with the Objective statement, Mr. Rowe's resume is "all purpose," designed to equip him with an exciting summary of his experience and achievements that doesn't define him too narrowly. You can see how an objective that reads "to benefit an organization that can use a resourceful and adaptable professional consistently described in performance evaluations as an action person who makes things happen" would give Mr. Rowe the flexibility to job hunt in virtually any field.

An all-purpose resume designed for maximum flexibility

In the Experience section you will notice that the emphasis is on communicating, in plain English that "translates" military experience into civilian language, Mr. Rowe's background and achievements in a variety of areas. You will see that Mr. Rowe held "staff" (planning, advising, and consulting) and teaching jobs, was also a company commander, managed aviation assets and a flying program, directed air support in a combat environment, and was involved in product development as well as research and development. Whew! Like most military professionals, he gained skills and experience in many different areas while serving his country, and his resume has been written to showcase his abilities in those versatile areas without defining him too narrowly.

A cover letter designed for aviation

While Mr. Rowe's resume is "all purpose" and designed to emphasize knowledge in several functional areas, his three cover letters were written to aggressively focus his resume on specific fields that particularly interested him. The aviation cover letter written for Mr. Rowe describes his company command experience in an aviation organization, mentions his Commercial Rotorcraft License and Single-Engine Land Private-Pilot License, and talks about his role in fielding new aviation products for military use.

A bodybuilding cover letter

In his spare time, Mr. Rowe enjoyed bodybuilding and had a yearning to make a career out of his favorite hobby. So you will find a bodybuilding cover letter that focuses his resume in such a way that he could explore opportunities in gymnasium management, health club operations, and numerous other niches within the growing fitness industry.

A cover letter for management

The management cover letter was written to emphasize Mr. Rowe's leadership by example, communication and strategic planning skills, and problem-solving abilities. The cover letter mentions that he had advanced to the rank of major while serving his country, so he had the credentials to prove his skills at the middle management/executive levels. The letter is designed to be a general and all-purpose letter of introduction to accompany Mr. Rowe's resume. The management letter was written so that it could open doors in any field or industry. As you may be aware by now, Mr. Rowe, like many military professionals, was unsure exactly what he wanted to do (or what he could do!) when he left military service. He thought he could probably find something to do in the aviation field, but he hoped the management skills he'd gained as a military officer were transferable to nearly any industry. The management letter was designed to help Mr. Rowe "go fishing" for management jobs in virtually any type of organization.

Not everyone needs three different cover letters in a job hunt.

Most of the resumes you will read in Part Two will be accompanied by only one cover letter, and usually that cover letter will be an "all-purpose" letter designed to be as versatile as possible. In general the resumes you see in this book were designed to be flexible in order to allow the customer to "fish" in many fields. You will see a chart in Part One of this book which will reveal that "lack of exact experience" is the last reason why people don't get hired in many situations. Employers are often seeking a person with a track record of accomplishment in any field rather than specific skills, so your all-purpose resume should simply market you in a general and exciting way so that many different types of employers and companies can see your potential to learn and to excel in their particular type of business.

The model cover letters in this book usually have two suggested endings.

You will notice on most of the cover letters in Part Two that there will be two suggested endings. Most people find that one model cover letter will work most of the time in a job hunt, and they simply put that cover letter into a computer so that they can word process the letter individually each time the resume is mailed. The cover letter is a way of personalizing the approach to each company. Choose the ending paragraph that says you'll be following up on the resume by calling the company soon, or the paragraph that asks the company to call or write you to suggest a time for you to meet. The purpose of a model cover letter is to give you a generic or prototype letter that you can use each time you send your resume so you don't have to "reinvent the wheel" and think up a cover letter each time you want to send your resume.

How to read the resumes and cover letters in Part Two

Now that you've been introduced to the general principle that many of the resumes in this book are "all purpose" and designed to allow the customer maximum flexibility in his or her job hunt, you are ready to read the resumes and cover letters in Part Two. They are arranged in several broad categories and are generally in alphabetic order by type of field or background, except that resumes not accompanied by cover letters or two-page resumes have been placed at the back of each section. Bear in mind that, since the military professional by definition tends to have a varied background, you may find resumes of people like yourself in several different areas of Part Two. For example, if you have an aviation background, you may find similar backgrounds in the Aviation section, the Communications and Electronics section, the Management section, and the Supply section. For example, Mr. Myatt's resume emphasizing weapons systems expertise is in the Management section but it could have been placed in the Law Enforcement and Security section. Where a resume was placed was often a judgement call, so look over resumes in various sections to make sure you're making maximum advantage of the book. You might find someone with an engineering background in the Engineering, Maintenance, or Management sections, for example. Just keep this in mind so you can make best use of the book. And good luck with your transition from military service!

RICK V. ROWE II
1110½ Hay Street, Fayetteville, NC 28305   (910) 483-6611

OBJECTIVE

To benefit an organization that can use a resourceful and adaptable professional consistently described in performance evaluations as an "action person who makes things happen."

EDUCATION & TRAINING

Earned **Bachelor of Science** (B.S.) degree, University of Alabama, Tuscaloosa, AL, 1977.
* Was named **Distinguished Military Graduate**.
Completed extensive graduate-level training as a military officer related to operations management, financial administration, production control, and leadership.

EXPERIENCE

PLANS OFFICER. U.S. Army, Ft. Bragg, NC (1993-present). Continuously brief top-level officers on plans for projects that pool Army, Navy, Air Force, and Marine Corps resources.

DIRECTOR OF SUPPORT OPERATIONS. U.S. Army, Ft. Bragg, NC (1991-92). Managed a variety of service operations supporting the overall mission of an 800-person organization; organized and directed special projects which required relocating personnel and assets; planned and supervised training programs; managed the safe implementation of an 11,000-hour flying-hour program to include 1,000 accident-free flying hours flown in a 30-day period during the Hurricane Andrew Relief Effort.
* Was praised for thrifty management of human resources and multimillion-dollar assets which included 50 aircraft, 51 wheeled vehicles, and other air/ground support equipment.

RESOURCES MANAGER. U.S. Army, Ft. Bragg, NC (1991). Was evaluated in writing as a "multi-talented self starter and team player" because of the multiple contributions I made, on my own initiative, to the largest aviation brigade in the U.S. Army; developed a strategic plan forecasting the organization's needs for equipment and personnel into the 21st century.
* Controlled resources including schools and training and supplies such as ammunition.

AVIATION STAFF OFFICER. U.S. Army, Saudi Arabia (1991). During the war in the Middle East, played a key role in planning and orchestrating the air support which is credited with "winning the war" while coordinating strategic and tactical aviation issues with the French, British, and Royal Saudi land forces.
* Operated with poise in an environment in which there was "no room for error."

ASSISTANT PROFESSOR OF MILITARY SCIENCE. Univ. of Puerto Rico, PR (1988-91). Was responsible for the recruiting, administration, and training of 187 college cadets and was the primary instructor for freshmen and senior cadets; was described as "endowed with matchless leadership, managerial, and instructor abilities."

GENERAL MANAGER ("COMPANY COMMANDER"). U.S. Army, Ft. Rucker, AL (1987-88). Was the chief executive officer of an aviation organization with 23 officer pilots and 15 flight instructors; became respected for my pro-active approach to problem solving while identifying solutions for backlogs and finding ways to optimize the use of scarce resources.
* Continuously lived by the concept of "leadership by example."

FORCE DEVELOPMENT STAFF OFFICER. U.S. Army, Ft. Rucker, AL (1987). Played a key role in the fielding of a new helicopter; coordinated material requirements with industry representatives, coordinated training related to equipment testing and monitored activities at an Experimentation Center; earned a reputation as an outstanding writer and briefer while briefing industry executives and government officials.

Highlights of other experience: Gained expert knowledge related to aviation.
* *Research & Development*: Determined user-oriented priorities for helicopter research, development, and acquisition; managed engineering change proposals (ECP's) and product improvement proposals (PIP's).
* *Operations management*: Maintained over 135 sets of flight records.
* *Aircraft/crew management*: Managed operations for an attack helicopter organization.

PERSONAL

Am a body builder. Bilingual in Spanish and English. Use WordPerfect and Harvard Graphics.

Date

Exact Name of Person
Exact Title of Person
Exact Name of Company
Street and/or Box Address
City, State, Zip

Dear Exact Name: (or Dear Sir or Madam:)

I would appreciate an opportunity to talk with you soon about how I could contribute to your organization through my expertise related to the aviation industry.

As you will see from my resume, I have been involved in most aspects of the aviation industry. In one job I managed an aviation organization as "company commander" and supervised its 23 officer pilots and 15 flight instructors while also performing as helicopter flight instructor. In another job I played a key role in fielding a new helicopter which has since been integrated into the Army inventory; I have also developed user-oriented priorities for helicopter research, development, and acquisition. During the war in the Middle East, I was instrumental in planning and implementing the air strategy that is credited with rapidly winning the war.

I hold a Commercial Rotorcraft License and a Single Engine Land Private Pilot License. I have managed flight hour programs which required a skilled planner and thinker in order to allocate resources in the most efficient and safest manner so that multiple organizational goals could be achieved under tight deadlines.

You would find me to be a versatile professional with the ability to "think" in aviation terms for both rotary and fixed-wing aircraft. I have held a Top Secret security clearance with BI.

I hope you will write or call me soon to suggest a time when we might meet to discuss your needs and goals and how I might contribute to them. Thank you in advance for your time.

Yours sincerely,

Rick V. Rowe II

Alternate last paragraph:
I hope you will welcome my call soon when I try to arrange a brief meeting at your convenience to discuss your needs and goals and how I might meet them. Thank you in advance for your time.

Date

Exact Name of Person
Exact Title of Person
Exact Name of Company
Street and/or Box Address
City, State, Zip

Dear Exact Name: (or Dear Sir or Madam:)

I would appreciate an opportunity to talk with you soon about how I could contribute to your organization through my knowledge of fitness and bodybuilding.

While achieving the rank of Major in the U.S. Army, I have developed a health-conscious life-style while also cultivating the art of bodybuilding. I am familiar with the "nuts and bolts" of gym-nasium management and health club operations from the customer's point of view, and I feel my insights could greatly contribute to increased profitability and market share in this growing industry.

You would find me to be a versatile professional who offers exceptionally strong communica-tion, motivational, and leadership skills. I can provide outstanding personal and professional refer-ences upon your request.

I hope you will write or call me soon to suggest a time when we might meet to discuss your needs and goals and how I might contribute to them. Thank you in advance for your time.

Yours sincerely,

Rick V. Rowe II

Alternate last paragraph:
I hope you will welcome my call soon when I try to arrange a brief meeting at your convenience to discuss your needs and goals and how I might meet them. Thank you in advance for your time.

Date

Exact Name of Person
Exact Title of Person
Exact Name of Company
Street and/or Box Address
City, State, Zip

Dear Exact Name: (or Dear Sir or Madam:)

I would appreciate an opportunity to talk with you soon about how I could contribute to your organization through my management experience and leadership ability.

As you will see from my resume, I have excelled in a "track record" of accomplishments while being promoted to the rank of Major in the U.S. Army. On numerous occasions I was selected for "hotseat" jobs that required an articulate communicator with outstanding strategic planning, problem solving, and motivational skills. In one job I developed the organization's first strategic plan forecasting personnel and equipment needs into the 21st century. In my current job as a plans officer I brief top-level government officials on plans for pooling the resources of Navy, Army, Air Force, and Marine Corps forces in special projects worldwide.

A physically fit and health-conscious person who enjoys body building in my spare time, I practice "leadership by example" in everything I do. In one job as an assistant professor at the University of Puerto Rico, I became a popular instructor and leader whom the college cadets wanted to emulate. In another job as a "company commander," I set the example for other officers to follow through my resourceful problem-solving style and ability to find new ways to maximize scarce resources.

You would find me to be a loyal and selfless person who is accustomed to making personal sacrifices so that the organization's goals can be achieved. I am single and would relocate according to your needs. I can provide outstanding personal and professional references upon your request.

I hope you will welcome my call soon when I try to arrange a brief meeting with you at your convenience to discuss your needs and how I might serve them. Thank you in advance for your time.

Yours sincerely,

Rick V. Rowe II

Alternate last paragraph:
I hope you will write or call me soon to suggest a time when we might meet to discuss your needs and goals and how I might meet them. Thank you in advance for your time.

Acknowledgments

Special thanks and acknowledgments are due to several people who helped to "midwife" the book into its final state. Patty Sleem, Stacy Martin, and Janet Abernethy were the writers, analysts, and organizers at PREP who helped in numerous ways. The graphic artist Kathi Quesenberry was the creator of the cover. We wish to thank the Cumberland County Library and Julie Stoddard for guidance regarding the materials available to jobhunters in libraries. Finally, appreciation is expressed to all customers of PREP Resumes through the years who gave us an opportunity to write their resumes and cover letters in order to help them transition into new careers in the public and private sectors. It has truly been a pleasure through the years to serve the career needs of the military professionals who serve our country with unselfishness, skill, and honor.

Introduction

Finding a job is always a job in itself, even in times of economic prosperity. And certainly finding a job tends to get more difficult in periods of recession or in an era when companies are "downsizing." But for the military professional, job hunting at any age or in any era poses unique technical difficulties which must be overcome. The main problem facing the military professional in a job hunt is explaining to potential employers, simply and understandably, what he/she has done!

WHAT'S UNIQUE ABOUT THE MILITARY PROFESSIONAL?

Let's look at the unique profile of the military professional. First, the good news: The military professional is more versatile and cross-trained than his/her civilian counterpart at almost any age. In military service, generally young people get an opportunity to gain management experience earlier than their civilian counterparts, and the military professional is usually cross-trained in numerous functional areas while working both "line management" and "staff" advisory or consulting jobs. But now, the bad news: The military professional has been working in a foreign language! Language such as "platoon leader," "petty officer," "deployment," "reserve component," "SOP's," "suspense dates," "battalion," "battlefield simulation," "brigade," "fitness reports," "NCO," "TDY," "exercise," and other similar military lingo does not communicate well outside the military world. What that means, as a practical matter, is that the military professional is greatly in need of a resume that "translates" his/her experience into "civilian language" or "plain English." If you have served your country in the armed forces and are looking toward the time when you will be seeking a civilian job or embarking on your "second career" after extensive military service, here are some tips that can help you from PREP, Professional Resume and Employment Placement, Box 66, Fayetteville, NC. PREP has served the military professional since 1981 and has specialized in "military translation."

Part One of the book is designed to walk you step-by-step through your job hunt.

Your job campaign will probably seem less overwhelming if you proceed logically through four steps.
* Step One: "Planning Your Job Campaign and Assembling the Right Tools."
* Step Two: "Using Your Resume and Cover Letter."
* Step Three: "Preparing for Interviews."
* Step Four: "Handling the Interview."

Part Two of the book shows resumes and cover letters used by actual military professionals to transition to civilian jobs.

In the second part of the book you will find resumes and cover letters of military professionals who have given permission to PREP to publish their documents. Their names and addresses have been changed to disguise their identity. If you write your own resume, you will certainly find lots of useful models!

Part One

STEP ONE
Planning Your Job Campaign and Assembling the Right Tools

WHAT IF YOU DON'T KNOW WHAT YOU WANT TO DO?

Your job hunt will be more comfortable if you can figure out what type of job you want to do. But you are not alone if you have no idea what you want to do next! You may be an infantry soldier wondering what on earth you have done or can do that will "translate" into a job in the civilian world. Or you may know that you have knowledge and skills in certain areas but want to get into another type of work. A pilot after a 20-year career may not want to fly airplanes for another 20 years, or perhaps declining eyesight prevents continuing such a career. You may be wondering what a career as a missile launch officer has prepared you to do in the civilian world. One of PREP's customers in 1986 was a very good computer programmer who said that he refused to sit in another windowless office performing tasks he was good at but didn't enjoy, and he wanted a resume that would help him become a forest ranger! What *The Wall Street Journal* has discovered in its research on careers is that most of us end up having at least three distinctly different careers in our working lives; it seems that, even if we really like a particular kind of activity, twenty years of doing it is enough for most of us and we want to move on to something else!

That's why at PREP we strongly believe that you need to spend some time figuring out *what interests you* rather than taking an inventory of the skills you have. You may have skills that you simply don't want to use, but if you can build your career on the things that interest you, you will be more likely to be happy and satisfied in your job. Realize, too, that interests can change over time; the activities that interest you now may not be the ones that interested you years ago. For example, some military professionals may decide that they've had enough of managing people and want a job managing only themselves, even though they have earned a reputation for being an excellent manager of human resources. We strongly believe that interests rather than skills should be the determining factor in deciding what types of jobs you want to apply for and what directions you explore in your job hunt. Obviously one cannot be a lawyer without a law degree or a secretary without secretarial skills; but a military professional can embark on a next career as a financial consultant, property manager, plant manager, production supervisor, retail manager, or other occupation if he/ she has a strong interest in that type of work and can provide a resume that clearly demonstrates past excellent performance in *any* field and *potential* to excel in another field. As you will see in a chart shown later in this booklet, "lack of exact experience" is the last reason why people are turned down for the jobs they apply for.

BUT HOW CAN YOU HAVE A RESUME PREPARED IF YOU DON'T KNOW WHAT YOU WANT TO DO?

You may be wondering how you can have a resume prepared if you don't know what you want to do next. The approach to resume writing which PREP has used successfully for many years is to develop an "all-purpose" resume that translates your skills, experience, and accomplishments into language employers can understand. What most people need in a job hunt is a versatile resume that will allow them to apply for numerous types of jobs. For example, you may want to apply for a specific job as a railroad conductor but you may also want to have a resume that will be versatile enough for you to apply for jobs in the construction, electronics, or health-care industry. Based on nearly 15 years of serving the military professional, we at PREP strongly believe that an all-purpose resume and specific cover letters tailored to specific fields is your best approach to job hunting rather than trying to create different resumes for different occupational areas. Usually, you will not even need more than one "all-purpose" cover letter, although the cover letter rather than the resume is the place to communicate your interest in a narrow or specific field. An all-purpose resume and cover letter that translate your military experience into plain English are the tools that will maximize the number of doors that open for you while permitting you to "fish" in the widest range of job areas.

DO YOU REALIZE THAT YOUR RESUME WILL PROVIDE THE SCRIPT FOR YOUR JOB INTERVIEW?

When you get down to it, your resume has a simple job to do: Its purpose is to blow as many doors open as possible and to make as many people as possible want to meet you. So a well-written resume that really "sells" you is a key that will create opportunities for you in a job hunt.

This statistic explains why: The typical newspaper advertisement for a job opening receives more than 245 replies. And normally only 10 or 12 will be invited to an interview.

But here's another purpose of the resume: it provides the "script" the employer uses when he interviews you. If your resume has been written in such a way that your strengths and achievements are revealed, that's what you'll end up talking about at the job interview. Since the resume will govern what you get asked about at your interviews, you can't overestimate the importance of making sure your resume makes you look and sound as good as you are.

SO WHAT IS A "GOOD" RESUME?

Very literally, your resume should motivate the person reading it to dial the phone number you have put on the resume. (By the way, that's one reason you should think about putting a local phone contact number on your resume, if possible, when your contact address is several states away; employers are much more likely to dial a local telephone number than a long-distance number when they're looking for potential employees.)

If you have a resume already, look at it objectively. Is it a limp, colorless "laundry list" of your job titles and duties? Or does it "paint a picture" of your skills, abilities, and accomplishments in a way that would make someone want to meet you? Can people understand what you're saying? Is your military experience translated into terminology that nonmilitary people can understand?

HOW LONG SHOULD YOUR RESUME BE?

One page, maybe two. Usually only people in the academic community have a resume (which they usually call a *curriculum vitae*) longer than one or two pages. Remember that your resume is almost always accompanied by a cover letter and a potential employer does not want to read more than two or three pages about a total stranger in order to decide if he wants to meet that person! Besides, don't forget that the more you tell someone about yourself, the more opportunity you are providing for the employer to screen you out at the "first-cut" stage. A resume should be concise and exciting and designed to make the reader want to meet you in person!

SHOULD RESUMES BE FUNCTIONAL OR CHRONOLOGICAL?

Employers almost always prefer a chronological resume; in other words, an employer will find a resume easier to read if it is immediately apparent what your current or most recent job is, what you did before that, and so forth in reverse chronological order. A resume that goes back in detail for the last 10 years of employment will generally satisfy the employer's curiosity about your background. Employment more than ten years old can be shown even more briefly in an "other experience" section at the end of your "Experience" section. Remember that your intention is not to tell everything you've done but to "hit the high points" and especially hit the employer with what you learned, contributed, or accomplished in each job you describe.

The functional resume is to be avoided except in specific circumstances. Employers don't like it when you tell them about yourself in vague categories like "management" and "production operations" and "logistics" without giving chronological details because they can't read the resume quickly and see "what you did when." Employers distrust functional resumes and they (usually correctly) fear that if you can't or won't give the dates of your employment history, there must be a problem you're trying to hide such as a five-year gap when you weren't working, etc. Don't use a functional resume just because you want to "cover up" a problem period in your past. Most gaps in employment can be explained to the employer's satisfaction — for example, if you haven't worked for the past five years because you were having a family. As we said earlier, the resume provides the "script" for the interview and most people find the interview to be a miserable experience with a functional resume because that resume format creates an attitude of suspicion on the employer's part and the interview will usually feel more like an interrogation.

WHAT IS NEEDED IN ORDER TO PREPARE YOUR RESUME?

Whoever prepares your resume needs to get to know you as well as possible, so it's wise to provide whatever documentation you have from military service. A professional resume writer at PREP who specializes in military translation would want to read copies of your formal military evaluations (OER's, NCOER's, EER's, APR's, EPR's, fitness reports, etc.). In addition to or in place of military paperwork, if not available, PREP customers complete a *Personal Review Form* which asks questions about goals, work history, accomplishments, strengths, weaknesses, and so forth. (Copies of the *Personal Review Form* used in the resume writing process at PREP are available for $3.00 by writing PREP, Box 66, Fayetteville, NC 28302). Writers at PREP are fond of saying that "we're good at reading between the lines but we have to have enough lines to read between!"

STEP TWO
Using Your Resume and Cover Letter

ONCE YOU GET YOUR RESUME, WHAT DO YOU DO WITH IT?

You will be using your resume to answer ads, as a tool to use in talking with friends and relatives about your job search, and, most importantly, in using the "direct approach" described in this book.

When you mail your resume, always send a "cover letter."

A "cover letter," sometimes called a "resume letter," is a letter that accompanies and introduces your resume. Your cover letter is a way of personalizing the resume by sending it to the specific person you think you might want to work for at each company. Your cover letter should contain a few highlights from your resume — just enough to make someone want to meet you.

1. Learn the art of answering ads.

There is an "art," part of which can be learned, in using your "bestselling" resume to reply to advertisements.

Sometimes an exciting job lurks behind a boring ad that someone dictated in a hurry, so reply to any ad that interests you. Don't worry that you aren't "25 years old with an MBA" like the ad asks for. Employers will always make compromises in their requirements if they think you're the "best fit" overall.

What about ads that ask for "salary requirements?"

Now what if the ad you're answering asks for "salary requirements?" The first rule is to avoid committing yourself in writing at that point to a specific salary. You don't want to "lock yourself in."

There are two ways to handle the ad that asks for "salary requirements."

First, you can ignore that part of the ad and accompany your resume with a cover letter that focuses on "selling" you, your abilities, and even some of your philosophy about work or your field.

Second, if you feel you must give some kind of number, just state a range. If you've been in military service and are making a transition to the "civilian" world, add another amount, say $10,000, to your salary to include your medical, dental, and other benefits. You might state, for example, "my current compensation, including benefits and bonuses, is in the range of $30,000 - $40,000."

Analyze the ad and "tailor" yourself to it.

When you're replying to ads, a finely-tailored cover letter is an important tool in getting your resume noticed and read.

On the next page is a cover letter which has been "tailored to fit" a specific ad. Notice the "art" used by PREP writers of analyzing the ad's main requirements and then writing the letter so that the person's background, work habits, and interests seem "tailor-made" to the company's needs. Use this cover letter as a model when you prepare your own reply to ads. (The person for whom PREP prepared this letter got an interview and then landed the job.)

January 20, 1983

Mr. Arthur Wise
Chamber of Commerce of the U.S.
9439 Goshen Lane
Burke, VA 22105

Dear Mr. Wise:

I would appreciate an opportunity to show you in person, soon, that I am the energetic, dynamic salesperson you are looking for as a Membership Sales Representative of the Chamber of Commerce.

Here are just three reasons why I believe I am the effective young professional you seek:

 * *I myself am "sold" on the Chamber of Commerce* and have long been an admirer of its goal of forming a cohesive business organization to promote the well-being of communities and promote business vigor. As someone better known that I put it long ago, "the business of America is business." I wholeheartedly believe that the Chamber's efforts to unite, solidify, and mobilize American business can be an important key in unlocking the international competitiveness and domestic vitality of our economy. I am eager to contribute to that effort.

* *I am a proven salesperson* with a demonstrated ability to "prospect" and produce sales. In my current job as a sales representative, I contact more than 50 military and business professionals per week and won in 1982 my company's award for outstanding summer sales performance. Previously, I excelled as a recruiter in promoting the advantages of an Army career.

* *I enjoy traveling and am eager to assist in the growth of North Carolina and vicinity.* I am fortunate to have the natural energy, industry, and enthusiasm required to put in the long hours necessary for effective sales performance.

You will find me, I am certain, a friendly, good-natured person whom you would be proud to call part of the Chamber's "team."

I hope you will call or write me soon to suggest a convenient time when we might meet to discuss your needs further and how I might serve them.

Yours sincerely,

Your Name

2. Talk to friends and relatives.

Don't be shy about telling your friends and relatives the kind of job you're looking for. Looking for the job you want involves using your network of contacts, so tell people what you're looking for. They may be able to make introductions and help set up interviews.

About 25% of all interviews are set up through "who you know," so don't ignore this approach.

3. Use the "direct approach."

More than 50% of all job interviews are set up by the "direct approach." That means you actually send a resume and a cover letter to a company you think might be interested in employing your skills.

To whom do you write?

In general, you should write directly to the <u>exact</u> <u>name</u> of the person who would be hiring you: say, the vice-president of marketing or data processing. If you're in doubt about whom to address the letter to, address it to the president by name and he or she will make sure it gets forwarded to the right person within the company who has hiring authority in your area.

How do you find the names of potential employers?

You're not alone if you feel that the biggest problem in your job search is finding the right names at the companies you want to contact.

You could select a list of, say, 50 companies you want to contact **by locations** from the lists that the U.S. Chambers of Commerce publish yearly of their "major area employers." Your nearest library will have the book which lists the addresses of all chambers.

If you're willing to travel and relocate, you could select a list of companies to contact **by industry**. You can find the right person to write and the address of firms by industrial category in *Standard and Poor's, Moody's,* and other excellent books available in public libraries.

Many people feel it's a good investment to actually call the company to either find out or double-check the name of the person they want to send a resume and cover letter to. It's important to do as much as you feasibly can to assure that the letter gets to the right person in the company.

On pages 33-36 at the end of Part One, you will find some advice about how to conduct library research and how to locate organizations to which you could send your resume.

What's the correct way to follow up on a letter you send?

There is a polite way to be aggressively interested in a company during your job hunt. It is ideal to end the cover letter accompanying your resume by saying "I hope you'll welcome my call next week when I try to arrange a brief meeting at your convenience to discuss your current and future needs and how I might serve them." Keep it low key, and just ask for a "brief meeting," not an interview. Employers want people who show a determined interest in working with them, so don't be shy about following up on the resume and cover letter you've mailed.

STEP THREE
Preparing for Interviews

But a resume and cover letter by themselves can't get you the job you want. You need to "prep" yourself before the interview. Step Three in your job campaign is "Preparing for Interviews." First, let's look at interviewing from the company's point of view.

WHAT ARE THE BIGGEST "TURNOFFS" FOR COMPANIES?

One of the ways to help yourself perform well at an interview is to look at this table which reveals the main reasons why companies <u>don't</u> hire the people they interview, according to the companies that do the interviewing.

Notice that "lack of appropriate background" (or lack of experience) is the <u>last</u> reason for not being offered the job.

---

*The 14 Most Common Reasons Jobhunters
Are Not Offered Jobs (according to the
companies who do the interviewing and hiring)*

1. Low level of accomplishment
2. Poor attitude, lack of self-confidence
3. Lack of goals/objectives
4. Lack of enthusiasm
5. Lack of interest in the company's business
6. Inability to sell or express yourself
7. Unrealistic salary demands
8. Poor appearance
9. Lack of maturity, no leadership potential
10. Lack of extracurricular activities
11. Lack of preparation for the interview, no knowledge about company
12. Objecting to travel
13. Excessive interest in security and benefits
14. Inappropriate background

Department of Labor studies since the 1950's have proven that smart, "prepared" job hunters can increase their beginning salary while getting a job in *half* the time it normally takes. (4 1/2 months is the average national length of a job search.) Here, from PREP, are some questions that can prepare you to find a job faster.

ARE YOU IN THE "RIGHT" FRAME OF MIND?

It seems unfair that we have to look for a job just when we're lowest in morale. Don't worry <u>too</u> much if you're nervous before interviews (Johnny Carson says he usually is, too!). You're supposed to be a little nervous, especially if the job means a lot to you. But the best way to kill unnecessary fears about job hunting is through 1) making sure you have a great resume and 2) preparing yourself for the interview. Here are three main areas you need to think about before each interview.

DO YOU KNOW WHAT THE COMPANY DOES?

Don't walk into an interview giving the impression that "if this is Tuesday, this must be General Motors."

Find out before the interview what the company's main product or service is. Where is the company heading? Is it in a "growth" or declining industry? (Answers to these questions may influence whether or not you want to work there!)

Information about what the company does is in annual reports as well as newspaper and magazine articles. Just visit your nearest library and ask the reference librarian to guide you to materials on the company. The appendix at the back of this book will give you many ideas about how to research companies.

DO YOU KNOW WHAT YOU WANT TO DO FOR THE COMPANY?

Before the interview, try to decide how you see yourself fitting into the company. Believe it or not, "lack of exact background" the company wants is usually the <u>last</u> reason people are not offered jobs.

Understand before you go to each interview that the burden will be on you to "sell" the interviewer on why you're the best person for the job and the company.

HOW WILL YOU ANSWER THE CRITICAL INTERVIEW QUESTIONS?

Put yourself in the interviewer's position and think about the questions you're most likely to be asked. Here are some of the most commonly asked interview questions:

Q: *"What are your greatest strengths?"*

A: Don't say you've never thought about it!

Go into an interview knowing the three main impressions you want to leave about yourself, such as "I'm hard-working, loyal, and an imaginative cost-cutter."

Q: *"What are your greatest weaknesses?"*

A: Don't confess that you're lazy or have trouble meeting deadlines!

Confessing that you tend to be a "workaholic" or "tend to be a perfectionist and sometimes get frustrated when others don't share my high standards" will make your prospective employer see a "weakness" that he likes. Name a weakness that your interviewer will perceive as a strength.

Q: *"What are your long-range goals?"*

A: If you're interviewing with Microsoft, don't say you want to work for IBM in five years!

Say your long-range goal is to be _with_ the company, contributing to its goals and success.

Q: *"What motivates you to do your best work?"*

A: Don't get dollar signs in your eyes here!

"A challenge" is not a bad answer, but it's a little cliched. Saying something like "trouble-shooting" or "solving a tough problem" is more interesting and specific. Give an example if you can.

Q: *"What do you know about this company?"*

A: Don't say you never heard of it until they asked you to the interview!

Name an interesting, positive thing you learned about the company recently from your research. Remember, company executives can sometimes feel rather "maternal" about the company they serve. Don't get onto a negative area of the company if you can think of positive facts you can bring up. Of course, if you learned in your research that the company's sales seem to be taking a nose-dive, or that the company president is being prosecuted for taking bribes, you might politely ask your interviewer to tell you something that could help you better understand what you've been reading. Those are the kinds of company facts that can help you determine whether you want to work there or not.

Q: *"Why should I hire you?"*

A: "I'm unemployed and available" is the wrong answer here!

Get back to your strengths and say that you believe the organization could benefit by a loyal, hard-working cost-cutter like yourself.

In conclusion, you should decide in advance, before you go to the interview, how you will answer each of these commonly asked questions.

Have some practice interviews with a friend to role-play and build your confidence.

STEP FOUR
Handling The Interview

Now you're ready for Step Four: actually handling the interview successfully and effectively. Remember, the purpose of an interview is to get a job offer.

EIGHT "DO'S" FOR THE INTERVIEW

According to the leading U.S. companies, here are the eight most important areas involved in interviewing success. You can fail at an interview if you handle just one area wrongly.

(1) DO Wear Appropriate Clothes.

You can never go wrong by wearing a suit to an interview.

(2) DO Be Well Groomed.

Don't overlook the obvious things like having clean hair, clothes, and fingernails for the interview.

(3) DO Give a Firm Handshake.

You'll have to shake hands twice in most interviews: first, before you sit down, and second, when you leave the interview. Limp handshakes turn most people off.

(4) DO Smile and Show a Sense of Humor.

Interviewers are looking for people who would be nice to work with, so don't be so somber that you don't smile.

(5) DO Be Enthusiastic.

Employers tell PREP they are "turned off" by lifeless, unenthusiastic job hunters who show no special interest in that company. The best way to show some enthusiasm for the employer's operation is to find out about the business beforehand.

(6) DO Show You Are Flexible and Adaptable.

An employer is looking for someone who can contribute to his organization in a flexible, adaptable way. No matter what skills and training you have, employers know every new employee must go through initiation and training on the company's turf. Certainly show pride in your past accomplishments in a specific, factual way ("I saved my last employer $50.00 a week by a new cost-cutting measure I developed"). But don't come across as though there's nothing about the job you couldn't easily handle.

(7) DO Ask Intelligent Questions about the Employer's Business.

An employer is hiring someone because of certain business needs. Show interest in those needs. Asking questions to get a better idea of the employer's needs will help you "stand out" from other candidates interviewing for the job.

(8) DO Show an Ability to "Take Charge" when the Interviewer "Falls Down" on the Job.

Go into every interview knowing the 3 or 4 points about yourself you want the interviewer to remember. And be prepared to take an active part in leading the discussion if the interviewer's "canned approach" does not permit you to display your "strong suit." You can't always depend on the interviewer's asking you the "right" questions so you can stress your strengths and accomplishments.

AN IMPORTANT "DON'T"

Don't ask questions about salary or benefits at the first interview.

Employers don't take warmly to people who look at their organization as just a place to satisfy salary and benefit needs. Don't risk making a negative impression by appearing greedy or self-serving.

The place to discuss salary and benefits is normally at the second interview, and the employer will bring it up. Then you can ask any questions you like without appearing excessively interested in what the organization can do for you.

"SELL YOURSELF" BEFORE TALKING SALARY

Make sure you've "sold" yourself before talking salary. First show you're the "best fit" for the employer and then you'll be in a stronger position from which to negotiate salary.

Interviewers sometimes throw out a salary figure at the first interview to see if you'll accept it. Don't commit yourself. You may be able to negotiate a better deal later on. Get back to finding out more about the job. This lets the interviewer know you're interested primarily in the job and not the salary.

NOW. . .NEGOTIATING YOUR SALARY

You must avoid stating a "salary requirement" in your initial cover letter, and you must avoid even appearing **interested** in salary before you are offered the job.

Never bring up the subject of salary yourself. Employers say there's no way you can avoid looking greedy if you bring up the issue of salary and benefits before the company has identified you as its "best fit."

When the company brings up salary, it may say something like this: "Well, Mary, we think you'd make a good candidate for this job. What kind of salary are we talking about?"

Never name a number here, either. Put the monkey back on the interviewer. Act as though you hadn't given the subject of salary much thought and respond something like this: "Ah, Mr. Jones, salary. . .well, I wonder if you'd be kind enough to tell me what salary you had in mind when you advertised the job?" Or ... "What is the range you have in mind?"

Don't worry, if the interviewer names a figure that you think is too low, you can say so without turning down the job or locking yourself into a rigid position. The point here is to negotiate for yourself as well as you can. You might reply to a number named by the interviewer that you think is low by saying something like this: "Well, Mr. Lee, the job interests me very much, and I think I'd certainly enjoy working with you. But, frankly, I was thinking of something a little higher than that." That leaves the ball in your interviewer's court again, and you haven't turned down the job, either, in case it turns out that the interviewer can't increase the offer and you still want the job.

LAST, SEND A FOLLOW-UP LETTER

Finally, send a letter right after the interview telling your interviewer you enjoyed the meeting and are certain (if you are) you are the "best fit" for the job.

Again, employers have a certain maternal attitude toward their companies, and they are looking for people who want to work for _that_ company in particular.

The follow-up letter you send might be just the deciding factor in your favor if the employer is trying to choose between you and someone else.

A sample follow-up letter prepared for you by PREP is shown below. Be sure to modify it according to your particular skills and interview situation.

And, finally, from all of us at PREP, best wishes in your job hunt and in all your future career endeavors.

Date

Exact Name of Interviewer
Exact Title or Position
Company Name
Address
City, State, Zip

Dear Exact Name of Interviewer:

I just wanted to let you know how much I enjoyed meeting with you yesterday, March 21st, at your office at 1110½ Hay Street.

I am even more certain now than I was before our meeting that I can make valuable contributions to you and to the XYZ Company. I feel quite enthusiastic abaout the exciting industrial product line I would be representing, and I'm sure that my highly motivated nature, combined with my proven sales know-how, would translate into sales and satisfied customers.

It would be a pleasure, too, to work with you and under your direction as part of your personal team in contributing to your company's success.

Thank you for your time and hospitality yesterday. I hope to have the pleasure of talking with you again soon.

Yours sincerely,

Your name

SOME ADVICE ABOUT COMPANY INFORMATION AVAILABLE AT LIBRARIES

Figuring out the names of the organizations to which you want to mail your resume is part of any highly successful job campaign. Don't depend on just answering ads, waiting for the ideal job to appear in a newspaper or magazine. Aggressively seek out a job in the companies you want to work for. Here is some information which you can use in researching the names of organizations you might be interested in working for.

Most libraries have a wide variety of information available on various organizations throughout the U.S. and worldwide. Most of these materials are only available for use in the reference room of the library, but some limited items may be checked out. Listed below are some of the major sources to look for, but be sure and check at the information desk to see if there are any books available on the specific types of companies you wish to investigate.

THE WORLDWIDE CHAMBER OF COMMERCE DIRECTORY

Most chambers of commerce annually produce a "list of major employers" for their market area (or city). Usually the list includes the name, address, and telephone number of the employer along with information about the number of people employed, kinds of products and services produced, and a person to contact about employment. You can obtain the "list of major employers" in the city where you want to work by writing to that chamber. There is usually a small charge.

The *Worldwide Chamber of Commerce Directory* is an alphabetical listing of American and foreign chambers of commerce. It includes:
All U.S. Chambers of Commerce (with addresses and phone numbers)
American Chambers of Commerce abroad
Canadian Chambers of Commerce
Foreign Chambers of Commerce in principal cities worldwide
Foreign Embassies and Consulates in the U.S.
U.S. Consulates and Embassies throughout the world

STANDARD AND POOR'S REGISTER OF CORPORATIONS, DIRECTORS, AND EXECUTIVES

Standard and Poor's produce three volumes annually with information concerning over 38,000 American corporations. They are:

Volume I - **Corporations**. Here is an alphabetical listing of a variety of information for each of over 38,000 companies, including:
name of company, address, telephone number
names, titles, and functions of several key officers
name of accounting firm, primary bank, and law firm

stock exchange, description of products or services
annual sales, number of employees
division names and functions, subsidiary listings

Volume 2 - **Directors and Executives.** This volume lists alphabetically over 70,000 officers, directors, partners, etc. by name.
Information on each executive includes:
principal business affiliation
business address, residence address, year of birth
college and year of graduation, fraternal affiliation

Volume 3 - **Index.**

MOODY'S MANUALS
Moody's manuals provide information about companies traded on the New York and American Stock Exchanges and over the counter. They include:

Moody's Industrial Manual
Here, Moody's discusses detailed information on companies traded on the New York, American, and regional stock exchanges. The companies are listed alphabetically. Basic information about company addresses, phone numbers, and the names of key officers is available for each company listed. In addition, detailed information about the financial and operating data for each company is available. There are three levels of detail provided:

Complete Coverage. Companies listed in this section have the following information in Moody's:
* *financial information* for the past 7 years (income accounts, balance sheets, financial and operating data).
* *detailed description of the company's business* including a complete list of subsidiaries and office and property sites.
* *capital structure information,* which includes details on capital stock and long term debt, with bond and preferred stock ratings and 2 years of stock and bond price ranges.
* *extensive presentation of the company's last annual report.*

Full Measure Coverage. Information on companies in this section includes:
* *financial information for the past 7 years* (income accounts, balance sheets, financial and operating data).
* *detailed description of company's business,* with a complete list of subsidiaries and plant and property locations.
* *capital structure information,* which includes details on capital stock and long term debt, with bond and preferred stock ratings and 2 years of stock and bond price changes.

Comprehensive Coverage. Information on companies in this section includes:

* *5 years of financial information* on income accounts, balance sheets, and financial and operating ratios.

* *detailed description of company's business,* including subsidiaries.

* *concise capital structure information,* including capital stock and long term debts, bond and preferred stock ratings.

Moody's OTC Manual

Here is information on 2,700 U.S. firms which are unlisted on national and regional stock exchanges. There are three levels of coverage: complete, full measure, and comprehensive (same as described above).

Other Moody's manuals include: **Moody's Public Utility Manual, Moody's Municipal and Government Manual,** and **Moody's Bank and Finance Manual.**

DUN'S MILLION DOLLAR DIRECTORY

Three separate listings (alphabetical, geographic, and by products) of over 120,000 U.S. firms. There are three volumes:

Volume 1 - The 45,000 largest companies, net worth over $500,000
Volume 2 - The 37,000 next largest companies
Volume 3 - The 37,000 next largest companies

MacRAE'S BLUE BOOK

Five volumes of information on companies and their products.
Volume 1 - Alphabetical corporate index.
Volume 2-4 - Alphabetical listing, by product, of manufacturers.
Volume 5 - Manufacturer's catalog data.

U.S. INDUSTRIAL DIRECTORY

Two volumes of information on specific products, corporate product literature, and the addresses and telephone numbers of industrial companies.

THOMAS' REGISTER OF MANUFACTURERS

16 volumes of information about manufacturing companies.

Volumes 1-8 - Alphabetical listing by product.
Volumes 9-10 - Alphabetical listing of manufacturing company names, addresses, telephone numbers, and local offices.
Volumes 11-16 - Alphabetical company catalog information.

INFORMATION ABOUT FOREIGN COMPANIES

Directory of Foreign Manufacturers in the U.S.
Alphabetical listing of U.S. manufacturing companies which are owned and operated by parent foreign firms. The information provided includes the name and address of the U.S. firm, the name and address of the foreign parent firm, and the products produced.

Directory of American Firms Operating in Foreign Countries
Alphabetical listing of the names, addresses, chief officers, products, and country operated in of U.S. firms abroad.

Jane's Major Companies of Europe
1,000 major European businesses indexed in three ways: by business line, by country, and alphabetically. Countries included are: Australia, Belgium, Denmark, Finland, France, Federal Republic of Germany, Ireland, Italy, Luxembourg, Netherlands, Norway, Portugal, Spain, Sweden, Switzerland, and United Kingdom.

INFORMATION AVAILABLE FROM THE INTERNET

Information about companies is also available through the Internet. A new interactive business directory called Big Yellow, a comprehensive on-line yellow-page service, has the names, addresses, and telephone numbers of more than 16 million businesses nationwide. It is available free to consumers at http://www.bigyellow.com.

Part Two

Date

Exact Name of Person
Title or Position
Name of Company
Address (no., street)
Address (city, state, zip)

Dear Exact Name of Person: (or Dear Sir or Madam if answering a blind ad.)

I would appreciate an opportunity to talk with you soon about how I could contribute to your organization through my expert management and communication skills as well as my ability to conceive new ideas and make them "come to life."

While serving my country in the U.S. Coast Guard, I have excelled in a "track record" of accomplishments related to planning, developing, and implementing new programs, systems, and equipment. Regarded as an "expert" in planning and administering training programs, I was recently selected to direct the training of 225 diversified specialists. While controlling an inventory of training assets, I utilized resources which reduced training costs. In a previous job, I was selected to develop a standardized training/maintenance program for a state-of-the-art aircraft.

With FAA private pilot and airframe and powerplant licenses, I am highly skilled in inspecting and providing quality control for aircraft maintenance. I have played a key role in designing money-saving technical systems and testing newly fielded equipment.

You would find me to be an enthusiastic and energetic professional with proven motivational skills. A proven innovator, I once built an aeriel advertising business "from scratch" into a thriving operation.

I hope you will welcome my call soon to arrange a brief meeting at your convenience to discuss your current and future needs and how I might serve them. Thank you in advance for your time.

Sincerely yours,

Jerry Garfinkle

Alternate last paragraph:
I hope you will call or write me soon to suggest a time convenient for us to meet and discuss your current and future needs and how I might serve them. Thank you in advance for your time.

JERRY GARFINKLE

1110½ Hay Street, Fayetteville, NC 28305   (910) 483-6611

OBJECTIVE

To benefit an organization that can use a talented manager and communicator who offers a strong background in aviation as well as the organizational ability needed to make new ideas "come to life."

EXPERIENCE

TRAINING & MAINTENANCE MANAGER. U.S. Coast Guard, Elizabeth City, NC (1987-present). Regarded as one of the Coast Guard's "training experts," was handpicked to direct training for 225 diversified aviation professionals and managing a 13-person team maintaining five aircraft.

* Played a key role in designing and developing an improved fuel depot; manage purchasing/distribution of 300,000 gallons of fuel monthly.
* Develop short-term and long-range training plans; coordinated with the U.S. Marine Corps to provide no cost professional training.
* Recognized the need and developed guidelines for a professional board to evaluate the skills of specialized personnel.
* Increased administrative efficiency by improving recordkeeping.
* Was described as a "clear and confident" speaker and "outstanding" writer.

SENIOR INSTRUCTOR/PROJECT COORDINATOR. U.S.C.G., Mobile, AL (1981-87). Was selected to develop a standardized training/maintenance program for personnel maintaining state-of-the-art HU-25A Falcon 200 aircraft; planned and presented a two-week training program while supervising up to four instructors and nine technicians.

* Created training/testing programs for aircraft technicians; programmed computerized flights simulators.
* Rewrote an outdated chapter in a popular training manual.
* Traveled to ten geographical locations to train personnel in new procedures; evaluated programs to determine problems and solutions.
* Developed an improved oxygen system which saved over a quarter-million dollars; tested and advised top executives on new equipment.
* In a part-time role, built a day-and-night aeriel advertising business "from scratch" into a thriving operation.

Other experience: (1970-81).
FLIGHT ENGINEER. Because of my excellent aviation skills, was selected to oversee aircraft inspections and quality control while supervising a team of 13 people maintaining and troubleshooting C-130 aircraft.

* Earned 2,400 hours flight time as a flight engineer.

MAINTENANCE SUPERVISOR. Became known as an expert mechanic and troubleshooter while performing scheduled and unscheduled maintenance and inspections on aircraft.
RADIO SUPERVISOR. Supervised up to four communications technicians while operating and maintaining sophisticated equipment.

Success in Solving Problems, Reducing Costs, & Managing Personnel

EDUCATION & TRAINING

Completed course work in History and General Studies, University of South Alabama, 1985. Excelled U.S. Coast Guard management training related to: aviation operations/maintenance, communication, and personnel training.

LICENSES

Hold FAA Private Pilot and Airframe and Powerplant licenses.
* Am skilled in performing aircraft inspections and safety checks.

PERSONAL

Am highly skilled in maintaining and troubleshooting aircraft systems. Attend to minute details while keeping sight of the "big picture." Believe in "doing the job right the first time." Adapt easily to rapid changes.

Date

Exact Name of Person
Title or Position
Name of Company
Address (no., street)
Address (city, state, zip)

Dear Exact Name of Person: (or Dear Sir or Madam if answering a blind ad.)

I would appreciate an opportunity to talk with you soon about how I could contribute to your organization through my experience and training as an airframe and power plant mechanic known for outstanding mechanical skills and leadership abilities.

During my approximately ten years in the U.S. Air Force I have become quite knowledgeable of the procedures and techniques needed to make maintenance operations run smoothly and on time. As you will see from my resume, my experience covers both small and long air carriers.

I have supervised as many as 60 people and in my most recent job, was selected to act as the liaison between local and U.S.-based Air Force reserve personnel training in Turkey. This included supervising the visiting mechanics who were using our maintenance facilities.

I am a hard working, dedicated professional who offers a broad base of knowledge and skills related to aircraft maintenance. I feel that I can make valuable contributions to an aircraft maintenance facility through my mechanical skills as well as my leadership abilities.

I hope you will welcome my call soon to arrange a brief meeting at your convenience to discuss your current and future needs and how I might serve them. Thank you in advance for your time.

Sincerely yours,

Patrick Angelis

Alternate last paragraph:
I hope you will call or write me soon to suggest a time convenient for us to meet and discuss your current and future needs and how I might serve them. Thank you in advance for your time.

PATRICK ANGELIS
1110½ Hay Street, Fayetteville, NC 28305   (910) 483-6611

OBJECTIVE

To offer my experience as an airframe and power plant mechanic to an organization that can use a well-trained and experienced professional who can handle long hours and hard work in order to see that the job is done right.

EXPERIENCE

AIRCRAFT MAINTENANCE SPECIALIST. U.S. Air Force, Turkey (1993-95).
Placed in charge of all phases of C-130 maintenance, was selected to serve as point of contact for reserve units from the U.S. who were participating in training exercises.
* Supervised groups of approximately 60 people when reserve personnel used my organization's facilities.
* Earned a reputation as a very knowledgeable professional while inspecting, troubleshooting, repairing, and servicing a wide range of aircraft including:
   C-130E/B/H   C-5   C-141   DC-8   DC-9   MD-11   727   L1011
* Named as an invaluable asset to the unit for accomplishments which earned the unit excellent ratings in a major inspection: troubleshot an engine problem to the defective starter control valve, and replaced the defective part in minimum time.

SUPERVISORY MAINTENANCE SPECIALIST. USAF, Middle East (1990-91).
Was awarded the Air Force Commendation Medal for my outstanding service in support of combat operations during the war in the Middle East.
* Handed the details of setting up the tents, dining facility, and work sites for over 1,000 people to use while in the Middle East.
* Was cited as a key player in removing and replacing four engines and three propellers within one 12-hour period.
* Officially commended for "untiring efforts," contributed to outstanding results including a 95.8% launch reliability rate, 1,912 missions completed, and 35,252 tons of cargo delivered.

Advanced to leadership roles while polishing my mechanical skills, USAF, Pope AFB, NC:
DEDICATED CREW CHIEF. (1987-93). Promoted to oversee the maintenance and servicing of one assigned C-130 aircraft, ensured engine changes, time changes on components, and inspections were done thoroughly and in a timely manner.
* Was selected to attend special training programs in advanced systems and engine run procedures.

MAINTENANCE SPECIALIST. (1985-87). Performed inspections, troubleshooting, and repair on aircraft including C-141, C-130E/B/H, C-5, and L100.
* Gained valuable experience while earning a reputation as a knowledgeable and skilled mechanic.

AIRCRAFT EXPERTISE

Through training and experience, can inspect, troubleshoot, repair, and service components on a wide range of aircraft including the following:

| C-130E/B/H | L100 | C-141 | C-5 | DC-8 | DC-9 | DC-10 | MD-11 | L1011 |
| 727 | C-12 | C-17 | C-20 | C-21 | C-22 | C-26 | C-27 | T-39 |

* Am skilled in using all tools and equipment of my trade including the following:
amp meters	multimeters	tensiometers	auxiliary power units
air compressors	light carts	bleed air units	electrical carts
hydraulic test carts	heaters	air conditioners	

TRAINING

Completed military training programs including:
   C-130 Self-contained Navigational Systems   Airlift Aircraft Maintenance
   C-130E/B/H Aircraft Systems Technician's Course   Supervisory Techniques
   C-130E/B/H Airlift Aircraft Maintenance Specialist Course & Engine Run Supervisor Course
   C-5 flaps/slats troubleshooting/repair & C-5 cargo ramp & doors troubleshooting/repair

PERSONAL

Have been entrusted with a Secret Security Clearance. Am a highly skilled mechanic with well-developed leadership and motivational abilities. Will relocate.

Date

Exact Name of Person
Title or Position
Name of Company
Address (no., street)
Address (city, state, zip)

Dear Exact Name of Person: (or Dear Sir or Madam if answering a blind ad.)

I would appreciate an opportunity to talk with you soon about my desire to become a valuable part of your organization through my experience in production/maintenance management, administration, quality/safety control, and personnel supervision.

As you will see from my resume, I have excelled in "hot seat" jobs in which one error of judgement can result in multimillion-dollar liability. I am accustomed to working in environments in which nothing is "routine" during the day except an attitude of constant vigilance and attention to detail. While thriving on the challenge of such positions, I have cultivated an attitude in which I view every problem as an opportunity for improving internal operations, and I have always instilled in my associates a belief that "quality and quantity production result in customer satisfaction."

My resume provides some insight into my ability to boost productivity while cutting costs. For example, while managing aircraft maintenance at Pope Air Force Base, I saved $420,000 of a $1.6 million budget by carefully eliminating unnecessary items. My bookkeeping techniques have been adopted by other agencies, and I am proud of the money-saving initiatives proposed by junior employees I trained.

In aircraft maintenance, there's always "an accident ready to happen," so many of my achievements have to do with things that never happened! I am, however, proud of the fact that, in March of 1994 following an F-16 mishap, a toxic chemical was contained in only four minutes using a plan I authored for responding to hydrazine emergencies.

I hope you will give me the opportunity to meet with you in person. At that time I could tell you about other accomplishments related to solving refueling dilemmas, reducing downtime, troubleshooting vent tank malfunctions, diagnosing "impossible" problems, and continuously improving repair and maintenance techniques. Known as a vibrant supervisor who enjoys working with others and who believes in "leadership by example," I also enjoy handling paperwork (believe it or not!) and I am known for my meticulous attention to detail and enthusiasm when handling huge volumes of technical documentation.

I hope you will welcome my call soon when I try to arrange a brief meeting with you to discuss your current and future needs and how I might serve them. I can assure you in advance that you would actually save money by hiring me because I am confident I can contribute significantly to your bottom line within a short period of time. Thank you in advance for your time.

Sincerely yours,

Michael Zercher

Alternate last paragraph:
I hope you will call or write me soon to suggest a time convenient for us to meet and discuss your current and future needs and how I might best serve them. Thank you in advance for your time.

MICHAEL ZERCHER
1110½ Hay Street, Fayetteville, NC 28305   (910) 483-6611

OBJECTIVE   To offer my expertise in production management, maintenance, quality assurance, and inventory control to an organization that can use a seasoned cost-cutter and creative problem solver known for "making things happen" while developing highly productive workers.

EDUCATION   Completing Associate's degree, Community College of the Air Force, Pope AFB, NC.
Received diplomas for completing three separate executive development programs lasting nearly two years in **Supervision/Management**, Air University; 1990, 1988, and 1987.
Earned numerous certificates from training programs studying advanced maintenance techniques, state-of-the-art quality control methods, and supervision.

HONORS & PUBLICATIONS   Named outstanding **Production Superintendent** based on performance reports, 1994.
Received seven prestigious medals for exceptional performance, 1982-94.
Authored and published Air Force Regulation 66-18, "Maintenance Methods & Procedures."

EXPERIENCE   **AIRCRAFT MAINTENANCE MANAGER.** U.S. Air Force, Pope AFB, NC (1990-94). At one of the Air Force's busiest airlift centers worldwide, supervise 49 people and control $2 million in assets while managing safety programs and instilling in all employees the philosophy that "quality and quantity production result in customer satisfaction"; am known for my belief that every problem is an opportunity to improve operations.
* *Creative problem solving:* When Congress began closing military bases and our work load increased due to consolidation, personally designed and drew up blueprints for a new facility which increased maintenance capability by 50%.
* *Aggressive cost control:* Trained junior supervisors in cost efficiency, assisted financial experts in establishing budgetary guidelines, created a new "working group" to brainstorm about money-saving proposals, and saw my bookkeeping techniques adopted by other agencies.
* *Safety management:* Wrote and implemented a plan for responding to hydrazine emergencies that outlines steps for disposing of this toxic chemical in 17 minutes maximum; following the 1994 crash of an F-16 when hydrazine spilled, the chemical was contained in four minutes, avoiding potentially costly liability.

ASSISTANT SHOP CHIEF. U.S. Air Force, Pope AFB, NC (1989-90). Was rapidly promoted to the job above after excelling in managing 49 people and a monthly budget of $135,000.
* *Prudent cost cutting:* Saved $420,000 of a $1.6 million budget.
* *Personnel development:* Became respected for my ability to train and motivate.

MAINTENANCE SHIFT SUPERVISOR. U.S. Air Force, Pope AFB, NC (1985-89). Supervised and evaluated 20 personnel while advising on technical problems, reviewing and editing computer input/output for accuracy, and scheduling/prioritizing work loads.
* *Maintenance know-how:* In formal presentations to as many as 400 people, demonstrated improved methods of repairing aircraft.
* *Troubleshooting ability:* Modified emergency evacuation plans and taught "buddy care" to 28 people.

QUALITY CONTROL INSPECTOR. U.S. Air Force, Philippines (1984-85). Evaluated and inspected 117 personnel in performing jobs related to aircraft maintenance.
* *Safety management:* Developed a safety training module for semiannual review by workers that increased employee safety consciousness and attention to detail.
* *Inspection expertise:* Maintained aircraft continuously "free of discrepancies."

MAINTENANCE MECHANIC. U.S. Air Force, Langley AFB, VA (1978-84). Removed, repaired, inspected, installed, and modified aircraft fuel distribution systems while originating numerous ideas that streamlined/modernized maintenance and improved safety.

Other experience: Gained experience in working in a job shop while assembling furniture.

PERSONAL   Offer exceptionally strong analytical skills and pride myself on my ability to quickly "cut to the heart" of a problem. Live by the highest standards of personal and professional conduct. Have been entrusted with a Top Secret security clearance. Have maintained aircraft of McDonnell Douglas, Boeing, Lockheed, General Dynamics, and Fairchild Republic.

Date

Exact Name of Person
Title or Position
Name of Company
Address (no., street)
Address (city, state, zip)

Dear Exact Name of Person: (or Dear Sir or Madam if answering a blind ad.)

I would appreciate an opportunity to talk with you soon about how I could benefit your organization through my outstanding technical skills in aviation maintenance as well as my ability to supervise and motivate others.

While serving my country in the U.S. Air Force, I have gained experience in all aspects of aircraft maintenance. I supervised a team involved in fueling, launching, and recovering aircraft while performing pre- and postflight inspections and servicing aircraft systems. Previously I led an inspection team to achieve a 98% quality assurance rating while inspecting aircraft in record time.

I am familiar with a wide range of aircraft systems and shop equipment. I hold a current FAA Airframe and Power Plant maintenance license and achieved scores of 98% on written and 100% on oral certification knowledge exams.

You would find me to be a dedicated professional with the ability to find creative solutions to tough mechanical problems. I am single and could relocate to nearly any area in the world.

I hope you will welcome my call soon to arrange a brief meeting at your convenience to discuss your current and future needs and how I might serve them. Thank you in advance for your time.

Sincerely yours,

Barry Zachary

Alternate last paragraph:
I hope you will call or write me soon to suggest a time convenient for us to meet and discuss your current and future needs and how I might serve them. Thank you in advance for your time.

BARRY ZACHARY

1110½ Hay Street, Fayetteville, NC 28305   (910) 483-6611

OBJECTIVE
To benefit an organization through my excellent technical skills in aircraft maintenance along with my proven ability to supervise and motivate others.

LICENSE
FAA Airframe and Power Plant License, 1986.
* Earned 98% on written and 100% on oral knowledge examinations.

EXPERIENCE
CREW CHIEF. U.S. Air Force, Tyndall AFB, FL (1989-90). Supervised a team of five involved in launching and recovering aircraft and in making pre- and postflight inspections; inspected engine bays; oversee towing and fueling procedures.
* Provided service to aircraft systems including:

    landing gear   canopy   secondary power systems
    tires   brakes   primary flight controls

* Removed and replaced engines and hydraulic components.
* Played a major role in achieving a 97% "mission capable" aircraft status.
* Learned in-depth weight and balance procedures.
* Identified and corrected serious component failures.

INSPECTION TEAM CHIEF. U.S.A.F., Kadena AB, Okinawa, Japan (1987-89). Achieved a 98% quality assurance pass rating while overseeing eight inspectors performing "first-line" checks of aircraft.
* Was credited with improving employees' technical knowledge of aircraft.
* Received a written commendation for inspecting aircraft in record time.

MAINTENANCE INSPECTOR. U.S.A.F., Korea, and Williams AFB, AZ (1985-87). Made post-maintenance aircraft inspections; removed and repaired components.
* Troubleshot flight control systems; inspected landing gear and flight control surfaces on the T-37 Trainer.
* At Williams AFB, played a key role in the team winning "Inspection Dock of the Year."

MACHINIST SPECIALIST. U.S.A.F., Travis AFB, CA, and Nellis AFB, NV (1977-84). Made aircraft parts from blueprints and shop design drawings.
* Designed tools which made routine tasks easier.
* Fueled, launched, and recovered aircraft; changed tires/inspected brakes.
* Performed preflight, thru-flight, and postflight inspections.

AIRCRAFT EXPERTISE
Have maintained McDonnell Douglas F-4 and F-15, Cessna T-37, Fairchild Republic A-10, General Dynamics F-16, and Lockheed C-5 and C-141 aircraft.
* Install, maintain and repair to the component level systems including:

    computerized flight control components   servo-cylinders
    pitch-roll channel assemblies   switching valves

EDUCATION & TRAINING
Graduated with an A.A. degree from the Basic Machinist Course, U.S. Army Ordnance Center, Aberdeen Proving Ground, MD, 1983.
Completed 390 hours of college-level U.S.A.F. training in aircraft maintenance.
Earned diploma from Embry-Riddle Aero-University's A&P course (4.0 GPA).
Am currently pursuing a B.A.S. in Aviation Maintenance Technology.

PERSONAL
SECRET clearance. Would relocate to South America, the South Pacific, or Asia.

Date

Exact Name of Person
Title or Position
Name of Company
Address (no., street)
Address (city, state, zip)

Dear Exact Name of Person: (or Dear Sir or Madam if answering a blind ad.)

I would appreciate an opportunity to talk with you soon about how I could contribute to your organization through my expertise as an aircraft mechanic and experience as a crew chief.

As you will see from my resume, I hold the FAA Airframe & Powerplant Mechanic License, and I am considered an expert in troubleshooting and repairing aircraft systems and engines.

On numerous occasions I have creatively applied my knowledge and technical skills to save downtime and money. For example, during a borescope inspection of a Pratt & Whitney F100 engine, I discovered a massive burnthrough of a combuster liner that, if undetected, would have caused a major fire. On another occasion while working with a colleague, I conceived of a way to change a component of a GE110 engine without removing the engine from the aircraft, and that procedure reduced the number of people needed for the task from five to two while saving 40 manhours of work.

While serving my country in the Air Force, I was promoted ahead of my peers to F-16 Crew Chief, and I usually wore other "hats" as well such as Flight Chief, Crew Chief Expediter, and Line Chief. Known for my dedication to quality standards while emphasizing safety, I can provide excellent personal and professional references, and I will cheerfully travel and relocate worldwide as your needs require.

I hope you will call or write me soon to suggest a time convenient for us to meet and discuss your current and future needs and how I might serve them. Thank you in advance for you time.

Sincerely yours,

Tyler Keneally

Alternate last paragraph:
I hope you will welcome my call soon to arrange a brief meeting at your convenience to discuss your current and future needs and how I might serve them. Thank you in advance for your time.

TYLER KENEALLY

1110½ Hay Street, Fayetteville, NC 28305   (910) 483-6611

OBJECTIVE

To offer my skills as an aircraft mechanic and my experience as a crew chief to a company that can use a skilled troubleshooter who offers a proven ability to work gracefully under pressure while correcting stubborn problems affecting aerospace powerplant systems.

LICENSE

FAA Airframe and Powerplant Mechanic, #429 53 7582

AIRCRAFT EXPERTISE

* Expert in troubleshooting and repairing F-16 aircraft systems — A,B,C,D models
* Familiar with Pratt & Whitney engines including F100 PW 200
* Experienced with General Electric engines including F110-GE100 and F110-GE129
* Offer ability to operate jet engine trim box, F-16 test cell

EXPERIENCE

F-16 CREW CHIEF. U.S. Air Force, Germany (1991-94).
Supervised other technicians while also performing as F-16 Crew Chief Expediter, Flight Chief, and Line Chief in addition to handling maintenance staff functions.
* Inspected, installed, repaired, maintained, troubleshot, serviced, and modified tactical aircraft system components including airframe and powerplant.
* Interpreted and provided advice on maintenance procedures and policy.
* Planned and conducted on-the-job training.
* Analyzed layouts, blueprints, and technical orders to diagnose problems.
* Conducted preflight and postflight inspections.
* Removed, installed, repaired, troubleshot, and serviced components/systems such as:

hydraulic systems	electrical systems
oxygen systems (gaseous and liquid)	powerplant
environmental systems	oil
ventilation and heating systems	fuel
auxiliary power units	wheels
flight surfaces and controls	brakes
landing gear; anti-icing systems	tires

* Analyzed and made recommendations regarding such features as these:

parts	clearances	fuel leaks
cracks	tolerances	corrosion
tire wear	skin damage	aircraft performance

Highlights of accomplishments:
* Was involved in 48 engine changes in a 60-day period.
* With a co-worker, conceived of a way to change a component of a GE110 engine without removing the engine from the aircraft; this reduced the number of people needed for this task from five to two and saved 40 manhours of work.
* During a NATO inspection, received five perfect personal evaluations, which played a key role in the unit's receiving an excellent rating and the "Outstanding Unit" award.
* During a borescope inspection of a Pratt & Whitney F100 engine, discovered a massive burnthrough of a combuster liner that, if undetected, would have caused a major fire.
* Spent eight months in Turkey and two months in Italy on special projects.

F-16 CREW CHIEF. U.S.A.F., Germany (1988-91).
Performed most of the tasks above while learning to expertly operate F-16 engines.
* Earned a respected medal for my contributions to the war in the Middle East.

F-16 CREW CHIEF. U.S.A.F., Japan (1986-88).
Earned an unusually rapid promotion to Crew Chief as an E-3, and became known for my emphasis on teamwork and "safety first, last, and always."
* Achieved a 100% pass rate on all quality assurance inspections.

EDUCATION

Excelled in more than two years of technical training related to aircraft maintenance, F129 engine operation, F110 engine operation, and other technical areas; also excelled in management and leadership development courses for maintenance managers and crew chiefs.

PERSONAL

Will cheerfully travel and relocate worldwide as needed. Can provide outstanding personal and professional references upon request.

Date

Exact Name of Person
Title or Position
Name of Company
Address (no., street)
Address (city, state, zip)

Dear Exact Name of Person: (or Dear Sir or Madam if answering a blind ad.)

I would appreciate an opportunity to talk with you soon about how I could benefit your organization through my expertise in air traffic control, my ability to supervise and motivate others, and my background in working with people from many cultures.

While serving my country in the U.S. Air Force, I gained extensive experience as an air traffic controller, tower supervisor, and instructor. While providing control support to multi-million-dollar aircraft and ensuring safety for hundreds of passengers daily, I have earned a reputation for my attention to detail and ability to smoothly handle any crisis.

With a "knack" for getting along with people from different cultures, I was recently selected to supervise American and Canadian controllers during a major international project. I have worked in worldwide locations including Japan, Turkey, and England. I have trained dozens of air traffic controllers who are now considered "expert."

You would find me to be a dedicated professional who offers a wide range of skills and adapts easily to any situation. Single, I am willing to relocate to any location in the world.

I hope you will welcome my call soon to arrange a brief meeting at your convenience to discuss your current and future needs and how I might serve them. Thank you in advance for your time.

Sincerely yours,

William Shivar

Alternate last paragraph:
I hope you will call or write me soon to suggest a time convenient for us to meet and discuss your current and future needs and how I might serve them. Thank you in advance for your time.

WILLIAM SHIVAR

1110½ Hay Street, Fayetteville, NC 28305   (910) 483-6611

OBJECTIVE
To benefit an organization that can use an experienced air traffic controller with the ability to supervise and motivate as well as a background in working with many cultures.

LICENSE & SPECIAL SKILLS
FAA Control Tower Operator License in 1982, 1986, and 1989.
Am certified and experienced in air traffic control operations related to:

     tower control   radar control   non-radar control
     tower supervision   training   flight data progress strips

Have been certified at radar approach control levels I, II, and III.
Operate APN-42 **Approach Surveillance Radar** and TPN-22, TPN-60, TPN-16, and TPN-19 **Radar Precision Approach Systems.**

EXPERIENCE
LEVEL II TOWER CONTROLLER. U.S. Air Force, Moody AFB, GA (1989-90). Supervise the performance of up to ten junior controllers while providing control support and safety for multimillion-dollar aircraft and hundreds of passengers daily; because of my reputation as an expert controller and safety-conscious decision maker, was selected for special projects including:

Extensive International Experience in Countries Including the United States, Canada, Japan, England, and Turkey

MOBILE RADAR UNIT SUPERVISOR. U.S.A.F., Grand Forks AFB, ND (1990). Was selected to lead a team of ten professionals controlling air operations from a state-of-the-art mobile radar unit.
* Played a key role in the implementation of a multimillion-dollar tanker/bomber air craft project.

LEVEL I TOWER CONTROLLER. U.S.A.F., Greenland (1990). Was picked to manage nine American and Canadian controllers during a major international training project.
* Refined my skills in motivating and supervising others.

RADAR SUPERVISOR/AIR TRAFFIC CONTROLLER. U.S.A.F., England (1987-89). After receiving my radar approach certification, was chosen to train five junior control while supervising a radar crew of 17.

AIR TRAFFIC CONTROLLER. U.S.A.F., Turkey (1986-87). Worked with Turkish controllers; received non-radar approach certification.

INSTRUCTOR and **AIR TRAFFIC CONTROLLER.** U.S.A.F., Shaw AFB, SC (1984-86). Was chosen to provide on-the-job training for an officer who took over the role of Chief of Air Traffic Control; played a key role in the reconstruction of the air traffic control training program including non-radar techniques.

TRAINING MANAGER and **AIR TRAFFIC CONTROLLER.** U.S.A.F., Okinawa (1982-84). Was certified as a tower coordinator while providing tower support to aircraft.
* Received "trainer" qualification; was in charge of the training regulations program.
* Was named "Controller of the Quarter" twice.

EDUCATION
Completing degree in **Air Avionics**, Community College of the Air Force.
Graduated from college-level U.S.A.F. training in management, safety, and survival.
Received Certificate of Training, Air Traffic Control Technical School, 1981.

PERSONAL
Hold SECRET security clearance. Am single and willing to relocate worldwide.

Date

Exact Name of Person
Title or Position
Name of Company
Address (no., street)
Address (city, state, zip)

Dear Exact Name of Person: (or Dear Sir or Madam if answering a blind ad.)

I would appreciate an opportunity to talk with you soon about how I could contribute to your organization through my background which includes approximately 12 years in airfield management.

As you will see from my resume, while serving in the U.S. Air Force I gained experience in working with flight plans, FAA and military air traffic control regulations, airway systems, and all other aspects of airfield management.

During this period I was awarded two achievement medals, a commendation medal, an outstanding unit award, and the Humanitarian Service Medal. My reputation has consistently included praise for my adaptability, willingness to work long hours without complaint, cheerful and pleasant personality, and leadership skills.

My experience encompasses all aspects of flight data and air operations such as processing international, civil, and local flight plans; presenting briefings to air crew members on runway, flight, and weather conditions; and ordering, maintaining, and distributing flight publications.

I feel that through my history of finding ways to streamline and improve operational procedures and my reputation as a dependable and enthusiastic professional, I could make valuable contributions to your organization as I have to the U.S. Air Force. Furthermore, I am willing to relocate at my own expense.

I hope you will call or write me soon to suggest a time convenient for us to meet and discuss your current and future needs and how I might serve them. Thank you in advance for your time.

Sincerely yours,

Christopher Presthus

Alternate last paragraph:
I hope you will welcome my call soon to arrange a brief meeting at your convenience to discuss your current and future needs and how I might serve them. Thank you in advance for your time.

CHRISTOPHER PRESTHUS

1110 ½ Hay Street, Fayetteville, NC 28305   (910) 483-6611

OBJECTIVE   To apply my expertise and experience in the area of airfield operations to an organization that can use an adaptable and dependable professional who can handle pressure and emergencies, lead employees to outstanding results, and display technical knowledge.

EXPERIENCE   **AIRFIELD MANAGEMENT SUPERVISOR.** U.S. Air Force, Pope AFB, NC (1993-94). Implemented improvements in operational procedures in the flight control center of a major air force base while coordinating air traffic with the FAA (Federal Aviation Administration) using the FAA Service B computer system to plan domestic and international flights.
* Cited for my ability to maximize scarce resources, reduced time required for distributing publications by 60% and gained 50% more work space through a renovation project.

SUPERVISORY AIRFIELD MANAGEMENT SPECIALIST. USAF, Patrick AFB, FL (1991-93). Earned a reputation as an exceptional performer with superior technical knowledge in a position which covered responsibilities ranging from inspecting flight facilities, to processing flight data, to reviewing flight data, to providing support for space shuttle launches.
* Expertly processed more than 2,500 international and domestic flight plans in two years.
* Played an important role in coordinating the evacuation of multimillion-dollar NASA, Department of State, and rescue squadron aircraft during Hurricane Andrew.

RANGE OPERATIONS SUPERVISOR. USAF, Korea (1990). Handled major operational areas simultaneously: managed a $250,000 inventory of simulators used to provide realistic training for American and Korean air crews and served as primary contact for emergency responses to aircraft incidents and accidents.
* Cut normal response times in half during one situation through my timely actions.

FLIGHT OPERATIONS SUPERVISOR. USAF, Shaw AFB, SC (1988-89). Promoted on the basis of my performance as a Weapons Range Specialist, was placed in a supervisory position which included planning and coordinating airfield operations.
* Used my technical knowledge and communication skills to rewrite standard operating procedures for flightline activities and general operations.

WEAPONS RANGE SPECIALIST. USAF, Shaw AFB, SC (1987-88). Ensured safety procedures were followed while working in a control center where weapons were tested and automated equipment used to plan activities and check results.
* Earned praise for my attention to detail, high degree of self motivation, and leadership.

AIRFIELD DISPATCHER. USAF, Korea (1986). Refined my ability to handle stress in a flight center where I was involved in checking and transmitting flight plans, coordinating air traffic information, responding to aircraft declaring emergencies, and dispensing information about weather conditions and training exercises.

EDUCATION & TRAINING   Am studying Resource Management, Community College of the Air Force; received certification with 59 hours of study in Airway Science.
Excelled in numerous training programs in airfield management and leadership.

SPECIAL KNOWLEDGE   Offer experience with the following computer hardware, software, and operating systems:

COMED system	Alden systems	FAA "B" circuit computer terminal
GTE modem	Data Products 8500 printer	pilot-to-dispatch radios
Western Union 8100 keyboard display terminal		Model 43 teleprinter
Sun type 4 and 5 keyboards		P3120 Marathon hard disc drive
Racal Milgo 24 LSI modem		Automated Weather Distribution System (AWDS)

Coordinated servicing and flight planning for ten space shuttle launches, most types of Army helicopters and a wide range of aircraft such as:

B-1	B-2	F-117	C-17	C-5	KC-10	B-747	C-141
F-4	F-111	C-130	F-16	F-15	F-14	F-18	T-39
T-38	T-37	A-6	A-7	A-10	C-12	C-21	Air Force 1 and 2

PERSONAL   Am known for my honesty and strong work ethic. Have frequently been described as a team player who can be counted on. Volunteer often for community improvement projects. Have been entrusted with a Top Secret security clearance with BI.

Date

Exact Name of Person
Title or Position
Name of Company
Address (no., street)
Address (city, state, zip)

Dear Exact Name of Person: (or Dear Sir or Madam if answering a blind ad.)

I would appreciate an opportunity to talk with you soon about how I could contribute to your organization through my versatile background which includes experience in petroleum quality assurance, laboratory procedures, and supply and inventory control operations.

While serving in the U.S. Marine Corps, I built a reputation as a professional knowledgeable in all aspects of bulk fuel operations ranging from sampling and gauging multithousand-gallon fuel tanks, to training and working with others as a firefighter, to accounting and inventory control, to shipboard refueling operations.

As you will see from my resume, I hold certifications as a Petroleum Laboratory Technician, Petroleum Supply Specialist, and Firefighter. While excelling in more than 850 hours of specialized technical training programs, I was honored as being among the very best students in each class from among personnel in all the military services.

My military experience also allowed me the opportunity to develop and polish my leadership abilities. By applying my own high standards of performance in each job, I have been successful in finding ways to improve operational procedures and guide my subordinates to provide expert support services.

I hope you will welcome my call soon to arrange a brief meeting at your convenience to discuss your current and future needs and how I might serve them. Thank you in advance for your time.

Sincerely yours,

William D. Archbell

Alternate last paragraph:
I hope you will call or write me soon to suggest a time convenient for us to meet and discuss your current and future needs and how I might serve them. Thank you in advance for your time.

WILLIAM D. ARCHBELL
1110½ Hay Street, Fayetteville, NC 28305   (910) 483-6611

OBJECTIVE

To contribute to an organization that can use a talented and enthusiastic professional with a broad base of knowledge in the petroleum industry and strong experience in areas including quality assurance, laboratory operations, bulk fuel handling, and administration.

TRAINING

Excelled in more than 850 hours of technical training programs emphasizing petroleum handling, supply operations, computer applications, and hazardous material safety.
* Consistently placed at the top in intensive technical training programs made up of highly qualified students from all the military services.

EXPERIENCE

SUPERVISORY BULK FUEL SPECIALIST. U.S. Marine Corps, Okinawa, Japan (1992-94).
Earned a reputation as an adaptable, well-organized professional while meeting the demands of three job specialties simultaneously: handled inventory control and accountability actions, inspection and testing, and quality assurance as the supervisor for six specialists.
* Guaranteed proper procedures were followed in order to determine and maintain both the physical and chemical quality of bulk fuels and lubricants.
* Controlled documentation regarding the receipt, dispensing of, and accounting for fuel.
* Provided leadership which allowed my department to reach high performance standards despite severe personnel shortages due to force reductions and military downsizing.

SENIOR BULK FUEL SPECIALIST. U.S. Marine Corps, Kaneohe Bay, HI (1989-92).
Supervised 10 technicians using aircraft hydrant refueling and tactical airfield dispensing systems; oversaw activities including sampling, gauging, and testing aviation fuels; ensured safe maintenance during the storage, handling, and dispensing of hazardous wastes.
* Known for my strict attention to detail and proper procedures, ensuring that operations were safe not only for aircrews and refueling personnel, but also for the environment.
* Initiated improvements to the procedures for accounting for fuel levels.

BULK FUEL TEAM LEADER. U.S. Marines, Saudi Arabia (1990-91).
Received several awards and medals for my contributions to allied war efforts as the supervisor of a nine-person team which set up and operated three fuel sites simultaneously.
* Excelled in providing the leadership for a nine-man team working closely together under adverse conditions in the harsh desert climate before and during the Middle East war.
* Serviced over 100 aircraft a day despite only having nine people for 15 refueling points.

BULK FUEL SPECIALIST. U.S. Marine Corps, Okinawa, Japan (1987-89).
Refueled ground and air transportation equipment as the operator of Forward Area Refueling/Rearming Points (FARRP) and maintained related equipment including pumps, hoses, fuel monitors, up to 20,000-gallon fuel bladders, 500-gallon fuel pods, and testing kits.
* Gained valuable experience in site survey procedures, multiple system set up and maintenance, and the recommended procedures for sampling, gauging, and testing.
* Acted as the unit's chief firefighter and fire training specialist.

FIRE FIGHTER. U.S. Marines, Okinawa, Japan (1985-86).
Selected to attend fire fighting training at a fire, crash, and rescue school and a fire department; assumed responsibility for fire prevention, training, and equipment maintenance.
* Received a prestigious Meritorious Mast and commendation for participating in controlling a fire — over a million dollars worth of computer equipment was saved.

CERTIFICATION

Hold certification as a Petroleum Laboratory Technician (1993), Petroleum Supply Specialist (1985), and Firefighter (1985).
* Am experienced in all pipeline transfer and receiving operations, site surveys, and the set up of Amphibious Assault Fuel Systems (AAFS), Tactical Airfield Fuel Dispensing Systems (TAFDS), and Helicopter Expedient Refueling Systems (HERS).
* Perform various laboratory tests on fuels and oils ranging from reed vapor pressure, to distillation, to flash/fire points, to APIs; use Mark II and III water/sediment test kits.
* Am skilled in refueling procedures for a wide variety of fixed and rotary wing aircraft.

PERSONAL

Secret security clearance. Am available to relocate worldwide according to the needs of my employer. Teach English to Japanese children along with sports which emphasize team efforts and physical conditioning. Have approximately two years of college-level studies, and currently enrolled in the Marine Corps National Apprenticeship Program.

Date

Exact Name of Person
Title or Position
Name of Company
Address (no., street)
Address (city, state, zip)

Dear Exact Name of Person: (or Dear Sir or Madam if answering a blind ad.)

I would appreciate an opportunity to talk with you soon about how I could contribute to your organization through my expertise related to petroleum products and cryogenics.

As you will see from my resume, I am considered one of the military's leading fuels systems specialists and I have supervised personnel and fuels distribution operations. Most recently I created a team of fuels specialists and then supervised those nine technical specialists while also operating 6,000 gallon aircraft servicing and refueling units.

In a previous job as a Cryogenics Supervisor, I maintained six storage tanks containing more than 50,000 gallons of liquid oxygen and nitrogen, which included overseeing the receipt, storage, issuance, and inventorying of those products. In a job as a Fuels Storage Operator, I was cited for error-free performance while receiving, storing, transferring, inventorying, and documenting transactions for approximately 34 million gallons of bulk aviation fuels annually.

While serving my country in the U.S. Air Force, I have received numerous honors and awards and have excelled in state-of-the-art training in my field.

You would find me to be a dedicated individual who is known for my safety-conscious attitude and attention to detail. I would be delighted to provide outstanding personal and professional references upon request.

I hope your will write or call me soon to suggest a time when we might meet to discuss your needs and goals and how I might serve them. Thank you in advance for your time.

Sincerely yours,

Stephen Anthony Albright

Alternate last paragraph:
I hope you will call or write me soon to suggest a time convenient for us to meet and discuss your current and future needs and how I might serve them. Thank you in advance for your time.

STEPHEN ANTHONY ALBRIGHT
1110½ Hay Street, Fayetteville, NC 28305   (910) 483-6611

OBJECTIVE

To offer my reputation as a dependable, enthusiastic, and hard-working young professional to an organization that can use my experience in the specialized field of aircraft fueling operations along with my exposure to maintenance, supply, and quality control activities.

EXPERIENCE

Through training and experience, have gained a strong base of knowledge and am succeeding as a **FUELS SYSTEMS SPECIALIST,** *stationed with the U.S. Air Force at Pope AFB, NC (1990-present). I have also served as a* **FUELS SYSTEMS SUPERVISOR,** *supervising up to 10 specialists, and am currently holding two jobs simultaneously*:

Special Operations Team Leader. Created a team of fuels specialists designated as the Forward Area Refueling/Rearmament Point (FARRP) team and have been the supervisor of nine specialists for approximately 2½ years; controlled a $50,000 supply account.
* Evaluated potential team members; made selections; scheduled training for personnel coming into the special team.
* Conducted regular inspections and ensured equipment was properly maintained.
* Contributed to the success of numerous international projects vital to national security.

Fuels Distribution Operator. Throughout my four years at Pope AFB, have driven and operated 6,000 gallon aircraft servicing and refueling units.
* Personally pumped more than 60 million gallons of aircraft fuel in a 1½-year period — an average of 40 million gallons a year — to several thousand aircraft.
* Used mobile and hydrant equipment to dispense fuels and oil products; maintained equipment; prepared required documentation.

Was involved in other aspects of aircraft fuel operations including the following:
Cryogenics Supervisor. Maintained six storage tanks containing more than 50,000 gallons of liquid oxygen and nitrogen: oversaw receipt, storage, issuance, and inventorying.
* Conducted regular odor tests and laboratory analyses to ensure quality of products.
* Maintained accurate and up-to-date records of all preventive maintenance performed on storage tanks, purging units, vacuum pumps, and cosmodyne samplers.

Fuels Storage Operator. Was cited for error-free performance while receiving, storing, transferring, inventorying, and documenting transactions for approximately 34 million gallons of bulk aviation fuels annually.

Preventive Maintenance Supervisor. Worked closely with vehicle maintenance personnel in order to schedule safety inspections as well as scheduled/unscheduled maintenance on mobile refueling equipment.

Fuels Lab Technician. Obtained samples and conducted laboratory tests on equipment and fuel facilities in order to ensure fuels were not contaminated.
* Verified that five aircraft crashes had not resulted in contamination of fuel supplies.

HONORS

Received a respected Air Force Achievement Medal for outstanding job performance as well as numerous performance awards for my professionalism and job skills:
> "Airman of the Month" <u>nine</u> times and "Airman of the Quarter" twice in four years
> "Pumper of the Month" <u>ten</u> times and "Pumper of the Year" one time

TRAINING

Completed approximately 29 weeks of training: 14 weeks (560 hours) related to fuel operations including air transportable and bulk fuel delivery systems and a four-week lab program and another 16 weeks of leadership, survival, and resistance/interrogation training.

EQUIPMENT EXPERTISE

Am qualified to operate R-5, R-9, R-11, and R-12 Mack and Dodge aircraft refueling vehicles. Operate virtually all Air Force forklifts and many of the Army's fuel servicing units.

PERSONAL

Received special training in graphic arts and printing in high school. Am an extremely reliable, dependable, and responsible individual known for my outgoing personality and ability to get along with everyone I meet. Took the H & R Block course for tax preparers.

Date

Tom Mozingo
AMR Services
P.O. Box 80665
Raleigh, NC 27623

Dear Mr. Mozingo:

I would appreciate an opportunity to talk with you soon about how I could contribute to your organization through my expertise in maintaining and troubleshooting diesel engines, aerospace equipment, and electronics systems.

While serving my country in the U.S. Air Force, I have gained extensive experience diagnosing, inspecting, troubleshooting, maintaining, and repairing a wide range of aerospace ground equipment. With a "knack" for fixing any mechanical system, I have been repeatedly commended for my initiative and "eye for detail." Skilled in detecting and repairing malfunctions before they become serious, I have "saved" many high-priority flights and received perfect scores on numerous evaluations.

With a U.S.A.F. certificate in Aerospace Ground Equipment Maintenance, I am skilled in working with a wide range of equipment including generators, engines, air conditioners/heaters, and compressors. I have operated construction equipment, tractor trailers, and flightline tugs. Known for my integrity, I hold a Secret security clearance.

You would find me to be an enthusiastic and safety-oriented worker who motivates others to achieve high goals.

I hope you will call or write me soon to suggest a time convenient for us to meet and discuss your current and future needs and how I might serve them. Thank you in advance for your time.

Sincerely yours,

John Hatcher

JOHN HATCHER

1110½ Hay Street, Fayetteville, NC 28305 (910) 483-6611

OBJECTIVE
To benefit an organization that can use a self-motivated and safety-oriented professional who offers proven expertise related to troubleshooting and maintaining diesel engines, aerospace equipment, and electronics systems.

CLEARANCE & LICENSES
Hold SECRET security clearance.
Hold U.S. Air Force certificates for aerospace ground equipment maintenance.
Hold Illinois Tractor-trailer Driver's License.

EXPERIENCE
AEROSPACE GROUND EQUIPMENT SPECIALIST. U.S.A.F. Pope AFB, NC (1988-present). Have become known for my "knack" for diagnosing and repairing malfunctions in mechanical and electrical systems while maintaining sophisticated equipment; was hand-picked to train and supervise four mechanics.
* Inspect, troubleshoot, and maintain equipment including engines, generators, and compressors; control equipment corrosion.
* Use manufacturers' manuals and schematic drawings; maintain records.
* Was repeatedly commended for my enthusiasm and initiative as well as my ability to use those qualities to motivate others.
* Have saved labor hours and equipment costs by detecting and repairing malfunctions before unit failure.
* Received **perfect** scores on 15 detailed inspections.
* "Rescued" many high-priority flights by troubleshooting problems.

GROUND EQUIPMENT MECHANIC. U.S.A.F., Pope AFB, NC (1987-88). Minimized downtime of diesel generators while refining my troubleshooting and maintenance skills; learned aircraft marshalling and wing-walking procedures.
* Was named "Apprentice of the Quarter" for work excellence, 1988.

Other experience:
TRACTOR-TRAILER DRIVER. Stan's Cartage, Addison, IL (1986).
CARPENTER. Norton & Norton Construction, Chicago, IL (1985).
FORKLIFT EQUIPMENT OPERATOR. Gamon Books, Chicago, IL (1983-85).

EQUIPMENT EXPERTISE
* Am certified to operate, troubleshoot, and maintain equipment including:
diesel engines: work with brands such as Allis Chalmers, Dayey, John Deere, Hatz, Onan, Petter, and Detroit Diesel
generators: 86 Hobart or Hollingsworth, MEP 006, MEP 25
gas turbine engines/generators: -60, -75, and -95 with bleed air
nonpowered support equipment: platforms, hoists, winches, and carts
construction equipment: bulldozers, forklifts, front-end loaders
compressors: ranging from MC2A 125 psi to MC1A 3,500 psi
air conditioners: MA-3, MA-3D
heaters: Davey, Hunter, Petter
* Use hydraulic testing equipment; operate Bobtail flightline tug; drive tractor-trailers.

EDUCATION & TRAINING
Graduated with a U.S.A.F. Certificate in Aerospace Ground Equipment Maintenance, 1987. Excelled in 284 hours of college-level training in specialized equipment maintenance, employee training, and management.
* In Basic Training was chosen as a squad leader for my leadership potential.
* Completed tractor-trailer driver training, 1987.

PERSONAL
Am known as a perfectionist who never leaves a job "half done." Offer the ability to plan and organize projects and motivate others to give "110%."

Date

Exact Name of Person
Title or Position
Name of Company
Address (no., street)
Address (city, state, zip)

Dear Exact Name of Person: (or Dear Sir or Madam if answering a blind ad.)

I would appreciate an opportunity to talk with you soon about how I could contribute to your organization through my experience in airfield operations including loading, repair parts supply support, and refueling with special emphasis on ground support equipment maintenance, repair, and inspection.

You will see when you look at my enclosed resume that I earned a reputation as a skilled technician and mechanic while proudly serving in the U.S. Navy. My ability to rapidly absorb new information and pass my knowledge on to others earned me the praise of my superiors and caused them to select me for special projects. In my most recent military assignment I not only accounted for a 2,300-line-item inventory of ground support equipment but also participated in training others in inspection techniques, contributed my troubleshooting and repair skills, and became the work station's safety specialist.

In earlier jobs I contributed my initiative and abilities while developing a money-saving training facility, was one of two people selected for a three-month project in the Middle East, and completed a six-week arc and gas welding course at a community college on my own time.

My current job as the Operations Manager and Maintenance Technician for a company with five geographically scattered laundromats allows me more of an opportunity to build on my supervisory skills and customer service abilities.

You would find me to be a congenial person who offers a high degree of self motivation and dedication to excellence. I am a natural leader who inspires others to join me in order to accomplish our group's peak levels of performance.

I hope you will welcome my call soon to arrange a brief meeting at your convenience to discuss your current and future needs and how I might serve them. Thank you in advance for your time.

Sincerely yours,

Dennis Wolfe

Alternate last paragraph:
I hope you will call or write me soon to suggest a time convenient for us to meet and discuss your current and future needs and how I might serve them. Thank you in advance for your time.

DENNIS WOLFE

1110½ Hay Street, Fayetteville, NC 28305   (910) 483-6611

OBJECTIVE   To offer a background which includes a strong base of experience in aviation ground support equipment repair to an organization that can use a talented, dedicated professional with a reputation for personal qualities of dedication and reliability.

SPECIAL KNOWLEDGE & SKILLS

Through training and experience gained while serving in the U.S. Navy, have become skilled in repairing, maintaining, and testing aircraft ground support equipment including:

tow tractors: TA-75A, B, and C; JG-40 and 75; TA-35

liquid oxygen carts: TMU-27 and TMU-70

hydraulic units: A/M27T-5, A/M27T-7, and AHT-63

nitrogen carts: NAN-2, NAN-2A, NAN-4, and NAN-9

mobile electric power plants: NC-8A, NC-2, NC-10 and MMG1A

air conditioning unit: AM32C-17

gas turbine compressors: GTC-85, NC-PP105, and AM47A-4

fire fighting unit: P-16

oxygen cart: O2

forklifts: 4, 6, & 20,000-lb.

aircraft lavatory pump unit

Repair and adjust fuel controls, flow dividers, oil and fuel pumps, generators, motors, relays, voltage regulators, thermostats, and air valves.

Licensed on ground support equipment; qualified in Hydraulic Contamination and Tire and Wheel.

Maintained aircraft including the following:

F-18A   A-6E   EA-6B   C-2   S-3   C-141   C-5   E-2

EXPERIENCE   **OPERATIONS MANAGER** and **MAINTENANCE TECHNICIAN.** Price Investments, various locations in southeastern North Carolina (1995-present). Make regular visits to each of five laundromats owned by the company to collect and count receipts, make bank deposits, complete any needed maintenance and repair, and handle any customer service or operational problems that have come up during my absence; supervised 11 employees.

Built a reputation as a talented technician/mechanic with leadership and supervisory abilities while advancing as an AVIATION SUPPORT EQUIPMENT MECHANIC, U.S. Navy:

EQUIPMENT CONTROL SPECIALIST and **SUPERVISOR.** NAS Whidbey Island, WA (1994). In addition to regular responsibilities as a supervisor and mechanic, was selected to oversee a support activity in which 2,300 items of equipment for 22 customer units were properly issued, received, and accounted for.

* Developed well-trained personnel who were thoroughly knowledgeable of pre- and post-operational inspection techniques.
* Implemented a system which made scanning repair/maintenance status boards (VIDS-MAF) easier to read at a glance and streamlined maintenance tracking activities.
* Was singled out for the critical position of work center safety petty officer.
* Applied expert troubleshooting skills which allowed for flightline repairs and eliminated aircraft downtime for repair.
* Made major contributor to the air station's selection for the 1993 Installation of Excellence Award.

EQUIPMENT REPAIR SPECIALIST. NAS China Lake, CA (1993). Applied my expertise to perform repairs on gas turbine compressors and preventive maintenance on all categories of ground support equipment.

* On my own initiative, spent 360 hours to create a state-of-the-art training facility which saved $40,000 in government funds by eliminating the need for outside labor.
* Completed a six-week arc and gas welding course at an area community college.

PREVENTIVE MAINTENANCE AND REPAIR SPECIALIST. The Philippines (1992). In addition to repair and maintenance on all classes of ground support equipment, gained experience in operating a 6,000-lb. forklift during a period of functional reorganization and change as activities were closed and the facility deactivated.

* Received an award for outstanding performance and learned to be a model of good will as a representative of the United States living and working in another country.
* Handpicked as one of two people to participate in a special project, learned the proper techniques for loading a C-2 aircraft and performed maintenance on 30 items of equipment in support of activities in the United Arab Emirates (April-June 1992).

EQUIPMENT REPAIR SPECIALIST. Japan (1990-91). Performed preventive maintenance on ground support and damage control equipment as well as becoming flight-deck qualified as a troubleshooter and member of the fire fighting party.

* Made contributions during the preparation of a Navy ship for decommissioning.

PERSONAL   Offer well-developed mechanical and technical skills. Have a strong interest in continuing to grow and develop new abilities related to aviation. Logged 20 flight hours in a C-2.

Date

Dear Sir or Madam:

I would appreciate an opportunity to talk with you soon about how I could contribute to your organization through my outstanding mechanical and supervisory skills and especially through my expertise with hydraulic systems.

Through training and experience I have become known as a top-notch performer who can be counted on to get things done no matter how difficult. I have consistently been singled out for special projects and for promotion ahead of my peers.

While serving my country in the U.S. Air Force, I have gained a reputation as an exceptionally talented young professional with abilities far above the average. Having been selected twice as the top performer in my organization — from a group of 100 employees — I was designated as one of the few supervisors with the authority to make the decision to ground aircraft for maintenance problems and then give the approval which will authorize them to fly.

I feel that I am a very mature and reliable individual who works well with others in both supervisory roles and as a contributor to team efforts. I participated in humanitarian missions in Saudi Arabia, Yemen, and Bosnia-Herzegovina where I was given the opportunity to see firsthand how rewarding helping others can be.

I hope you will call or write me soon to suggest a time convenient for us to meet and discuss your current and future needs and how I might serve them. Thank you in advance for your consideration.

Sincerely yours,

Davis Delaney

DAVIS DELANEY
1110½ Hay Street, Fayetteville, NC 28305   (910) 483-6611

OBJECTIVE
To offer my mechanical abilities, supervisory skills, and technical expertise to an organization that can use a well-trained young professional who consistently earns the highest evaluations and a reputation for performing at a level head and shoulders above my peers.

AREAS OF EXPERTISE
Through training and experience, have become skilled and qualified in the following areas:

airframes and power plants	production supervision
operational testing	in-flight refueling systems
mechanical control and valve repairs	maintenance supervision
precision inspection, testing, and grading	electrical and electronics repair

Am experienced as a maintenance technician on aircraft including:

C-130E	C-5	C-141	T-38

Have logged 200 flight hours as a crew chief.

EXPERIENCE
Earned a reputation as an exceptional performer with superior supervisory and technical abilities while earning promotions at an accelerated rate, U.S. Air Force, Pope AFB, NC:
SUPERVISORY HYDRAULIC MECHANIC. (1993-94). Was singled out for increased responsibilities in training and supervising the performance of 14 aircraft mechanics.

* Reached a level of inspection and decision-making responsibility in three years that traditionally would take eight years to achieve: earned "Red X Waiver Authorization," which allowed me to assess whether an aircraft was airworthy.
* Played an important role in the organization's success in completing humanitarian and contingency missions with perfect 100% reliability.
* Helped in the evacuation of 600 American citizens from civil war-torn Yemen.

HYDRAULIC MECHANIC. (1990-93). Selected by my peers as the top performer from among 75 employees, made important contributions during two 2-month trips to Germany while performing scheduled and unscheduled maintenance on 17 aircraft.

* Earned an achievement medal for my efforts in ensuring that aircraft were 100% airworthy and available when needed to fly humanitarian airlifts in aid of the people of Bosnia-Herzegovina.
* Learned that helping people survive in times of war or other emergency situations is very rewarding and gives you great personal satisfaction.
* Placed in the top 5% of Air Force personnel in my rank worldwide and received early promotion based on my initiative, expertise, and performance.
* Was part of a team selected to go to Saudi Arabia on three separate occasions in order to help move equipment and supplies to various locations.
* Voted by my peers as the top performer in a 100-person organization, also was honored as the employee of the quarter for the entire parent organization.

APPRENTICE. (1990-93). During my apprenticeship period, became highly skilled in troubleshooting, inspecting. overhauling, and performing operational checks on aircraft pneumatic components.

* Learned to handle the responsibility of working on multimillion-dollar aircraft and of ensuring that they were mechanically sound.
* Became known as a professional who always contributed to team efforts.

TRAINING
Excelled in more than 1,400 hours of training programs including a 720-hour pneudraulics systems technical school and other courses in hazardous waste handling, maintenance documentation, and troubleshooting hydraulics problems.

PERSONAL
Have been awarded two achievement medals in addition to recognition as employee of the quarter in 1992 and other "top performer" awards. Always give 100% effort.

Date

Exact Name of Person
Title or Position
Name of Company
Address (no., street)
Address (city, state, zip)

Dear Exact Name of Person: (or Dear Sir or Madam if answering a blind ad.)

I would appreciate an opportunity to talk with you soon about how I could contribute to your organization through my talents as an innovative leader and skilled communicator who has excelled serving my country in the U.S. Air Force. You will see from my resume that I offer superior technical skills and will go the "extra mile" to see projects through from start to finish.

In my most recent position as inventory manager, I was instrumental in establishing a unique tracking and identification system to account for aircraft tools and equipment. The system saved the Air Force hours of time-consuming paperwork to report lost tools and thousands of dollars required to repair engine damage caused by missing parts. As a crew chief, I directed maintenance operations on aircraft during domestic test flights and international emergency situations.

The recipient of an Air Force Commendation Medal, I have been officially evaluated as "a dedicated and exceptional performer" and was one of 10 airmen in the country to be selected for early advancement to the next rank. I feel certain I have the skills and abilities that could make me a valuable part of your team.

I hope you will welcome my call soon to arrange a brief meeting at your convenience to discuss your current and future needs and how I might serve them. Thank you in advance for your time.

Sincerely yours,

Ray Gulickson

Alternate last paragraph:
I hope you will call or write me soon to suggest a time convenient for us to meet and discuss your current and future needs and how I might serve them. Thank you in advance for your time.

RAY GULICKSON
1110½ Hay Street, Fayetteville, NC 28305   (910) 483-6611

OBJECTIVE

To contribute to an organization that can use an innovative thinker who has excelled through superior technical knowledge of aircraft operations and a natural talent for maximizing human, fiscal, and material assets.

HONORS & AWARDS

* *Commendation Medal*, 1994: Awarded for excellent service in USAF.
* *Below the Zone Promotion Award*, 1993: One of 10 airmen in the U.S. selected for early advancement to the next rank because of exceptional performance.
* *Honor Graduate*, 1992: Ranked first in a class of 12 studying aircraft maintenance as part of Qualification Training Program.
* *Good Conduct Medals*, 1991-1994: In recognition of outstanding service in USAF.

EXPERIENCE

INVENTORY MANAGER. USAF, Pope AFB, NC (1993-1994). Applied my attention to detail and outstanding motivational skills to ensure aircrafts flew with a full complement of serviceable and well-maintained parts and support equipment.
* Supervised three flightline technicians who inspected and supplied diagnostic equipment for aircraft repair.
* Spearheaded the installation of a tracking system for tools and equipment expenses, avoiding the high costs of engine damage caused by missing parts.
* Kept exacting documentation that enabled maintenance crews to render the aircraft ready in minimal time.

CREW CHIEF. USAF, Various locations (1992-1993). Handpicked to direct all aspects of inspection and maintenance on aircrafts during special assignments throughout the world.
* *California/Arizona*: Inspected test flights of an aircraft with a new radar system that was being considered for purchase on the entire Lockheed C-130E fleet; through my superior technical knowledge, enabled aircraft to achieve a 100% reliability rate.
* *Germany*: Participated in humanitarian missions flying to Bosnia to deliver food and medical supplies; flew into a hostile area to change a main landing gear tire, ensuring secure passage back to a U.S. military base.
* *Croatia*: Under hostile fire conditions, replaced a blown tire on a C-130E, enabling safe takeoff in only one hour.

MAINTENANCE TECHNICIAN. USAF, Pope AFB, NC (1991-1993). Acquired valuable technical know-how while excelling in this position to ensure readiness and safety of the aircraft at all times.
* Changed tires, brakes, engines, and other major components.
* Serviced aircrafts using liquid oxygen carts.
* Refueled aircraft prior to and in between flights.

CUSTOMER SERVICE SPECIALIST. Foley's Department Stores, Austin/San Antonio, TX (1989-90). In this fast-paced, "meet the public" position, was quickly promoted because of my exceptional public relations skills selling a variety of retail goods.
* Received *Salesperson of the Month Award* for increased sales in men's clothing by 15% in six months.
* Gained knowledge of consumer electronic products, including televisions, VCRs, and camcorders.

SECURITY OFFICER. Foley's Department Stores, College Station, TX (1988-89). Through my diligent observance and swift apprehension of shoplifters, was able to reduce loss of merchandise by 5%; maintained loss prevention systems, including ink tags and other electronic devices.

Other experience:
Groundskeeper. Country Club of Colorado and Pikes Peaks Towers, Colorado Springs, CO. (1985-1987). Helped to finance college education by performing building maintenance, landscaping, and painting during the summer.

EDUCATION

Liberal arts curriculum courses, University of Kansas, Lawrence, KS, 1986-88.
Completed several hours of college-level training in management and aircraft maintenance.

TECHNICAL EXPERTISE

* Have the ability to read technical data and schematics and work with all types of tools, including torque wrenches, OHM meters, and hydraulic jacks.
* Offer extensive experience using a variety of photography equipment and techniques.

Exact Name of Person
Title or Position
Name of Company
Address (no., street)
Address (city, state, zip)

Dear Exact Name of Person:`(or Dear Sir or Madam if answering a blind ad.)

I would appreciate an opportunity to talk with you soon about how I could contribute to your company through my proven expertise in aviation and management as well as my knowledge of government contracting procedures.

While serving my country in the U.S. Army, I acquired skills in helicopter flying instruction and management.`I have managed half-billion dollar training operations and played a major role in "maturing" the pilot and instructor training programs for the Army's most sophisticated helicopters and equipment.

With a Top Secret security clearance, I offer outstanding technical knowledge of helicopters as well as valuable insight into the Department of Defense's future needs in this area.

You would find me to be a knowledgeable aviation professional who is dedicated to producing quality work.`I am sure that my technical skills and management ability would make me a valuable asset to your company.

I hope you will welcome my call soon to arrange a brief meeting at your convenience to discuss your current and future needs and how I might serve them.`Thank you in advance for your time.

Sincerely yours,

Michael Parker

Alternate last paragraph:
I hope you will call or write me soon to suggest a time convenient for us to meet and discuss your current and future needs and how I might serve them.`Thank you in advance for your time.`

MICHAEL PARKER

1110½ Hay Street, Fayetteville, NC 28305   (910) 483-6611

OBJECTIVE

To benefit an organization that needs a dedicated professional with expertise in aviation management/helicopter operations along with knowledge of government contracting.

LICENSE

FAA Commercial Pilot license, rotorcraft, multi-engine and instrument rated.

EXPERIENCE

AIRCRAFT COMMANDER/OPERATIONS MANAGER. U.S. Army, Germany (1987-present). Manage a 23-person team operating $252 million of helicopters and ground equipment while directing a multimillion-dollar flying hour program using the AH-64, OH-58, and UH-60 aircraft.
* Set and maintain standards for excellence in aircraft and equipment readiness; ensure the team's ability for combat at any time.
* Trained and developed "from scratch" the team operating the AH-64, the Army's most sophisticated aircraft fighting machine.

GENERAL MANAGER. U.S. Army, Ft. Rucker, AL (1986-87). As a captain in a major's job, excelled in managing and "maturing" pilot and instructor training programs worth $524 million for newly fielded assets.
* Advised top-level executives on the implementation of the AH-64 Apache helicopter and the TH-1S Pilot Night Vision System Surrogate Trainer.
* Acted as liaison with civilian contractors and Army maintenance personnel.
* Persuaded top officials to implement the combat mission simulator.
* Was the "driving force" behind the training of 200 Apache pilots and 40 instructor pilots flying a total of over 13,500 hours.
* Identified and corrected an instructor pilot shortage which would have caused pilot training to cease within the year.

TRAINING MANAGER. U.S. Army, Ft. Rucker, AL (1984-85). Coordinated with civilian manufacturers and Army agencies in developing a flight training program hailed as the Army's "newest and most dynamic"; established instructional programs and revised instructional materials.
* Scheduled and maintained records of training; monitored the flight hour program; managed safety and standards programs.
* Developed procurement/maintenance programs for aircraft and equipment.

TRAINING SUPERVISOR. U.S. Army, Ft. Rucker, AL (1983-84). Oversaw the training of 180 aviators annually in AH-1S attack helicopter flight; supervised 12 instructors.

Other experience: U.S. Army, locations worldwide (1978-82). Was praised in writing as "articulate, aggressive, and knowledgeable" as a pilot and team leader.

AIRCRAFT EXPERTISE & FLIGHT TIME

Have flown UH-1H (Huey), AH-1S (Cobra), and AH-64 (Apache) helicopters.
* Am a certified instructor pilot for the AH-64 aircraft.
Operate TH-1S Pilot Night Vision System and a wide range of radio equipment.
Logged 1,287 hours in rotary-wing aircraft with 1,000 as pilot-in-command.

EDUCATION

B.S. in Education, The Citadel, Charleston, SC, 1977.
Completed Hughes Helicopter's AH-64 Production Planners' Course, 1984.

PERSONAL

Knowledgeable of future Department of Defense helicopter needs. Top Secret clearance.

Date

Exact Name of Person
Title or Position
Name of Company
Address (no., street)
Address (city, state, zip)

Dear Exact Name of Person: (or Dear Sir or Madam if answering a blind ad.)

I would appreciate an opportunity to talk with you soon about how I could contribute to your organization through my practical experience in law enforcement. As you will see from my resume, I offer a record of exceptional performance during 9 1/2 years with the Milwaukee (Wisconsin) Police Department.

During my years of service as a Police Officer in this city of approximately 750,000 people, I earned the respect of my superiors, peers, and members of the community for my dedication to excellence in every aspect of my responsibilities. I was often singled out for difficult and sensitive assignments in recognition of my exceptional communication skills and ability to deal with any situation through my fair but firm manner. During one eight-month period in 1987-88, I worked as an Undercover Narcotics Enforcement Officer, and I participated in activities which resulted in closing 25 inner-city drug houses.

I have demonstrated that I work well under pressure, can follow directions from superiors and official guidelines, and also use my own common sense and intelligence to take charge and make decisions. Additionally I offer excellent public relations abilities and understand the importance of maintaining a strong community presence.

I left the law enforcement field to try to reach another of my career goals and completed rigorous training to become a U.S. Army warrant officer aviator. Literally tens of thousands of applications are received each year and only 750 of the most highly qualified applicants are chosen for this training program. I am very proud to have completed this training and earned a position as a helicopter pilot and military officer.

I feel that through my success in these demanding roles, I have proven my adaptability and versatility. Both professions require a person to think on his feet and handle crisis situations on a daily basis. I feel that I offer a unique mix of abilities which could make me a valuable addition to an organization such as yours.

I hope you will welcome my call soon to arrange a brief meeting at your convenience to discuss your current and future needs and how I might serve them. Thank you in advance for your time.

Sincerely yours,

Masters McLaughlin

Alternate last paragraph:
I hope you will call or write me soon to suggest a time convenient for us to meet and discuss your current and future needs and how I might serve them. Thank you in advance for your time.

MASTERS MCLAUGHLIN
1110 ½ Hay Street, Fayetteville, NC 28305   (910) 483-6611

OBJECTIVE

To offer my exceptional communication and motivational skills to an organization that can use a mature professional who has excelled in the demanding fields of law enforcement and aviation through demonstrated intellectual skills and an aggressive, enthusiastic personality.

EXPERIENCE

AVIATOR/TRAINING PILOT and **OPERATIONS MANAGER**. U.S. Army, Ft. Bragg, NC (1990-present), Am excelling as a professional aviator operating a million-dollar aircraft: plan, coordinate, and carry out assigned missions as the senior member of an air crew operating under an 18-hour notice as part of the rapid deployment forces.
* Chosen to train and supervise a 16-person Nuclear/Biological/Chemical (NBC) defense team; provided specialized proficiency training to a 45-person company, earning commendable — the highest possible — ratings in two consecutive inspections.
* Oversee the physical security for $20 million worth of equipment.
* Placed third in a 9mm team pistol competition.

Served with distinction as a Police Officer known for my common sense approach and high moral values. Was effective in relating to people from diverse ethnic and cultural backgrounds by taking charge when the situation demanded, Milwaukee, WI:
POLICE OFFICER. (1984-90). Often singled out for highly sensitive and particularly demanding jobs, handled a range of activities including accident and crime investigations, enforcement of state and local laws, domestic dispute response and intervention, and "first responder" for first aid and emergency situations.
* Applied my public speaking skills while giving testimony in criminal and traffic court.
* Received special recognition for saving the life of a man whose clothing caught fire in his yard — smothered the flames and treated him for shock until the ambulance arrived.
* Contributed to the police department's public image while coaching neighborhood youth in Police Athletic League competition.

UNDERCOVER NARCOTICS ENFORCEMENT OFFICER. (1987-88). Handpicked for this sensitive assignment, spent approximately eight months on teams which executed search warrants resulting in the shut down of more than 25 inner-city drug houses.
* Received training in specialized techniques which included "sting" operations, the use of personal listening devices (wires), undercover narcotics purchases, and surveillance.
* Developed cases through informants and received additional training in chemical testing from the state's crime lab.

POLICE AIDE. (1980-84). After placing first from among 300 applicants, at age 17 was accepted for this position which gave me the opportunity to learn about the daily routines and inner workings of the department.
* Gained experience in areas such as fingerprinting and in-processing prisoners.
* Provided administrative assistance during medical exams for applicants and by maintaining medical records for applicants being processed into the department.
* Conducted warrant queries for street officers and maintained files of criminal warrants.

EDUCATION & TRAINING

B.S., Criminal Justice, Mount Senario College, Ladysmith, WI, 1989.
* Graduated *magna cum laude* with a 3.89 GPA.
Completed more than 4,800 hours of advanced programs including flight training and warrant officer professional development schools as well as law enforcement courses in training and evaluation techniques, narcotics identification, and radar speed detection.

LICENSES & SPECIAL SKILLS

FAA Commercial Pilot license, rotorcraft helicopter/ instrument helicopter, 1991.
"Law Enforcement Officer" certification, Wisconsin Law Enforcement Standards Board, 1984.
Am an experienced field training officer and undercover narcotics agent familiar with surveillance search warrants, sting operations, and undercover purchases from suspects.
Qualified as an Expert with the M-16 rifle and 9mm pistol.

PERSONAL

Offer approximately 900 accident-free flight hours in the UH-1H Iroquois (Bell Huey) and in the Cessna 150 with 300 hours as pilot-in-command. Have a Secret security clearance.

Date

Dear Sir or Madam:

I would appreciate an opportunity to talk with you soon about how I could benefit your organization through my technical and mechanical skills in maintaining hydraulic and related electrical systems, airframes, and powerplant systems.

Pneudraulic systems expertise

While serving my country in the U.S. Air Force, I have acquired extensive expertise in maintaining state-of-the-art pneudraulic systems on the B-52G, KC-135A, F-4G, and F-16C aircraft, including in-flight refueling systems. With a reputation as an hydraulic maintenance "expert," I offer superior skills in the use of schematics.

Airframe and powerplant maintenance know-how

After establishing myself as a pneudraulic systems specialist, I helped implement the Air Force's new Rivot Work Force maintenance program which expanded my duties to include airframe and powerplant maintenance for the F-4G. I have received written recognition of my outstanding supervisory skills and offer the ability to motivate a team for maximum efficiency.

You would find me to be a highly motivated worker with outstanding technical skills and the ability to maintain aircraft for safe flight.

I hope you will call or write me soon to suggest a time convenient for us to meet and discuss your current and future needs and how I might serve them. I will be in the Air Force until November 6, 1990. After I separate from the Air Force, I can be contacted at my home address which is on top of my resume.

Sincerely yours,

Raymond Stein

RAYMOND STEIN
1110½ Hay Street, Fayetteville, NC 28305   (910) 483-6611

OBJECTIVE

To contribute to an organization through my proven expertise in maintaining aircraft hydraulic and electrical systems, along with my technical and mechanical skills in airframe and powerplant maintenance.

LICENSE

Hold FAA Airframe and Powerplant License.

EXPERIENCE

PNEUDRAULIC SYSTEMS SPECIALIST/AIRCRAFT MECHANIC. U.S. Air Force, Germany (1987-90). Specialize in the maintenance, troubleshooting, and repair of state-of-the-art pneudraulic (hydraulic and pneumatic) systems while maintaining the airframe and powerplant systems for the sophisticated F-4G aircraft; perform preflight, thru-flight, and postflight checks.
   * Supervise up to 12 maintenance/repair professionals.
   * Maintain, troubleshoot, and repair in-flight refueling systems.
   * Inspect, make test runs, troubleshoot malfunctions, and replace components in engines; repair structural/mechanical airframe damage.
   * Have maintained some of the Air Force's most advanced hydraulic systems on both the McDonald Douglas F-4G and the General Dynamics F-16C aircraft.
   * After earning a reputation as a pneudraulic systems specialist, took part in the Air Force's new Rivot Work Force maintenance system which increased my duties to include airframe and powerplant maintenance.
   * Described in writing as an "hydraulic specialist, engine specialist, and crew chief, all in one," acquired expert skills on F-4G aircraft.
   * Received a respected award for my skill in supervising personnel and "keeping the shop at its highest level."
   * Earned a reputation for outstanding skill in utilizing the schematics of hydraulic and electrical systems.
   * Placed first in a competition which rated the battle damage repair abilities of participants in both written and hands-on tests.
   * As an hydraulic systems expert, can troubleshoot and repair any hydraulic malfunction, whether on aircraft or other machinery; have experience in overhauling, rebuilding, and operating test stands in-shop.

AIRCRAFT PNEUDRAULIC SYSTEMS TECHNICIAN. U.S. Air Force, (1986-87). Refined my skills in the inspection, maintenance, and repair of pneudraulic systems working on the Boeing B-52G and KC-135A aircraft; inspected and maintained all systems including in-flight refueling systems.

ADVANCED TECHNICAL TRAINING

Completed U.S.A.F. college-level training courses including these (1986-88):
Aircraft Pneudraulic Systems Mechanic Course (403 hours).
In-flight Refueling Systems Mechanic Course (86 hours).
   * Was **Honor Graduate** from this course.
Aircraft Pneudraulic Repair Technician Course (KC-135) (132 hours).
Aircraft Pneudraulic Repair Technician Course (F-16) (76 hours).
Aircraft Pneudraulic Repair Technician Course (F-4) (84 hours).
Aircraft Battle Damage Repair Technician Course (60 hours).

PERSONAL

Have a working knowledge of German and Spanish. Hold Secret security clearance. Pride myself in maintaining aircraft for safe flight. Take the initiative. Known for my versatile skills and positive attitude.

Date

Exact Name of Person
Title or Position
Name of Company
Address (no., street)
Address (city, state, zip)

Dear Exact Name of Person: (or Dear Sir or Madam if answering a blind ad.)

Can you use a talented and skilled computer technician who offers a strong background in the installation, repair, and servicing of both hardware and software systems?

Offering an eight-year history of accomplishments while serving my country in the U.S. Army, I have been awarded two achievement medals and numerous certificates of appreciation for my professionalism, technical abilities, and dedication to excellence.

My experience covers IBM, Unisys, Unix, Everex, Hewlett Packard, and Memorex Telex equipment. I have a broad base on which to build and continue to learn which includes inventory control, customer service, and training in addition to the practical technical skills.

I have been chosen to participate in several special projects including one in Puerto Rico where my team was sent to connect a computer network with one in the U.S. We had to install phone lines and configure dedicated lines for the transmission of information through a satellite system. The project required three days of intense efforts but was completed successfully. On another occasion I was involved in disassembling a complete microcomputer system, moving it from one city to another, and then reassembling it.

I feel that my attention to detail and insistence on getting the job done right from the beginning are among my most valuable qualities. I am known for my punctuality and ability to get along with others.

I hope you will welcome my call soon to arrange a brief meeting at your convenience to discuss your current and future needs and how I might serve them. Thank you in advance for your time.

Sincerely yours,

Terry Spell

Alternate last paragraph:
I hope you will call or write me soon to suggest a time convenient for us to meet and discuss your current and future needs and how I might serve them. Thank you in advance for your time.

TERRY SPELL
1110 ½ Hay Street, Fayetteville, NC 28305   (910) 483-6611

OBJECTIVE

To apply my excellent technical skills related to the installation, servicing, and repair of computer hardware and software to an organization that can benefit from my attention to detail, dedication, and ability to relate to and work well with others.

TECHNICAL EXPERTISE

Offer expertise in the operation, maintenance, and repair of computer systems including:
Memorex Telex cluster controllers and terminals   IBM cluster controllers
Racal-Milgo, Codex, and Unisys modems   Everex PCs
Hewlett Packard and Honeywell systems   IBM mainframes, dumb terminals, PCs, monitors
Unisys PCs, printers, spurs, cluster controllers, monitors, and minicomputers
Install all types of software including, but not limited to, the following:
WordPerfect Windows Norton Antivirus dBase IV Lotus PowerPoint Excel
Skilled in troubleshooting internal logic of the Theater Army Medical Material Information System (TAMMIS).
Offer basic knowledge of programming in Bourne Shell Scripting, JCL, and C languages.
Familiar with viruses, virus prevention, and notification to users to prevent contamination.

EXPERIENCE

Gained a reputation as a dependable and highly skilled computer technician, U.S. Army:
HARDWARE SPECIALIST. Germany (1994-95). Selected for a position usually held by a more experienced professional, achieved error-free control over issuing and receipt of a $70,000 inventory of computer equipment while training and supervising technicians.
*   Disposed of 75% of the organization's outdated, obsolete equipment.
*   Installed, troubleshot, repaired, and upgraded PC hardware and software.

MINICOMPUTER SYSTEM OPERATOR. Germany (1992-94). Handled activities ranging from installing, operating, and performing unit-level maintenance for a multi-user information system, to controlling input/output data, to taking care of bulk data storage operations.
*   Earned recognition as a key contributor to the smooth transition to a new medical management information system at the Army's Medical Material Center for Europe: the new system greatly improved the efficiency of supply operations and customer service.
*   Acted as an Assistant Instructor to train and provide guidance for operations personnel and applied my knowledge by preparing and carrying out lesson plans and outlines.
*   Was chosen to handle a project to disassemble a complete minicomputer system, move it to a location in another city, and reassemble it.

NETWORK TECHNICIAN and **SYSTEMS ANALYST.** Ft. McPherson, GA (1989-91). Was cited for my adaptability in learning procedures for connecting networks and troubleshooting problems while maintaining multiple mainframes.
*   Gained experience in customer service and fault isolation for circuit continuity.
*   Monitored system access and use to insure security for information.
*   Handpicked for a special project, traveled to Puerto Rico to connect computer systems: installed phone lines and configured dedicated line modems so that information could be received and transmitted through a satellite system.
*   Provided critical logistical support for humanitarian and military missions including the war in the Middle East, Somalia, and Rwanda.

COMPUTER OPERATOR. Ft. McPherson, GA (1987-89). Learned the importance of providing fast and efficient customer service while processing programmer and customer requests and input/output information for customers.
*   Maintained critical backup information in support of six mainframe computers.
*   Guaranteed that work was completed on schedule by working 12-hour shifts to overcome the problems of personnel shortages.

EDUCATION & TRAINING

Earned certification as a Computer/Machine Operator from the U.S. Army education system and completed training programs in the following areas:
Microsoft Word for Windows   electronic mail
WordPerfect for the Office and WordPerfect 5.1   German language and culture
applications software — hardware operations and system concepts
Completed college-level courses in Sociology and English while in Germany.

PERSONAL

Hold Secret security clearance. Was awarded two achievement medals and numerous certificates.

Date

Exact Name of Person
Title or Position
Name of Company
Address (number and street)
Address (city, state, and ZIP)

Dear Exact Name of Person: (or Dear Sir or Madam if answering a blind as.)

I would appreciate an opportunity to talk with you soon about how I could contribute to your organization through my technical expertise, wide base of knowledge in the electronics field, and supervisory abilities.

As you will see from my enclosed resume, I have been singled out for advanced technical training and promoted within the field of electronics warfare systems testing, repair, maintenance, and operation. My troubleshooting abilities have been applied in military intelligence organizations where response times were critical and equipment had to be kept up continuously and downtime virtually eliminated. I am skilled in rapidly learning new procedures and in finding ways to increase productivity and reduce operating costs. For instance, while in Korea I earned two achievement medals for my professionalism and dedication and saved the government over $1,688,000 by locating excess equipment inventories and arranging for their return.

I am especially interested in applying my abilities in repair and troubleshooting to an organization that can benefit from my experience in testing and my knowledge of electronic theory as well as my experience in reviewing and making recommendations on circuitry changes. I am experienced in using test equipment such as oscilloscopes, logic and test probes, and calibrators.

I hope you will welcome my call soon to arrange a brief meeting at your convenience to discuss your current and future needs and how I might serve them. Thank you in advance for your time.

Sincerely yours.

Ernest Leland Snider

Alternate last paragraph:
I hope you will call or write me soon to suggest a time convenient for us to meet and discuss your current and future needs and how I might serve them. Thank you in advance for your time.

ERNEST LELAND SNIDER

1110½ Hay Street, Fayetteville, NC 28305   (910) 483-6611

OBJECTIVE

To contribute to an organization that can use an adaptable quick learner who offers well-developed troubleshooting and technical electronics skills along with the ability to motivate others through my dedication and personal drive to succeed.

EXPERIENCE

Refined my technical skills and leadership abilities while building a strong base of experience in the specialized field of electronic warfare systems maintenance, U.S. Army:

SUPERVISORY ELECTRONIC WARFARE SYSTEM REPAIR TECHNICIAN. Korea (1993-95). Earned the praise and respect of my superiors for my diligence and technical skills displayed while finding ways to improve productivity and reduce repair turnaround time as the supervisor of six technical specialists in a military intelligence organization.

* Implemented a direct support repair section capable of completing component-level deficiencies, thereby eliminating the need to send numerous parts out for repair.
* On my own initiative, became cross trained in the repair of radar systems.
* Supervised the repair and maintenance of over 25 types of microwave, satellite, fiber optics, and high frequency systems.
* Provided security and access to more than $500,000 worth of communications security (COMSEC) materials; became skilled in repairing cryptoanalysis equipment.
* Gained exposure to the functional areas of personnel management, administration of shop and work area activities, quality control, and supply requisitioning.
* Was awarded two achievement medals for dedication and for efforts which resulted in a $1,688,000 savings for the government by reducing excess equipment inventories.
* Received a certificate of appreciation for my "exceptional efforts" in training personnel to a high level of competence in preparing for and presenting a fall 1995 seminar.

ELECTRONICS TECHNICIAN and **SHOP FOREMAN.** Ft. Irwin, CA (1991-93). Became proficient in activities necessary for the smooth operation of a military intelligence company while learning procedures for collecting vital information and for operation, maintenance, and repair procedures for surveillance, microwave, and computer equipment.

* Repaired a wide range of electronic warfare systems equipment including the following:

Trailblazers	Turkey 32	OG-181 ASAS	
Trojan	REMBASS radar	PPS-A5 radar	I-METS
CCS — Central Communication System		fiber optics	AN\TLQ-17

EDUCATION & TRAINING

Am studying **Electronic Digital Repair,** Fayetteville Technical Community College, NC. Attended specialized training programs including a one-year course (equivalent to 45 semester hours) for electronics Excelled in additional training including a professional leadership development course and earned certificates in state-of-the-art common and classified electronic warfare systems.

TECHNICAL EXPERTISE

Troubleshoot, test, repair, modify, operate, and maintain electronic equipment such as:
Radars: PPS-5A, REMBASS, and I-REMBASS
Satellite: Motorola LST5; Trojan Spirit I and II; Trojan Classic
Jamming equipment: AN/TLQ-17A
Direction finding equipment: Trailblazer (AN/TSQ-175), Tiger, Turkey 32, AN\TSQ-128
ASAS — All Source Analysis Systems
CCS — Central Communication System
Computer peripheral devices: UGC-144, Hewlett Packard, Sony
Other: high, very high, ultrahigh, and microwave receivers; narrow band recorders/ reproducers; tactical antennas, antenna control units, and radio frequency switches.

* Make detailed tests using equipment including voltmeters, ohmmeters, oscilloscopes, signal generators, power meters, spectrum analyzers, and other testing devices.
* Conduct electrical and mechanical tests using wiring diagrams, signal flow charts, technical manuals, troubleshooting charts, and other aids.
* Apply principles and theories of electrical circuitry, engineering mathematics, and physics as well as reviewing and recommending changes in circuitry of equipment.

CLEARANCE

Hold a Top Secret security clearance with SBI.

PERSONAL

Enjoy applying my technical skills while repairing amplifiers, VCRs, and other electronics devices.

Date

Exact Name of Person
Title or Position
Name of Company
Address (no., street)
Address (city, state, zip)

Dear Exact Name of Person: (or Dear Sir or Madam if answering a blind ad.)

Can you use an electronics technician with experience in specialized areas of robotics and electromechanical devices? I also offer a reputation as a mature young professional who can be counted on to get the job done and to motivate others to follow my own high performance standards.

When you look at my resume you will see that I have earned a reputation as a highly skilled technician. Consistently selected for critical leadership roles, I have been very successful both as a team player and leader during my years of service to my country in the U.S. Coast Guard. In my most recent role I was the direct supervisor of four electronics technicians and of up to 28 people involved in operating and maintaining sophisticated weapons systems.

My military experience allowed me the opportunity to gain five years in electronics troubleshooting and four years of simultaneous experience in microminiature soldering and repair. I excelled in advanced technical training programs and completed more than 3,680 hours in such programs as electronics, troubleshooting electromechanical systems, soldering and circuit board repair, and computer diagnosis/maintenance/repair as well as law enforcement.

I hope you will welcome my call soon to arrange a brief meeting at your convenience to discuss your current and future needs and how I might serve them. Thank you in advance for your time.

Sincerely yours,

Michael V. Rowe III

Alternate last paragraph:
I hope you will call or write me soon to suggest a time convenient for us to meet and discuss your current and future needs and how I might serve them. Thank you in advance for your time.

MICHAEL V. ROWE III
1110½ Hay Street, Fayetteville, NC   (910) 483-6611

OBJECTIVE

To offer excellent technical skills to an organization that can use a talented young professional with experience in the specialized areas of robotics and electromechanical devices as well as the ability to accept challenges and lead others to achieve outstanding results.

EXPERIENCE

Earned a reputation as a trustworthy, honest, and reliable young professional who could be counted on to get the job done while setting an example for others, U.S. Coast Guard:
TECHNICAL SUPERVISOR. Seattle, WA (1993-95). Used my knowledge and skills to find ways to improve and streamline procedures and reduce costs while supervising up to 28 people involved in the operation and maintenance of sophisticated weapons systems.

* Initiated a technical assistance program, which when approved and put into operation throughout the Coast Guard resulted in a $220,000 annual savings.
* Reduced downtime an impressive 35% through my suggestions for revamping maintenance procedures.
* Was singled out for leadership of a security force based on the U.S.'s command ship during the sensitive situation in Haiti and Cuba in 1994.
* Guided my team of security specialists to win a meritorious unit award for their accomplishments in Haiti.
* Supervised four technicians as the electronics shop foreman.
* Ranked first out of 53 technicians and earned 26 points more than the next highest grade on a test used to make decisions on career advancement and promotions.

ELECTRONICS TECHNICIAN. Honolulu, HI (1991-93). Applied my technical skills and eye for detail as the unit's leading microminiature soldering and repair technician.
* Provided leadership to other specialists in the operation and maintenance of high-tech weapons systems.
* Became proficient as a shop technician as well as a field service technician.

HONOR GUARD. Alexandria, VA (1988-89). Was handpicked to represent the Coast Guard as a member of the Presidential Honor Guard, one of the most elite assignments available.
* Participated in events at the White House, Tomb of the Unknown Soldier, the Pentagon, and in parades throughout the country.
* Placed in the top four of 200 people in consideration for this honor: selection criteria included appearance, stamina, and the ability to command and lead others.

TECHNICAL KNOWLEDGE

Through experience and training, offer the ability to troubleshoot and repair to the component level certain parts of the Navy 2M program, the MK-15 Phalanx close-in weapon system, and the MK-92 gun fire control system as well as the AN/UYK-7 computer.
Am thoroughly familiar with every item of test equipment used by the U.S. military including:

spectrum analyzers	oscilloscopes	voltmeters
signal generators	multimeters	power meters
frequency counters	electronic counters	fluke meters

TRAINING

Completed in excess of 3,680 hours of specialized technical training in programs such as:
basic and advanced electronics — 1,440 hrs.
electronic troubleshooting/basic and advanced electromechanical systems — 1,120 hrs.
law enforcement (maritime speciality) — 480 hrs.
basic and advanced soldering and circuit board repair — 320 hrs.
advanced computer diagnosis, maintenance, and repair — 320 hrs.

CLEARANCE

Was entrusted with a Top Secret security clearance with White House access.

PERSONAL

Have a strong personal drive to succeed. Adapt easily and quickly to new or rapidly changing circumstances. Consistently earned selection for the tough jobs.

Date

Exact Name of Person
Title or Position
Name of Company
Address (no., street)
Address (city, state, zip)

Dear Exact Name of Person: (or Dear Sir or Madam if answering a blind ad.)

I would appreciate an opportunity to talk with you soon about how I could contribute to your organization through my experience in supervision and inspection along with my expertise in copper and fiber optic cable installation, splicing, and termination.

As you will see from my resume, I have supervised teams on projects worldwide while planning, directing, and inspecting the repair and installation of copper and fiber optic cable systems. I am well known for my ability to figure out resourceful solutions for "impossible" problems. On numerous fiber optic installation jobs, I creatively overcame problems related to unavailable material, underground conduit systems, inexperienced personnel, and constantly changing customer requirements. I was described in writing as "the most outstanding team chief deployed to Desert Storm" during the war in the Middle East, where I was specially selected to supervise the most critical installations supporting air operations. On many projects I have averted potential work stoppages by fabricating missing parts and modifying others not meeting design specifications.

Although I have excelled in supervisory positions and in positions as a quality assurance inspector, I am equally comfortable in "hands-on" technical jobs if your organization is in need of a technical expert who can produce quality work with little or no supervision. A single person who has lived and worked all over the world, I am willing to relocate and travel as your needs require. I am a flexible person who thrives on new challenges. Confident of my ability to rapidly master emerging technologies, I would also welcome new training opportunities. I can provide excellent personal and professional references upon request.

I hope you will welcome my call soon to arrange a brief meeting at your convenience to discuss your current and future needs and how I might serve them. Thank you in advance for your time.

Sincerely yours,

George V. Whitfield

Alternate last paragraph:
I hope you will call or write me soon to suggest a time convenient for us to meet and discuss your current and future needs and how I might serve them. Thank you in advance for your time.

GEORGE V. WHITFIELD

1110½ Hay Street, Fayetteville, NC   (910) 483-6611

OBJECTIVE

To benefit an organization that can use a talented electronics professional who offers experience as a supervisor and inspector along with expertise in copper core and fiber optic cable installation, splicing, termination, and testing.

EXPERIENCE

ELECTRONICS TEAM CHIEF. U.S. Air Force, Griffiss AFB, NY (1991-95). On projects worldwide, supervised installation teams of eight to 24 people while planning, directing, and inspecting repair/installation of copper and fiber optic cable systems.
* Supervised 16 separate installations, and completed each one on time, within budget, and without a single deficiency during quality assurance inspections.
* While directing the simultaneous installation of six fiber optic cable projects, saved $100,000 in penalty costs by completing the projects in minimum time.
* Produced a cost savings of nearly $12,000 by saving 3,470 labor hours during the installation of more than 80,000 ft. of fiber optic cable.
* On one project, averted a potential work stoppage by fabricating missing parts and modifying others not meeting design specifications.
* Was named *Team Chief of the Year* for organizing and supervising several high-impact fiber optic installations with very tight deadlines.
* Described in writing as "the most outstanding team chief deployed to Desert Storm" during the war in the Middle East, was specially selected to supervise the most critical installations supporting air operations in several countries; played a key role behind the scenes in the U.S. display of air superiority.
* On large fiber optic installation jobs, creatively overcame problems related to back-ordered material, underground conduit systems, inexperienced personnel, and constantly changing customer requirements by researching material substitutes, engineering changes in cable route/repairing duct system, and prioritizing contractor requirements.

ELECTRONICS INSTALLATION CHIEF & INSPECTOR. USAF, Germany (1987-90). Named *Team Chief of the Year* for completing microwave antenna installations supporting the European long-haul link while planning, directing, and inspecting the installation of communications cable and antenna systems throughout Europe; trained and supervised teams with between six and 14 people.
* Saved $32,000 while supervising a massive antenna/waveguide replacement on the tallest tower in Air Force inventory; although contractors' bids had specified a two-month project and a 12-person crew utilizing an elevator to transport personnel/equipment to the top, we completed the job with an eight-person crew in 45 days with the elevator inoperable.
* Monitored maintenance of tools, vehicles, and heavy equipment.
* Engineered and implemented additional requirements at customers' request.

CABLE/ANTENNA MAINTENANCE TECHNICIAN. USAF, Vandenberg AFB, CA (1986). Developed and trained personnel in performing a preventive maintenance schedule that resulted in zero down time for all missile launch facilities.
* Was responsible for maintaining, troubleshooting, and repairing telephone and coaxial cable as well as UHF, VHF, HF, and microwave antennas.
* Trained maintenance personnel to use special purpose vehicles, thereby ensuring that quick reaction repair was flawless.
* Was named *Team Member of the Year* for my technical expertise and professionalism.

ELECTRONICS INSTALLATION TEAM MEMBER. USAF, worldwide (1980-85). Directed numerous on-site operations installing buried and underground cable systems.
* Identified problems with proposed cable routes and engineered changes.
* Installed, repaired, and removed outside plant telephone and antenna systems.
* Managed a project in New Mexico where experimental trenchers were being tested; trained personnel installing 32,000 ft. of buried cable in solid granite.

EDUCATION & PROFICIENCIES

Completed extensive college-level programs of instruction related to communications cable installation and splicing, fiber optics, and team supervision.

Proficient with test equipment such as Fiber Optic TDR, power meters, analyzers, fault locators, TDRs for copper cable, multimeters, and meggars.

Proficient in operating trenchers, boom trucks, winch trucks, backhoes, front loaders, cable plows, bull dozers, boring machines, cable reel trucks, cable trailers, and cranes.

PERSONAL

Proven ability to overcome engineering deficiencies and anticipate potential problems.

Date

Exact Name of Person
Title or Position
Name of Company
Address (no., street)
Address (city, state, zip)

Dear Exact Name of Person: (or Dear Sir or Madam if answering a blind ad.)

I would appreciate an opportunity to talk with you soon about how I could contribute to your organization through my versatile managerial and technical skills.

While serving my country in the U.S. Army, I have excelled in managing projects, people, and finances while earning a reputation as a sensitive supervisor who could "bring out the best in others." Through my experience as a mid-level manager, I have been involved in behavior, career, safety, and performance counseling, and I became known for my ability to positively impact the morale and productivity of employees working for me.

In addition to my effective management style, I offer a range of technical skills and knowledge which includes experience in supervising the installation and maintenance of multichannel radio operations. I have become skilled in managing production operations in environments where safety is a major consideration at all times. In my current job supervising 18 people operating and maintaining information transmissions systems, I have led my employees to maintain a perfect safety record. I recently received HAZMAT training and am knowledgeable of OSHA requirements.

You would find me in person to be a congenial individual who has an ability to establish rapport with people at all organizational levels.

I hope you will welcome my call soon to arrange a brief meeting at your convenience to discuss your current and future needs and how I might serve them. Thank you in advance for your time.

Sincerely yours,

Charles Hayward

Alternate last paragraph:
I hope you will call or write me soon to suggest a time convenient for us to meet and discuss your current and future needs and how I might serve them. Thank you in advance for your time.

CHARLES HAYWARD

1110½ Hay Street, Fayetteville, NC 28305   (910) 483-6611

OBJECTIVE

To benefit an organization that can use a skilled supervisor with an ability to sensitively manage human resources while solving stubborn problems related to production operations, employee training, strategic planning, inventory control, and financial accountability.

EDUCATION

Completing B.S. degree in Criminal Justice, Fayetteville State University (a campus of the University of North Carolina); degree expected in 1996.
Earned A.S. degree in Criminal Justice, Central Texas College, 1995.
Excelled in U.S. Army courses which refined my security and electronics knowledge as well as my analytical, supervisory, operations management, and strategic thinking skills.
* Earned Certificates in Security Management and Supervisory Management.
* Received HAZMAT training; became knowledgeable of OSHA.

CLEARANCE

Possess Secret security clearance; can pass rigorous background investigation.

EXPERIENCE

INFORMATION SYSTEMS SUPERVISOR & PRODUCTION MANAGER. U.S. Army, Ft. Bragg, NC (1993-present). Supervise 18 people involved in operating and maintaining information transmissions systems supporting the needs of the XVIII Airborne Corps; account for $3 million in equipment that includes vehicles, power generators, antenna systems, communications security (COMSEC) devices, and related radio signal equipment.

* Oversee the installation, operation, and maintenance of Mobile Subscriber Equipment (MSE), Line of Sight (LOS) radio systems, and radio communications networks.
* Am known for my emphasis on safety and training; am proud of my organization's perfect safety record and its expertly trained personnel.
* Am widely respected for my ability to train, motivate, and manage people; am skilled at listening to and counseling employees and resolving conflicts between individual needs and organizational goals.
* Write/distribute a wide range of production control documents, technical reports, and administrative records; both orally and in writing, evaluate the performance of associates who report to me.
* Planned, implemented, and supervised technical and tactical training programs to ensure expert technical proficiency of all employees.
* Have improved the attitude and morale of many people as their supervisor; have a knack for "bringing out the best in others" and believe strongly in leadership by example.

TEAM CHIEF. U.S. Army, Ft. Bragg, NC (1984-92). Managed a team of nine employees installing, operating, and performing maintenance on radio systems, antenna systems, power generation equipment, and multiplexing equipment including COMSEC devices.

* Received the prestigious Bronze Star Medal for service in the Gulf War (Desert Storm).
* Was involved in behavior, career, safety, and performance counseling; referred people for specialized alcohol and drug counseling, financial counseling, and family counseling.

Other experience: Received the highest evaluations of my performance and character as a multichannel communications equipment operator; was singled out for rapid promotion because of demonstrated management potential, and advanced quickly to Team/Section Chief.

COMPUTERS

Am proficient in using software for word processing; completed formal computer programming training in BASIC and COBOL.

PERSONAL

Can provide exceptionally strong references. Truly enjoy the challenge of helping young people develop to their fullest potential. Have an ability to establish rapport with people.

Date

Exact Name of Person
Title or Position
Name of Company
Address (no., street)
Address (city, state, zip)

Dear Exact Name of Person: (or Dear Sir or Madam if answering a blind ad.)

I would appreciate an opportunity to talk with you soon about how I could benefit your organization through my proven management ability as well as my extensive experience and formal education in information systems.

While serving my country in the U.S. Army, I have excelled in a "track record" of achievements in increasing the quality and efficiency of computer operations. Most recently I "turned around" a troubled organization into one cited as the "standard" for training. While implementing the organization's first computer system, I streamlined operations and dramatically improved the quality of vital intelligence reports. With a B.A. degree in Computer Science, I am pursuing graduate work in Information Systems Management.

Previously I refined my skills in information systems planning while implementing a system for an Army base in Germany. With a Top Secret SI clearance with SBI, I offer a strong knowledge of our nation's intelligence procedures and needs as well as experience in supervising the translation of Russian materials into English.

You would find me to be a dedicated professional with excellent written and oral communication skills as well as the ability to motivate workers and increase efficiency and productivity in any organization.

I hope you will welcome my call soon to arrange a brief meeting at your convenience to discuss your current and future needs and how I might serve them. Thank you in advance for your time.

Sincerely yours,

Marshall Henry, Jr.

Alternate last paragraph:
I hope you will call or write me soon to suggest a time convenient for us to meet and discuss your current and future needs and how I might serve them. Thank you in advance for your time.

MARSHALL HENRY, JR.

1110½ Hay Street, Fayetteville, NC 28305   (910) 483-6611

OBJECTIVE

To benefit an organization that can use a dedicated professional offering proven management ability and communication skills along with "hands-on" experience and formal education in information systems management.

CLEARANCE, LANGUAGES

Hold TOP SECRET SI security clearance with SBI.
Offer knowledge of Russian and German.

EDUCATION

Pursuing Master's degree in **Information Systems Management**, University of Southern California.
Earned B.A. degree in **Computer Science**, University of Maryland, 1986.
Received FCC General Radio Telephone License, Cleveland Institute of Electronics, 1986.
Completed other training in computer operations and management.
Excelled in advanced Russian language studies, Defense Language Institute, CA.

EXPERIENCE

ELECTRONIC OPERATIONS CHIEF. U.S. Army, Key West, FL (1987-present). Was handpicked for this job because of my expert understanding of the global intelligence community and products; supervised the introduction of this organization's first computer systems while managing 54 personnel involved in round-the-clock computer and electronics operations; provided electronic links with the Navy and Air Force.

Extensive
Expertise
in
the
Management
of
Information
Systems

* Led this "troubled" organization to set new training standards.
* Perform long-range planning for military intelligence operations, training programs, and computer operations.
* Dramatically improved organizational reporting: transformed reports containing data described as "untrustworthy and of little value."
* Streamlined operations while maximizing limited human and equipment resources.
* Increased employees' scores on knowledge tests by 25%.
* In a part-time **computer operator** job, train personnel to perform night-time computer operations on a mainframe computer.

COMPUTER SYSTEMS ACQUISITION MANAGER. U.S. Army, Germany (1985-86). Played a key role in designing and implementing an information systems plan for this major Army base; supervised computer professionals while coordinating and documenting changes to the existing system and planning integration for over 30 systems.
* Received a prestigious medal while earning a reputation as an "expert" on the interrelation of systems, data, and personnel.

RUSSIAN TRANSLATION SUPERVISOR. U.S. Army, Germany (1983-85). Oversaw a team of 26 intelligence professionals using a computer-based system to translate and transcribe Russian materials into English.
* Introduced the use of a data base for training.

COMPUTER OPERATIONS SUPERVISOR. U.S. Army, Hunter Army Airfield, GA (1981-83). Earned a reputation as an outstanding manager and technician while supervising 35 personnel using computer-based military intelligence systems.

Other U.S. Army experience: Used military intelligence computers.

COMPUTER SKILLS

Operate Data General Eclipse and Wang Alliance System as well as numerous U.S. military intelligence and other computers.

PERSONAL

Have the ability to evaluate data and develop plans. Known for my excellent written and oral communication skills. Believe in giving "110%" in any job.

Date

Exact Name of Person
Title or Position
Name of Company
Address (no., street)
Address (city, state, zip)

Dear Exact Name of Person: (or Dear Sir or Madam if answering a blind ad.)

I would appreciate an opportunity to talk with you soon about how I could contribute to your organization through my skills and experience related to communications.

While serving my country in the U.S. Army, I was promoted ahead of my peers and selected for numerous difficult assignments which required an excellent planner and decision maker who could safely organize and manage difficult projects. In one job as a Network Switching System Chief, I tested and fielded a new communications package and then wrote the Standard Operating Procedures for the system. In other jobs as a radio section chief, I managed teams of people while supervising the installation, operation, and maintenance of radio systems, HF systems, data systems, and computer networks.

I have put my technical know-how and management skills to work for our country in numerous historic crises; for example, in Iraq, Panama, and Honduras I played a key role in managing radio communications during the U.S. intervention. I have completed extensive technical training related to network switching systems operations, wire systems installation and operation, and switchboard programming, maintenance, and interfacing.

With an unblemished safety record in managing high-risk projects ranging from air mobile and airborne operations to tricky installations and repairs, I have trained and supervised dozens of people and multimillion-dollar equipment including radios, antennas, computers, generators, computers, and tactical vehicles.

You would find me in person to be a congenial individual with an ability to work well with people at all levels of the organization and with the general public. I am known for reliability, integrity, and loyalty as well as high personal and professional standards.

I hope you will call or write me soon to suggest a time convenient for us to meet and discuss your current and future needs and how I might serve them. Thank you in advance for you time.

Sincerely yours,

Edmond Warren

Alternate last paragraph:
I hope you will welcome my call soon to arrange a brief meeting at your convenience to discuss your current and future needs and how I might serve them. Thank you in advance for your time.

EDMOND WARREN

1110 ½ Hay Street, Fayetteville, NC 28305   (910) 483-6611

OBJECTIVE

To contribute to an organization that can use a dedicated professional with exceptionally strong skills related to technical communications systems installation, operation, maintenance, and management as well as law enforcement and emergency operations.

COMPUTERS

Knowledgeable of popular software including Harvard Graphics, Formtool, dBase III, Prowrite, WordPerfect, and Freelance; offer the ability to rapidly master new software.

EXPERIENCE

COMMUNICATIONS CONSULTANT. U.S. Army, Ft. Bragg, NC (1994-95). Handpicked for this top-level advisory/planning role with a 750-person signal organization; used my communications background while planning and managing, with a perfect safety record, numerous high-risk airborne operations.
* While managing jumpmaster training, increased the number of jumpmasters by 25%.
* Stepped into a job which was outside my field and excelled through applying my planning and management skills.
* Planned the air and sea movement of people and assets to Haiti for the U.S. intervention called Operation Uphold Democracy.

NETWORK SWITCHING SYSTEM CHIEF. U.S. Army, Ft. Bragg, NC (1992-94). Within the same organization, received a promotion from **Team Chief** in charge of eight people to **Section Chief** of 15 people during this time period; was responsible for nearly $8 million in equipment.
* *Installation*: Supervised installation of two line-of-sight multichannel radio terminals, two small extension switches, and four generator sets.
* *Operations*: Operated multichannel radio terminals, single channel tactical satellite radios, extension switches, and generator sets.
* *Fielding/testing*: Fielded and tested the Secure Enroute Communications Package (SECOMP); then troubleshot and managed this communications system.
* *Writing and publishing*: Wrote the Standard Operating Procedures for SECOMP.
* *Perfect safety record*: Emphasis on safety resulted in no accidents or injuries.

TRAINING/OPERATIONS MANAGER. U.S. Army, Ft. Bragg, NC (1992). Handpicked by the commander for this job planning and administering the details of air mobile and airborne operations.
* Handled a heavy load of paperwork such as preparing training schedules, status reports of airborne and air mobile operations, and documentation related to employee training.
* Increased jumpmaster personnel by 33% and air movement personnel by 25%.

SINGLE-CHANNEL RADIO SECTION CHIEF. U.S. Army, Ft. Bragg, NC (1988-92). Received several medals during this time period, and was handpicked by top executives to manage numerous projects involving providing communications support during airborne operations.
* Managed teams of people while supervising the installation, operation, and maintenance of single-channel tactical satellite radio systems, high-frequency (HF) systems, data systems, and computer networks which supported the mission of the 82nd Airborne Division to be able to relocate within 18 hours on "no notice" to any point on the globe.
* Played a key management role during several historic crises; for example, managed radio communications during the ground assault in Iraq; managed communications for invasion forces during assault on Tocumen-Torrijos Airport in Panama; and managed the team that was "first in, last out" providing satellite radio support in Honduras when Sandinistas invaded from Nicaragua.

WIRE SYSTEM OPERATOR/TEAM CHIEF. U.S. Army, Ft. Bragg, NC (1985-87). Installed, operated, and maintained semiautomatic and automatic switchboards, telephone central offices and auxiliary equipment, and power generators; installed wire and cable, and constructed pole lines.

EDUCATION

Completed two years of college-level, state-of-the-art technical training related to network switching systems operations, wire systems installation and operation, and switchboard programming, maintenance, and interfacing.
Completed two years of college, General Studies, Rocky Mountain College, Billings, MT.

PERSONAL

Received numerous letters, awards, and medals while serving my country in the Army.

Date

Exact Name of Person
Title or Position
Name of Company
Address (no., street)
Address (city, state, zip)

Dear Exact Name of Person: (or Dear Sir or Madam if answering a blind ad.)

I would appreciate an opportunity to talk with you soon about how I could benefit your company through my expertise in managing telecommunications operations as well as my exceptionally strong planning, problem-solving, decision-making, and motivational skills.

As a Captain in the U.S. Army, I was recently handpicked to manage 30 highly experienced technicians installing and maintaining a state-of-the-art telecommunications system serving a 900-person organization as well as a residential/business community of 1,200 people. Because of my outstanding leadership and motivational skills, my team was rated "best" in its parent organization.

Previously managing a 42-person communications maintenance facility, I have routinely briefed top-level executives on communications needs, trends, and capabilities. Because of my expert planning skills, I was once selected to develop emergency radio network plans. I have excelled in extensive graduate-level training designed to enhance my telecommunications skills and management "know-how."

You would find me to be a highly motivated executive with the ability to set goals and motivate personnel to achieve them. I am familiar with the operation and troubleshooting of a wide range of equipment.

I hope you will welcome my call soon to arrange a brief meeting at your convenience to discuss your current and future needs and how I might serve them. Thank you in advance for your time.

Sincerely yours,

Robert Kearnes

Alternate last paragraph:
I hope you will call or write me soon to suggest a time convenient for us to meet and discuss your current and future needs and how I might serve them. Thank you in advance for your time.

ROBERT KEARNES
1110½ Hay Street, Fayetteville, NC 28305   (910) 483-6611

OBJECTIVE

To benefit an organization that can use an experienced leader who offers expertise in telecommunications operations management along with strong planning, problem-solving, decision-making, and motivational skills.

EXPERIENCE

TELECOMMUNICATIONS DISTRICT MANAGER. U.S. Army, Germany (1987-90). As a Captain in the U.S. Army, was handpicked to manage a 30-person operation installing and maintaining a telecommunications system serving a 900-person organization and a 2,000-person community; improved a communications link for teams operating along the German/Czechoslovakian border.
* Advised executives on needs, trends, and equipment capabilities.
* Led the operation rated as "best" in the parent organization.
* Earned a respected medal for managing communications operations with no downtime during a major training project.
* Coordinated the implementation of a computer system which is now being modified to provide "electronic mail" and other communications links.
* Was praised in writing for being "technically superior to senior officers" and for developing outstanding training/maintenance programs.

COMMUNICATIONS MAINTENANCE MANAGER. U.S. Army, Ft. Hood, TX (1986-87). Managed a 42-person, multimillion-dollar maintenance facility servicing 110 sets of communications equipment for a 550-person organization; briefed a general and other executives on equipment status.
* Achieved a 95% availability rate — highest in the parent organization.

RADIO COMMUNICATIONS CONSULTANT. U.S. Army, Ft. Hood, TX (1986). Developed plans for the implementation of emergency communications networks for an organization of 550 people; coordinated personnel training.
* Monitored and advised executives on the performance of new equipment.
* Was selected to lead a 90-person operation during a month-long training project; oversaw the installation and operation of all radio systems.
* Received a special medal and a "Distinguished Leader" award.

EXECUTIVE AIDE and **OPERATIONS MANAGER.** U.S. Army, Ft. Hood, TX (1984-86). Wore two managerial "hats" as the "right hand" of the administrator of a 130-person organization and as the training/operations manager for a 35-person organization operating $20 million of communications equipment.

COMMUNICATIONS FACILITY MANAGER. U.S. Army, Korea (1982-83). Was awarded a medal for my superb management of an organization of 55 people providing vital 24-hour communications links to strategic planners and managers; oversaw a remote microwave facility.

**EDUCATION
&
EXECUTIVE
DEVELOPMENT
TRAINING**

B.A. in Public Administration, California State University at San Jose, 1982.
Earned Certificates upon graduation from these graduate-level schools designed to advance the skills/knowledge of telecommunications executives:
* Combined Arms Services Staff School: quantitative analysis/problem solving and group/team management.
* Signal Officer Advanced Course: communications-electronics management.
* Communications-Electronics Staff Officer School: staff coordination.
* Signal Officer Course: communications management.

PERSONAL

Member, Armed Forces Communications & Electronics Association. Hold SECRET security clearance. Offer a reputation for outstanding employee management. Operate and troubleshoot equipment including radios, computers, antennas, COMSEC equipment, switching systems, and digital message devices.

Date

Exact Name of Person
Title or Position
Name of Company
Address (no., street)
Address (city, state, zip)

Dear Exact Name of Person: (or Dear Sir or Madam if answering a blind ad.)

I would appreciate an opportunity to talk with you soon about how I could benefit your organization through my expertise in installing, operating, and maintaining telecommunications equipment along with my abilities as a supervisor and motivator.

While serving my country in the U.S. Army, I currently oversee a team of three involved in installing, operating, and maintaining automated switchboard systems and analog telephone systems. I have earned distinguished commendations for my work, and I was awarded a respected medal for installing a communications system in the U.S. Virgin Islands after the Hurricane Hugo disaster. During training projects, I have installed systems in many countries worldwide and maintained vital links for U.S. forces in Panama during the December 1989 mission.

I am knowledgeable of many manual, semiautomatic, and automatic switchboard systems as well as telephone systems. I have had experience in the fielding of automatic circuits. Known for my leadership abilities, I was promoted ahead of my peers to supervisory responsibilities.

You would find me to be a dedicated professional who "keeps going" until the job is done.

I hope you will welcome my call soon to arrange a brief meeting at your convenience to discuss your current and future needs and how I might serve them. Thank you in advance for your time.

Sincerely yours,

William Lennon

Alternate last paragraph:
I hope you will call or write me soon to suggest a time convenient for us to meet and discuss your current and future needs and how I might serve them. Thank you in advance for your time.

WILLIAM LENNON

1110½ Hay Street, Fayetteville, NC 28305   (910) 483-6611

OBJECTIVE   To benefit an organization that can use a dedicated professional who offers skills in installing, operating, and maintaining telecommunications equipment along with the proven ability to train, supervise, and motivate others.

EXPERIENCE   **TELECOMMUNICATIONS SUPERVISOR.** U.S. Army, Ft. Bragg, NC (1988-90). Was promoted to supervise a team involved in installing, operating, and maintaining automated switchboard systems and analog telephone systems providing vital communications links for military executives.
* Use traffic diagrams and route bulletins to plan circuit connections.
* Correct communications security (COMSEC) violations; coordinate work schedules; maintain work logs.
* Act as liaison with radio communications operators.
* Program automatic switchboard systems.
* In less than three years advanced to corporal, an unusually rapid promotion to a rank reserved for professionals who demonstrate outstanding management potential, technical expertise, and strong judgement.
* Earned a distinguished medal for installing a communications system which restored order in the U.S. Virgin Islands after the Hurricane Hugo disaster.
* Maintained a vital communications link for strategic planners and military personnel during the United States mission to Panama in December 1989.
* Established and maintained communications links for countries including Egypt, Jordan, England, Honduras, and Costa Rica during training projects.
* Developed my skills in motivating personnel to "do the job right the first time" and counseled employees on professional and personal problems.

SWITCHBOARD INSTALLER/OPERATOR. U.S. Army, Ft. Bragg, NC (1986-88). Earned a reputation as an outstanding technician while acquiring hands-on experience installing, operating, and maintaining switchboard systems and telephone central offices for the famed 82nd Airborne Division.
* Operated manual and semiautomatic switchboards; supervised automatic switchboard systems; performed troubleshooting on equipment.
* Refined my technical skills while developing my leadership ability.
* Earned a respected medal for my outstanding work.

EQUIPMENT   Install, operate, and maintain telecommunications equipment including:
EXPERTISE   automated switchboards   two- and four-wire telephone systems
                 26-pair telephone cable   telephone/switchboard test equipment
* Plan and set up field communications systems.

EDUCATION   Completing courses in **electronics**, North Carolina State University.
&   Completed college-level U.S. Army training in **cable/wire analysis** and **repair,** and **G.T.E.**
TRAINING   **government systems automatic switchboard repair.**
* Graduated from the Army's Advanced Airborne School, a physically and emotionally demanding course which trains young leaders to supervise parachute operations.

PERSONAL   Hold SECRET security clearance. Am an excellent leader who "keeps going" until the job is done. Am known for my planning and organizational skills.

Date

Exact Name of Person
Exact Title or Position
Name of Company
Address (no., street)
Address (city, state, zip)

Dear Exact Name of Person: (or Dear Sir or Madam if answering a blind ad.)

I would appreciate an opportunity to talk with you soon about how I could benefit your organization through my expertise in communications systems, leadership, and project management.

While serving my country in the U.S. Army, I have developed skills in areas related to communications security, inventory control, overseeing the operating, repairing, and troubleshooting a wide range of complex satellite systems, and developing and implementing professional development and training. I have also served as a liaison to top-level officials and have consistently been promoted above my peers. I offer a Bachelor of Science degree in Geography from Arizona State University along with a wide range of college-level continuing education courses.

You would find me to be a versatile, dedicated professional with a reputation for problem-solving and decision-making, as well as the ability to motivate and lead others. I believe my skills and abilities would make me a valuable part of your team.

I hope you will call or write me soon to suggest a time convenient for us to meet and discuss your current and future needs and how I might serve them. Thank you in advance for your time.

Sincerely,

Dale Richards

Alternate last paragraph:
I hope you will welcome my call soon to arrange a brief meeting at your convenience to discuss your current and future needs and how I might serve them.

DALE RICHARDS
1110½ Hay Street, Fayetteville, NC 28305   (910) 483-6611

OBJECTIVE   To benefit an organization in need of a hard-working professional with a background in management and leadership, technical abilities, and project management, who possesses a knack for decision-making, problem-solving, and motivating personnel.

EDUCATION   **Bachelor of Science degree** in Geography, with a minor in Geology, Arizona State University, Tempe, AZ, 1990.

Completed a wide range of college-level coursework in personnel supervision, equipment management, communications networks, microwave satellite communications, Mobile Subscriber Equipment (MSE), secure-voice networks, and counterterrorism.

CLEARANCE   Hold Secret security clearance through SBI with Top Secret security clearance pending.

EXPERIENCE   *Gained valuable leadership, planning, and technical experience while serving as an officer in the U.S. Army:*
DIRECTOR OF OPERATIONS. Ft. Bragg, NC (1993-present).
Hold a position usually reserved for more senior management, utilizing excellent planning, managerial, and technical skills supervising communications for a 435-person organization.
* Control a multimillion-dollar inventory consisting of 33 aircraft, communications and surveillance equipment, and ammunition.
* Direct the operation, repair, and troubleshooting of a variety of mobile subscriber equipment.
* Train, coordinate, and supervise a staff of 12 communications specialists.
* Selected to receive in-depth Mobile Subscriber equipment training.
* Act as departmental Planning and Training Manager, overseeing the professional development of entry-level and mid-level management personnel.
* Coordinate and assist in the implementation of secret air and ground missions.

COMMUNICATIONS SUPERVISOR/PERSONNEL MANAGER. Ft. Bragg, NC (1992-93).
Gained an excellent working knowledge of technical equipment while polishing my organizational and delegation skills supervising a team of 58 communications personnel.
* Directed the maintenance, repair, and operations of 32 vehicles and over $20 million in high-tech Mobile Subscriber equipment.
* Coordinated and implemented all technical and professional development training for 58 employees.
* Processed classified COMSEC key tapes, inventory, and hand receipts.\
* Ensured all organizational and professional standards were upheld.
* Earned a reputation for easily establishing a rapport with people from diverse cultural and socioeconomic backgrounds.
* Completed all assignments quickly and accurately while working under variable and dangerous conditions, including providing a vital communication link between front-line and rear echelon organizations during combat conditions.
* Scheduled all work orders and tracked the accountability of all equipment manifests.\

EXECUTIVE OFFICER. Seoul, Korea (1991-92).
Honed communication abilities while preparing and delivering highly detailed personnel readiness and operations reports to top-level management.
* Developed and implemented operating procedures and field exercises.
* Coordinated training programs for over 300 employees in addition to overseeing the maintenance and operation of 65 vehicles.
* Created and instituted a system that decreased vehicle repair time by 20%.

EQUIPMENT   Familiar with a wide range of communications systems, including COMSEC, CCI, Mobile Subscriber Equipment (MSE), FM SINCGARS, high-frequency AM radios, and DGM-TRI-TAC and other tactical satellites.

PERSONAL   Known as a dedicated, focussed professional able to motivate others to do their best. Work well as both a team leader and a team member. Am computer literate.

Date

Exact Name of Person
Title or Position
Name of Company
Address (no., street)
Address (city, state, zip)

Dear Exact Name of Person: (or Dear Sir or Madam if answering a blind ad.)

I would appreciate an opportunity to talk with you soon about how I could contribute to your organization through my skills in telecommunications and electronics engineering, as well as my experience troubleshooting and repairing complex communications equipment to the component level. I am currently relocating to Columbia, SC, and will be available for employment in mid-March. Currently in the process of job hunting and house hunting, I can make myself available for interviews at your convenience.

As you will see from my track record of success on the enclosed resume, while serving my country in the U.S. Army I gained valuable technical skills related to multimillion-dollar telecommunications systems.

Because of my technical and management know-how, I have been the recipient of numerous awards and medals. I was chosen to oversee several projects on different parts of the globe involving installing, troubleshooting, repairing, and maintaining electronic switching systems and computers.

I believe you would find me to be a young professional who is eager to excel and to benefit my employer. I also have a knack for motivating others through example.

I hope you will call or write me soon to suggest a time convenient for us to meet and discuss your current and future needs and how I might serve them. Thank you in advance for your time.

Sincerely yours,

Linda Matthews

Alternate last paragraph:
I hope you will welcome my call soon to arrange a brief meeting at your convenience to discuss your current and future needs and how I might serve them. Thank you in advance for your time.

LINDA MATTHEWS
1110½ Hay Street, Fayetteville, NC 28305   (910) 483-6611

OBJECTIVE

To contribute to an organization that can use a communications-electronics professional who offers expertise related to switchboard and communications-electronics installation and repair along with proven skills in interacting smoothly with customers, employees, and supervisors.

EXPERIENCE

PUBLICATIONS CLERK. U.S. Army, Germany (1993-94). Refined my administrative abilities and became skilled in customer relations while operating a wide range of printing equipment in a large U.S. Army Printing and Publications Center; in this job which required a Secret security clearance, maintained strict accountability of sensitive forms and other publications.
* Used my technical troubleshooting skills to minimize equipment downtime.

SALES ASSOCIATE. U.S. Army, Germany (1992-93). Received a cash award, numerous written compliments from customers, and a respected award for my outstanding customer service as a sales associate at one of the military's largest retail stores in Europe.

TELECOMMUNICATIONS SUPERVISOR. U.S. Army, Germany (1991-92). As Communications Supervisor for a medical organization, trained and supervised five people while directing the expert operation and maintenance of multimillion-dollar telephone equipment.
* Trained employees to use schematics and to troubleshoot electrical circuits.
* Acquired knowledge of international telephone operations and interface requirements.
* On my own initiative, developed a model employee proficiency test to ensure that newly assigned personnel were sufficiently skilled to work without supervision.
* Received four prestigious medals for exceptional managerial performance.

COMMUNICATIONS SECTION CHIEF. U.S. Army, Germany (1987-91). Trained and supervised seven communications-electronics specialists while directing maintenance performed on a NATO communications network which had to remain in operation 24 hours a day, seven days a week.
* Applied my "hands-on" technical expertise in creating and wiring a switchboard as a function of operating, maintaining, troubleshooting, and repairing the organization's communication system.
* Was responsible for ordering and maintaining accountability of $3 million in hardware.
* Controlled inventory and monitored the turn-in and procurement of equipment.
* Received three respected medals for troubleshooting ability and management skills.

WIRE SECTION CHIEF/SWITCHBOARD OPERATOR. U.S. Army, Ft. Ord, CA (1985-87). In an engineering organization, maintained the switchboard and accounted for more than 50 miles of telephone/communications cable while also repairing equipment malfunctions.

TELEPHONE OPERATOR, TELEPHONE LINE INSTALLER, LINE REPAIRER, & SWITCHBOARD OPERATOR. U.S. Army, various locations worldwide (1979-85). Developed expertise in all aspects of telephone operation, repair, and maintenance.

TECHNICAL SKILLS

Proficient in operating, maintaining, repairing, and troubleshooting equipment including:

frequency modulated radio	amptitude modulated radio
VHF and UHF antennas	digital multimeter/ohmmeter/volt meter
omni directional antennas	COMSEC equipment

Skilled in cable repair, telephone wire repair, and J-box/C-block installation.
Offer expertise in using Class A tone/pulse phones and soldering iron.

EDUCATION/ TRAINING

Completed classes in electronics and computer hardware/software repair; excelled in numerous U.S. Army courses related to management, supervision, and counseling as well as communications-electronics installation and repair.

PERSONAL

Am an adaptable, results-oriented professional with special abilities in telecommunication systems. Have a knack for motivating others. Am proud to have received numerous awards during my military career for heroism, valor and loyalty, and meritorious service; earned safe driver's award for having over 12,000 accident-free miles.

GREGORY WHISNANT

1110½ Hay Street, Fayetteville, NC 28305   (910) 483-6611

OBJECTIVE

To benefit an organization that can use a dynamic young professional who offers outstanding technical skills with state-of-the-art electronics equipment and the ability to supervise and motivate others.

EXPERIENCE

PRECISION MEASURING EQUIPMENT SUPERVISOR. U.S. Air Force, England (1988-90). Earned unusually rapid promotion to "sergeant" while supervising a six-person team in the operation, adjustment, calibration, and maintenance of precision measuring equipment vital to aviation, radar, and satellite operations.

* Received a distinguished medal for contributions to NATO: used spare parts to develop a test "jig" which reduced calibration time on specialized equipment by 20%.
* Ensured the quality of equipment by correcting calibration procedures when found to be faulty.
* Refined my skills in training and motivating others.

PRECISION MEASURING EQUIPMENT TECHNICIAN. U.S. Air Force, England (1985-88). Developed a wide range of technical skills while operating and maintaining an inventory of over 10,300 electronic testing items used to maintain equipment for over 255 work centers throughout England; obtained replacement parts.

* Earned a reputation as an expert electronics technician who can work with any piece of equipment; provided quick "turnaround" times for repairs.
* Reduced a backlog of weapon calibration test sets needing repairs; am known as the organization's expert on these vital sets.
* Provided flight line repairs during use of a new missile system.
* Received a 98.6% rating on quality inspections of my work.
* "Saved" an important mission by repairing three weapon programming units in one shift; was praised in writing for this "outstanding" effort.
* Dedicated much of my off-duty time to the study of electronics; was praised in written evaluations for my rapid advancement in my field.

EQUIPMENT EXPERTISE

Operate, troubleshoot, align, calibrate, and repair to the component level a wide range of precision measuring electronics equipment including:

8566 spectrum analyzers	3586 selective level meters
3325A synthesized function generators	oscilloscopes
signal generators	AN/APM-427 radar simulators
12A7541-813 weapons programmers	

* Repair and calibrate electronics equipment used in aviation, missile guidance, weapons programming, satellite and radar tracking, communications, and meteorology.
* Completed TACAN training.
* Worked with equipment on F-111A, EF-111A, and FB-111A Aardvark aircraft.

EDUCATION & TRAINING

Completed eight months of college-level U.S.A.F. training in precision measuring equipment operation and maintenance, 1986.

Graduated as a **Distinguished Graduate** from the U.S.A.F. NCO Preparatory Course emphasizing leadership and management skills, 1988.

Completed a course in Algebra, Community College of the Air Force, 1988.

PERSONAL

Hold Secret security clearance. Am known for "taking on" broken or complicated equipment and fixing it. Have excellent communication skills.

JASON KEELING
1110 ½ Hay Street, Fayetteville, NC 28305　　　　　　　　　　(910) 483-6611

OBJECTIVE
To offer my experience, knowledge, and strong interest in computer systems administration, analysis, and security to an organization that can use my creativity and enthusiasm along with my outstanding supervisory, leadership, and instructional skills.

TRAINING
Excelled in technical training programs including the following:
UNIX/(TCP/IP)/security on the Cisco routers/WAN security—how to set up an Internet on a LAN/WAN, security on a LAN/WAN, and shell programming in Telnet: vendor training sponsored by Cisco Systems, Inc.; Camp Lejeune, NC, 1995
small system/LAN administration/Banyan—performing small system troubleshooting, Banyan instructor certification, funding and administration of a LAN; Camp Lejeune,1994

TECHNICAL EXPERTISE
Through training and experience, have very good technical and logical knowledge in areas including systems administration, small computer operations, and systems security.
* Have worked in-depth with most applications-level programs commonly found in today's workplace and am a Windows Developer.
* Set up Windows for Workgroups networks for two area insurance companies.
* Built about 10 computers from scratch on my own time.
* Ordered all parts and built my own top-of-the-line PC for about half of the normal market cost to the average user.
* Am technically proficient in computer communications applications and trained on the most sophisticated systems in use today.
* Served as administrator of one of the world's largest LAN/WAN systems.

HARDWARE & SOFTWARE
Offer experience with the following:

Sparc 10 UNIX machines	Cisco 7000 routers	Windows NT
Windows for Workgroups	Sun UNIX machines	Cisco AGS+
Subnetting Internet networks	Lotus notes servers	Borland C++
DEC Pentium 100 Banyan servers	Synoptics fiber optics	16mb Token rings

EXPERIENCE
SYSTEMS ADMINISTRATION AND SECURITY SPECIALIST. U.S. Marine Corps, Camp Lejeune, NC (1992-95).
Selected for specialized technical schooling and a transfer to the computer field after three years as an Infantry Team Leader, earned advancement after my superiors discovered my background and strong interest in computer applications.

* Ran the systems administration and security for the Second Marine Expeditionary Force (IIMEF) for the East Coast which covered from Norfolk, VA, to Parris Island, SC.
* Learned to set up security for a WAN and advanced administration specific to the LAN/WAN.
* Personally set up the Internet (TCP/IP) for IIMEF along with the firewalls for the Cisco 7000 router.
* Maintained a server room with 25 dual DEC Pentium systems and built several servers.
* Achieved 100% success in ensuring data security.
* Was awarded a Top Secret security clearance.

INFANTRY TEAM LEADER. USMC, Camp Lejeune, NC (1989-92).
Earned a reputation as a natural leader with good communication skills and a talent for providing clear, easily understood instructions and guidance to my subordinates.
* Contributed to the success of a drug interdiction operation in the Florida Everglades which earned my team a Joint Meritorious Unit Citation and me a personal letter of appreciation.
* Received specialized training in leadership and instructional techniques as well as weapons and tactics.

PERSONAL
Am considered a very creative individual who is also a logical thinker with strong analytical skills. Spend my leisure time programming, building computers, and reading to keep up with the latest news in the computer industry. Am very physically fit and enjoy running.

Date

Exact Name of Person
Title or Position
Name of Company
Address (no., street)
Address (city, state, zip)

Dear Exact Name of Person: (or Dear Sir or Madam if answering a blind ad.)

I would appreciate an opportunity to talk with you soon about how I could contribute to your organization through my experience in heavy equipment operation and my "accident-free" driving record.

While serving my country in the U.S. Air Force, I became known as a skillful and safe driver and equipment operator. I earned an achievement medal for my contributions as a member of a civil engineering company in Germany. During the war in the Middle East I provided important support while removing 45 inches of snow from runways. Then I kept the runways free of snow and ice accumulation which allowed allied planes to complete their assigned missions.

In the aftermath of the war, I was honored with another achievement medal in recognition of my contributions during efforts to ensure the safe passage of Kurdish refugees along the Iraqi/ Turkish border. I took heavy equipment out along remote trails in a heavy downpour of rain and was described as "displaying exceptional courage which reflects favorably on himself and the image of the U.S. Air Force."

I hope you will welcome my call soon to arrange a brief meeting at your convenience to discuss your current and future needs and how I might serve them. Thank you in advance for your time.

Sincerely yours,

Ronald D. Eason

Alternate last paragraph:
I hope you will call or write me soon to suggest a time convenient for us to meet and discuss your current and future needs and how I might serve them. Thank you in advance for your time.

RONALD D. EASON
1110½ Hay Street, Fayetteville, NC 28305   (910) 483-6611

OBJECTIVE

To contribute my excellent skills in operating heavy equipment and my safe driving record to an organization that can use a hard-working young professional.

SPECIAL SKILLS

Through training and experience, am qualified to operate and drive vehicles and heavy equipment including, but not limited to, the following:

John Deere 410 backhoe	Case 580-B backhoe
dump trucks up to 20 tons (automatic)	Caterpillar 130-G motorized grader
8- to 12-ton vibratory roller	rough terrain forklift
John Deere 4½ cubic yard loader	John Deere 690-C pneumatic excavator

EXPERIENCE

*Developed a reputation as a highly skilled and competent **Heavy Equipment Operator** while serving in the U.S. Air Force:*

Sheppard AFB, TX (1992-93). Further developed my operating skills and reputation for dependability while involved in using equipment to help solve serious road and airstrip problems and make repairs.

* Helped construction crews and engineering company personnel with projects including preparations for laying concrete foundations.
* Was singled out for the honor of "best equipment operator in the R.E.O.T. School."

Sembach AB, Germany (1990-92). Earned two Air Force Achievement Medals for my contributions which were officially described as "distinctive" and "invaluable" to a civil engineering company.

* Excavated and removed 100 cubic meters of contaminated soil after an oil/water separator developed a leak: was commended for completing the project ahead of schedule.
* Played an important role in removing 45 inches of snow from runways so that flight lines were able to remain operational and in use in support of the war in the Middle East.
* Was named the community's "Technician of the Month, November 1991."
* Was credited with solving numerous major road and ground problems through my skills, knowledge, and important contributions.
* Made contributions during the construction of a concrete foundation for a skateboard ramp which provided a recreational outlet for community members of all ages.

Iraq and Turkey (1990-91). Performed with distinction in the harsh environment and dangerous conditions during the war in the Middle East.

* Was singled out for praise for "exceptional courage" displayed while transporting a front end loader through narrow remote trails in a downpour of rain in order to provide safe transport for Kurdish refugees on the only accessible trail.
* Received a certificate of appreciation for my "outstanding contributions in support of the security of Northern Iraq."

TELEPHONE CABLE INSTALLER. Army National Guard, Grove Hill, AL (1987-89).
Learned the technical details of installing cable and COMSEC (communication secure) telephones to allow constant contact between various departments and companies.

HEAVY EQUIPMENT OPERATOR. Scott Bridge, Inc., Opelika, AL (1988-89).
Operated a variety of equipment including backhoes, loaders, and small terrain forklifts.
* Passed my knowledge on to new employees by conducting training in equipment operating techniques and safety procedures.

TRAINING

Completed military training programs in heavy equipment operation.

PERSONAL

Secret clearance. Offer an "accident-free" driving history despite weather conditions including heavy snow in Germany and alternating heat and heavy rain in the Middle East.

Date

Exact Name of Person
Title or Position
Name of Company
Address (no., street)
Address (city, state, zip)

Dear Exact Name of Person: (or Dear Sir or Madam if answering a blind ad.)

I would appreciate an opportunity to talk with you soon about how I could benefit your organization through my outstanding leadership, communication, and management skills refined as a junior military officer.

As a lieutenant in the U.S. Navy, I have excelled in a wide range of management and public relations roles. In 1988 I completed a two-year qualifying/screening process and was selected as an executive aide/ operations manager managing activities on a 4,500-person "floating hotel," the USS Midway. In a previous job I managed the repair and maintenance of multimillion-dollar hydraulic, air conditioning, and heating systems. My leadership ability and decision-making skills have been tested and refined on hundreds of occasions where I have been responsible for rescue projects, "hostile water" operations, and other emergency/crisis situations.

I have been selected for numerous special projects related to promoting excellent relations with Japan. Because of my public relations expertise, I was chosen to plan and conduct high-visibility public relations events for international VIPs.

You would find me to be a dedicated professional who is accustomed to giving "110%" in any job. I am single and willing to relocate to areas including Hong Kong and Australia.

I hope you will welcome my call soon to arrange a brief meeting at your convenience to discuss your current and future needs and how I might serve them. Thank you in advance for your time.

Sincerely yours,

James Bass

Alternate last paragraph:
I hope you will call or write me soon to suggest a time convenient for us to meet and discuss your current and future needs and how I might serve them. Thank you in advance for your time.

JAMES BASS

1110½ Hay Street, Fayetteville, NC 28305   (910) 483-6611

OBJECTIVE

I offer proven leadership, communication, management, and decision-making skills to an organization that can use a dynamic and innovative professional who has excelled as a junior military officer.

EXPERIENCE

EXECUTIVE AIDE/OPERATIONS MANAGER. U.S. Navy, USS Midway (1988-present). After an intensive two-year qualifying/screening process, was promoted to oversee all internal operations as well as navigational safety for this "floating hotel" containing 4,500 people; as an executive aide, also function as the "right arm" of the commanding officer.
* Manage the operation and maintenance of navigation equipment.
* Control a budget; train junior executives.
* Refined my skills in problem solving and decision making while routinely working 18-hour days, seven days a week.
* Because of my outstanding public relations expertise, was chosen as **Honors Officer** to plan and conduct functions for international VIPs; managed 42 events.
* Refined my skills in organizing materials and personnel to increase efficiency while decreasing cost.
* Rewrote standard operating procedures for the organization.
* Earned respect for my "crisis management" skills while coordinating rescue projects and "hostile water" operations.
* Received a special award for "exceptional ship handling abilities."

DIRECTOR OF MAINTENANCE, ENGINEERING, AND REPAIR SERVICES. U.S. Navy, USS Midway (1987-88). Earned a respected medal while overseeing 241 technical personnel repairing damage and maintaining multimillion-dollar systems including:

air conditioning/heating   ventilation
fire fighting systems   hydraulic systems
* Reorganized the maintenance training program in order to maximize strategic, long-term efficiency.
* Reduced repair time to an all-time low.

Other management and public relations experience (1987-89): Because of my public relations skills and leadership ability, was handpicked for special projects including these:
PUBLIC RELATIONS/TRAINING OFFICER. Planned and presented daily instruction for 206 people on Japanese language and culture.
JAPANESE LIAISON OFFICER. For an "exchange" program, trained Japanese naval officers in radio communications procedures; in this "public relations" role, promoted good will between nations.
MARKETING DIRECTOR. Directed a fund-raising campaign which collected thousands of dollars for charity.

**EDUCATION &
TRAINING**

Bachelor of Arts degree in **Asian Studies**, University of Michigan, Ann Arbor, MI, 1986. Completed U.S. Navy training in leadership and management.
Graduated from the Dale Carnegie Interpersonal Relations Course.

COMPUTERS

Program in Basic; use dBase, Word Star and Lotus 1-2-3 software.

PERSONAL

Hold Secret NAC security clearance. Have lived in Japan since 1987. Willing to relocate to areas including the Far East and Australia. Am an outstanding communicator.

Date

Exact Name of Person
Title or Position
Name of Company
Address (number and street)
Address (city, state, and ZIP)

Dear Exact Name of Person: (or Dear Sir or Madam if answering a blind as.)

I would appreciate an opportunity to talk with you soon about how I could contribute to your organization through my expertise in logistics and distribution as well as through managerial, leadership, and motivational abilities refined as a junior military officer.

You will see by my enclosed resume that I have earned a reputation as an intelligent, articulate, and assertive professional who consistently excels at handling multiple simultaneous operations and activities. Through sound judgment, strong decision-making skills, and the ability to handle pressure I have been effective in improving procedures, streamlining operations, and molding employees into cohesive and productive teams.

I am especially interested in transforming my military management background into a position in logistics management in the import/export industry and in staying in the Pacific Rim. I have enjoyed living, working, and traveling in this part of the world and would like to make it my permanent home. I feel that I offer exceptional organizational, motivational, and communication skills which would make me a valuable asset to an organization in need of an honest, reliable, and dependable professional.

I hope you will welcome my call soon to arrange a brief meeting at your convenience to discuss your current and future needs and how I might serve them. Thank you in advance for your time.

Sincerely yours,

Leon Phillip Williams

Alternate last paragraph:
I hope you will call or write me soon to suggest a time convenient for us to meet and discuss your current and future needs and how I might serve them. Thank you in advance for your time.

LEON PHILLIP WILLIAMS
1110½ Hay Street, Fayetteville, NC 28305   (910) 483-6611

OBJECTIVE

To offer abilities refined as a naval officer known for an assertive, dynamic leadership style, high degree of initiative and perseverance, and the ability to provide exceptional human, material, and fiscal resource management.

EXPERIENCE

Consistently earned the respect and praise of senior management, my peers, and employees while advancing in positions of increasing responsibility and developing a reputation as a knowledgeable Surface Warfare Officer, U.S. Navy:

EXECUTIVE ASSISTANT/PROJECT MANAGER. Home port: Pearl Harbor, HI (1995-present). Was selected for a position on the staff of the Commanding Officer, Naval Station Pearl Harbor, on the basis of my performance in earlier managerial roles.

ENGINEERING OFFICER, TRAINING COORDINATOR, and **QUALITY ASSURANCE MANAGER.** USS Constellation (CV-64). Home port: San Diego, CA (1993-95). Often held multiple positions simultaneously and always led my people to exceed expectations and achieve success: was the officer in charge of over 110 employees along with six supervisors and managers.

* Earned praise for my hands-on style of leadership along with exceptional organizational and managerial skills.
* Displayed sound judgment and a level-headed approach to problem solving which earned praise during a challenging deployment to the Western Pacific and Arabian Gulf.
* Developed successful, highly regarded long-range training programs for a 600-person engineering department in what would usually be a permanent position, but which I filled simultaneously with a critical and demanding management role.
* Applied my diplomatic and communication skills while briefing and guiding more than 130 distinguished visitors on tours of USS Constellation (CV-64).
* Consistently earned formal evaluations placing me at or near the top of groups of competitive young officers.
* During two fiscal years tracked more than 750 changes to engineering operation sequencing systems and casualty control procedures along with more than 250 control work packages.
* Applied sound judgment and ingenuity to make lasting improvements in operational and material readiness in a fast-paced engineering department.
* Was officially evaluated as the guiding force behind significant improvements in material resource management for two main machinery spaces which resulted in a dramatic improvement in plant efficiency and combat readiness for a vital national asset.
* Oversaw a $50 million removal, overhaul, and reinstallation project as a Quality Assurance Manager.

WEAPONS OFFICER and **PUBLIC AFFAIRS REPRESENTATIVE.** USS Mobile (LKA-115). Home port: Long Beach, CA (1989-93). Rapidly earned a reputation as an adaptable, mentally sharp, dynamic young professional with a firm and fair style of leadership and the ability to handle heavy work loads and pressure in my first assignments as a military officer.

* Orchestrated a comprehensive plan of action and milestones for a $75 million shipyard overhaul in which all work was completed in 75% of the time allotted and within budget.
* Selected for Public Affairs roles, was praised for my diplomacy and informative style of keeping civilian entities informed of naval activities and accomplishments while presenting a "positive image" of the navy.
* Received a Navy Achievement Medal for my efforts during the war in the Middle East which included the unloading of over 1,400 tons of critical cargo, including vehicles and ammunition, during a 26-hour period.
* Trained and led flight deck crews through 1,500 incident-free shipboard helicopter operations in support of logistics efforts during Desert Shield and Desert Storm.

EDUCATION

B.A., Material Logistics Management, Michigan State University, East Lansing, MI, 1984.

COMPUTER KNOWLEDGE

Offer familiarity with computer software programs including the following:
WordPerfect 5.1 dBase IV   Lotus 1-2-3   Microsoft Word 6.0

PERSONAL

Have enjoyed several years of living, working, and traveling in the Pacific Rim area. Was entrusted with a Top Secret security clearance with SBI.

DAVID HORN

1110½ Hay Street, Fayetteville, NC 28305   (910) 483-6611

OBJECTIVE

I want to benefit an organization that can use a West Point-educated young executive who offers superior management and communication skills along with creative problem-solving and decision-making abilities.

EDUCATION & TRAINING

M.B.A. Candidate, A.B. Freeman School of Business, Tulane University, New Orleans, LA. Bachelor of Science (B.S.) degree in Political Science, U.S. Military Academy at **West Point**, 1985.
Completed U.S. Army training for officers; because of my judgement and integrity, was selected for training in nuclear weapons control.

EXPERIENCE

CONSTRUCTION SUPERINTENDENT/CONSTRUCTION ENGINEER. U.S. Army, Selfridge Air National Guard Base, MI (1989-90).
Managed all phases of planning and construction on several multimillion-dollar projects including a hotel, marina, and child care center; negotiated the purchase of equipment and services.
*   Managed quality control; directed inspections and made decisions to accept/reject work.

PERSONNEL OFFICER. U.S. Army, Germany (1988).
As personnel officer for a 500-person, nuclear capable Field Artillery Battalion, oversaw an 11-person staff involved in performing legal operations and public relations.

*   Reorganized the management of vital information pertaining to nuclear weapons control and strategic planning; created a standardized cataloging/ordering system.
*   Was described as "uncommonly mature and concerned" while aiding employees in legal and financial matters; established a model safety program.

DIRECTOR OF SUPPLY AND SERVICE OPERATIONS. U.S. Army, Germany (1987-88).
Was evaluated as "contributing immeasurably to the success" of this fast-paced organization while managing a variety of service operations including the maintenance/supply function.

*   Was cited as dramatically improving supply operations by reorganizing storage areas and streamlining inventory control.
*   Led the maintenance section to be rated as "best" within the parent organization; it was chosen to compete for higher honors worldwide.

EXECUTIVE OFFICER. U.S. Army, Germany (1987).
While holding a Top Secret security clearance with BI, was praised for my management ability as second-in-command of this 125-person nuclear capable organization.
*   Implemented the smooth transition to new transportation equipment while leading the organization in meeting its busiest-ever schedule.

FIRST-LINE SUPERVISOR. U.S. Army, Germany (1985-87).
Was recognized as having top executive potential while training and managing a team of eight operating state-of-the-art electronics systems.

*   Managed maintenance and electronics teams rated "best" in the parent organization.
*   Developed innovative training techniques which improved vital nuclear, biological, and chemical (NBC) training.

PERSONAL

Am known for giving unselfishly of my time. Was an Eagle Scout.

DAVID JAMES LAWSON
1110½ Hay Street, Fayetteville, NC 28305   (910) 483-6611

OBJECTIVE

To contribute to an organization that can benefit from a motivated junior executive offering a background in mechanical engineering coupled with leadership and logistics management skills refined during six years of commissioned Naval service.

EDUCATION & TRAINING

Bachelor of Science in Mechanical Engineering (B.S.M.E.), University of Toledo, OH, 1983. Designated an Aerospace Engineering Duty Officer after completing U.S. Navy training in leadership, aviation maintenance, and logistics management.

EXPERIENCE

ASSISTANT DEPARTMENT DIRECTOR. U.S. Navy, NAS Adak, AK (1989-present). Because of my technical knowledge and management skills, was chosen as the "right hand" of an executive overseeing a 136-person aviation maintenance facility.
* Identified and filled personnel deficiencies and established procedures to respond to future departmental requirements.
* Developed a comprehensive program which standardized compilation and extraction of personnel training data for the department.
* Resourcefulness saved over 20% of $75,000 budget I managed.
* Decreased inoperative component diagnostic units from five to zero

A "Track Record" of increasing efficiency and productivity

PRODUCTION DIRECTOR. U.S. Navy, NAS Adak, AK (1988-89). Managed a seven-person team directing the maintenance of aircraft components and systems.
* Reduced component "turnaround" time to an all time low of 6.9 days.

QUALITY ASSURANCE PROGRAM MANAGER. U.S. Navy, NAS Adak, AK (1988). Directed a quality assurance program designed to improve performance and productivity and decrease defects in the maintenance of aircraft components and ground support equipment; provided unparalleled quality and customer support.
* Refined inspection criteria and enhanced monitoring programs.
* Reduced component re-repair 30%; discovered 23 product material flaws.

QUALITY ASSURANCE/MAINTENANCE MANAGER. U.S. Navy, NAS Lemoore, CA (1987-88). Vastly improved caliber of aircraft maintenance through an intensified quality assurance program while overseeing a maintenance division of 29 people; received "flawless" scores on inspections.

FLIGHT DIVISION DIRECTOR. U.S. Navy, NAS Kingsville, TX (1986). Oversaw aircraft inspections, launch and recovery operations, and maintenance troubleshooting activities on 60 aircraft. Made procedural changes that increased efficiency and safety enabling this organization to handle its busiest-ever flight schedule.

BUDGET/MATERIAL MANAGER. U.S. Navy, NAS Kingsville, TX (1984-86). Successfully managed $3.5 million operating budget, controlled aircraft maintenance material inventory, and monitored fuel/flight costs.

AIRCRAFT EXPERTISE

Experienced with Lockheed P-3C "Orion," McDonnell Douglas F/A-18 Hornet and TA-4J Skyhawk aircraft, and the Allison T56A-14, General Electric F404-GE-400, and Pratt and Whitney J52 power plant systems

PERSONAL

Comfortable with computers, Computer Aided Design (CAD). Secret security clearance.

Date

Exact Name of Person
Title or Position
Name of Company
Address (no., street)
Address (city, state, zip)

Dear Exact Name of Person: (or Dear Sir or Madam if answering a blind ad.)

I would appreciate an opportunity to talk with you soon about how I could contribute to your organization through my ability to set up new operations, improve the efficiency of existing systems and procedures, and manage people and finances for maximum productivity.

While serving my country for three years as an officer in the U.S. Army, I have had an opportunity to be selected for "hotseat" jobs which have thoroughly tested my creativity, endurance, and problem-solving skills as well as my ability to manage complex operations where one wrong decision could cost someone his or her life. For example, on a special project in Cuba, I was selected as "camp commander" of a 2,000-person migrant camp which had no systems for providing food and clothing and where daily riots were commonplace. I quickly established all logistical systems and procedures, set up an internal government, installed a medical facility, and maintained law and order. In another assignment, I managed the provision of all goods and services for 10,000 migrants in eight camps.

With a reputation as a strong and resourceful leader, I have also had considerable experience as a comptroller in planning and administering budgets during an era when every dollar had to be stretched to its maximum utility. Experience has taught me that organizational skills are a vital key to success because achieving any goal usually depends on the ability to prioritize tasks and follow through in spite of all obstacles.

I feel confident you would find me to be a congenial individual with multiple talents that could benefit your organization and help you achieve your objectives. I can provide outstanding personal and professional references upon request.

I hope you will welcome my call soon to arrange a brief meeting at your convenience to discuss your current and future needs and how I might serve them. Thank you in advance for your time.

Sincerely yours,

Brian Fencing

Alternate last paragraph:
I hope you will call or write me soon to suggest a time convenient for us to meet and discuss your current and future needs and how I might serve them. Thank you in advance for your time.

BRIAN FENCING
1110½ Hay Street, Fayetteville, NC 28305   (910) 483-6611

OBJECTIVE

To add value to an organization that can use a versatile junior executive who offers proven abilities related to managing people, projects, and finances along with specialized experience in planning and coordinating logistics, distribution, and production activities.

EDUCATION

Bachelor of Arts (B.A.) degree, Political Science major with a minor in Psychology, Hofstra University, Hempstead, NY, 1991.
As a junior officer, attended Ranger School, the military's "stress test" management school designed to test the mental and physical limits of the military's top leaders; excelled in this school which has a 60% dropout rate, 1992-93.
Completed the four-month Military Police Officer Basic Course, 1992.

EXPERIENCE

COMPTROLLER and **LOGISTICS & OPERATIONS MANAGER**. U.S. Army, Ft. Bragg, NC (1994-present). For an airborne military police organization, coordinate a wide range of service operations and functions including these:
* *Finance and budgeting:* Plan and manage a $400,000 operating budget, which involves meticulous research of historical data to forecast needs and then strict attention to detail to avoid overspending; prepare a consolidated weekly budget "status report" in order to brief the chief executive officer.
* *Transportation and maintenance services:* Coordinate the utilization of a 220-vehicle fleet, and assure that vehicles and radios are maintained in excellent condition in order to respond to crises and emergencies.
* *Inventory control:* Purchase supplies and equipment ranging from clothing to repair parts, and oversee the distribution of supplies; inspect the efficiency of supply procedures and systems within the parent organization, and have implemented numerous checklists to maintain vigilance at all supply levels.
* *Fuel management:* Carefully plan and manage the purchasing of the organization's fuel supply, and coordinate its warehousing and distribution.
* *Supply management:* On a daily basis, work with subordinate supply managers in order to oversee proper accounting for 1000 transactions monthly.
* *Written communications:* Rewrote the organization's standard operating procedures (SOPs) governing both budgeting/financial control and supply management; after considerable research, implemented timesaving procedures that reduced operational costs.
* *Accountability and comptrollership:* When the organization relocated to Haiti for a special project, justified and was reimbursed for 100% of the $600,000 we spent.

FIRST-LINE SUPERVISOR. U.S. Army, Ft. Bragg, NC (1994). Trained and managed a 30-person platoon and controlled equipment and vehicles valued at $750,000 while also acting as the law enforcement supervisor of the world's largest U.S. military base, which is also North Carolina's fourth largest community; set up security measures and traffic control for the 1994 Ft. Bragg Fair which catered to 35,000 people with zero injuries or accidents.
* On a special project in Cuba, was handpicked as commander of a 2000-person migrant camp; established all service operations and logistical systems for the migrants which included setting up a feeding system, providing clothing and shoes, establishing a medical facility, setting up a camp government, and overseeing law and order.
* Was handpicked for another special project because of my reputation as a "logistical expert": acted as supply officer providing supplies to eight camps housing 10,000 migrants.

FIRST-LINE SUPERVISOR. U.S. Army, Korea (1993-94). Managed a 30-person platoon involved in peacekeeping over a 15,500-square mile area while personally accounting for and maintaining vehicles, radios, and weapons valued at half a million dollars.
* Designed and built a new machine gun firing position which was described as "brilliant" and the dimensions of which were used to design the one officially adopted by the Army.

PERSONAL

Familiar with software including WordPerfect 5.1 and Harvard Graphics. Believe that organizational skills are critical to success in any task because most activities depend on the ability to prioritize, research, and follow through. Offer exceptional writing ability; have written three plays in my spare time. Have a proven talent for establishing congenial relationships.

Date

Exact Name of Person
Title or Position
Name of Company
Address (no., street)
Address (city, state, zip)

Dear Exact Name of Person: (or Dear Sir or Madam if answering a blind ad.)

I would appreciate an opportunity to talk with you soon about how I could contribute to your organization through my experience in managing finance and accounting operations.

As an officer in the U.S. Army, I have acquired experience overseeing finances at many levels. Recently as a staff accountant, I identified over $1.5 million in funds that were available for program directors. With a knowledge of several computer software packages, I played a key role in implementing an on-line query to the accounting data base and have overseen automatic data processing (ADP) operations.

In a previous job I managed payroll accounting for over 15,000 personnel and was promoted within two months to manage the disbursal of payroll, pay entitlements, and travel payments. I accounted for over $1 million in cash monthly in both U.S. and foreign currency with 100% accountability of all funds.

You would find me to be an enthusiastic and dedicated professional willing to give "110%" to excel in any job.

I hope you will welcome my call soon to arrange a brief meeting at your convenience to discuss your current and future needs and how I might serve them. Thank you in advance for your time.

Sincerely yours,

Rosemary Hill

Alternate last paragraph:
I hope you will call or write me soon to suggest a time convenient for us to meet and discuss your current and future needs and how I might serve them. Thank you in advance for your time.

ROSEMARY HILL

1110½ Hay Street, Fayetteville, NC 28305 (910) 483-6611

OBJECTIVE
To benefit an organization in need of an intelligent, enthusiastic young professional with expertise in managing financial and accounting operations along with management skills refined as a junior military officer.

EXPERIENCE
FINANCE MANAGER. U.S. Army, Ft. Bragg, NC (1989-present). At the nation's largest military base, supervise a staff of five while managing all administrative matters for a 90-person company which must be ready to relocate instantaneously to any location in the world.
* Plan and conduct financial training; oversee financial reporting.
* Account for an inventory of assets; oversee budgeting for maintenance.
* Prepare monthly financial statements for top management.
* Was selected to lead finance teams providing support in worldwide locations including the U.S. Virgin Islands following the hurricane Hugo disaster.
* Earned outstanding scores on top-level inspections and was praised for my contribution to training projects.

STAFF ACCOUNTANT. U.S. Army, Ft. Bragg, NC (1988-89). For an organization overseeing thousands of personnel, analyzed and prepared financial reports while performing strategic planning and automating many manual accounting processes.
* Earned a reputation as a shrewd analyst by identifying over $1.5 million in funds which could be used by program directors.
* Played a key role in the implementation of an on-line query to the accounting data base.
* Gained insight into the auditing process.

FINANCE OFFICER/FOREIGN EXCHANGE SPECIALIST. U.S. Army, Korea (1987). Excelled as "payroll chief" while overseeing a 50-person section processing payroll for 15,000 employees.
* Was promoted within two months to the role of "disbursing officer"; supervised a staff of nine funding payrolls and disbursing pay entitlements and travel payments.
* Accounted for over $1 million monthly in U.S. and Korean currency.
* Trained a section manager to effectively oversee the disbursing section.
* Learned the complex Army payroll computer system.

OPERATIONS MANAGER. U.S. Army, Korea (1986-87). Was chosen to supervise a team of six overseeing supply, training, housing, and administrative duties for 90 personnel in the organization operating closest to the Korean DMZ.
* Maintained a 100% accountability of assets.

EDUCATION & TRAINING
Bachelor of Science in Business Administration (B.S.B.A.) in **Accounting**, Shippensburg University, Shippensburg, PA, 1986.
Completed Army and college course work in areas including:

budgeting	tax accounting	cost accounting
managerial accounting	auditing	resource management

COMPUTERS
Operate Lotus 1-2-3, Enable, Wordstar, and Multimate software.

PERSONAL
Hold Secret security clearance. Work well with people from all backgrounds.

Date

Exact Name of Person
Title or Position
Name of Company
Address (no., street)
Address (city, state, zip)

Dear Exact Name of Person: (or Dear Sir or Madam if answering a blind ad.)

I would appreciate an opportunity to talk with you soon about how I could contribute to your organization through my keen analytical skills, communication and decision-making abilities, and my management experience gained as a finance executive.

Management and administrative expertise
After earning unusually rapid promotion to the rank of Captain, I currently manage an operation of 70 employees updating/maintaining 20,000 payroll accounts daily and processing 30,000 additional payroll and travel documents monthly. Previously I managed a disbursing operation which distributed over $70 million yearly without a single loss of funds in two years.

Project planning and "sales" ability
I was chosen for a Department of the Treasury award for my development of an employee savings/financial investments purchase program which was a "top seller" for three years.

Public relations and communication skills
I have made presentations to thousands of junior executives about financial careers and have briefed Department of the Treasury VIPs.

You would find me to be a dedicated professional with the enthusiasm, adaptability, and "can-do" attitude to excel in any job.

I hope you will welcome my call soon to arrange a brief meeting at your convenience to discuss your current and future needs and how I might serve them. Thank you in advance for your time.

Sincerely yours,

Brian Bolton

Alternate last paragraph:
I hope you will call or write me soon to suggest a time convenient for us to meet and discuss your current and future needs and how I might serve them. Thank you in advance for your time.

BRIAN BOLTON

1110½ Hay Street, Fayetteville, NC 28305   (910) 483-6611

OBJECTIVE

To benefit an organization that can use a dedicated young executive who offers keen analytical skills, outstanding communication and decision-making abilities, as well as management experience gained as a finance executive.

EXPERIENCE

CHIEF, PAY AND EXAMINATION DIVISION. U.S. Army, Germany (1989-present). As a captain in the U.S. Army, was promoted to train, supervise, and evaluate 70 employees involved in updating/maintaining 20,000 payroll accounts daily and data processing 30,000 additional documents monthly related to payroll and travel allowances.
* Developed and implemented a program combining employee training and document analysis which increased data processing accuracy to 99.2%.
* Earned a reputation for outstanding "crisis" management during a 25% increase in government employee travel.
* Took pride in increasing efficiency and accuracy of payroll processing for thousands of Americans living overseas.
* Became knowledgeable of foreign currency conversion.

FINANCE OFFICER/SAVINGS PROGRAM MANAGER. U.S. Army, Ft. Bragg, NC (1987-88). Developed and implemented a finance training program while coordinating an employee savings plan and financial investments purchase program which was a "top seller" for three years.

* Earned a Department of the Treasury award for developing sales training and "workshop" presentations into a program which increased employee participation in this savings plan from 38% to 62%.
* Created a bond purchase reporting program now used nationwide.
* Because of my public relations skills, was selected to escort Department of the Treasury executives during visits.
* Trained and led 100 financial managers to earn top scores on evaluations.

DISBURSEMENT MANAGER. U.S. Army, Ft. Bragg, NC (1986-87). Was selected to oversee the daily processing of $1.5 million of Treasury checks, traveller's checks, and cash; disbursed $70 million yearly without a single loss of funds.

* Implemented a cashier training program which resulted in two years of operation with perfect accountability of all money.
* Because of my public speaking skills, was chosen to speak to 3,000 ROTC cadets on financial careers in the military.
* Refined my personnel management skills supervising eight employees.

EDUCATION & TRAINING

Bachelor of Science in **Corporate Finance**, University of Alabama, Tuscaloosa, AL, 1985.
* Member, **Jasons**: a leadership and scholarly honorary society.
Completed Army training in budgeting, finance, and management.
* Was **Honor Graduate**, Finance Officer Advanced Course, 1989.
* Graduated from the Army's Advanced Airborne School, a physically and emotionally demanding course which trains executives to supervise parachute operations.

PERSONAL

Hold Secret security clearance. Familiar with Army budgeting procedures. Can creatively analyze and find solutions for the toughest problems.

Date

Exact Name of Person
Title or Position
Name of Company
Address (no., street)
Address (city, state, zip)

Dear Exact Name of Person: (or Dear Sir or Madam if answering a blind ad.)

I would appreciate an opportunity to talk with you soon about how I could contribute to your organization through my strong interest in applying my analytical skills and financial expertise to a business that can use a mature professional with these skills.

You will see from my enclosed resume that I served my country as a U.S. Army officer after graduating from The United States Military Academy at West Point. Graduating from West Point was one of my greatest accomplishments — to complete an engineering degree at this demanding school requires a high level of perseverance and great personal dedication to excel. It also gave me an opportunity to refine my natural leadership abilities.

I left military service recently and am very interested in making a change to the financial industry. I have been handling my own investments successfully for about five years and am very familiar with key investment vehicles such as stocks, bonds, mutual funds, and options and can evaluate companies as prospective investments.

I feel that I have demonstrated a keen intellect and strong analytical skills as a Pilot, Operations Manager, and Personnel Administration Manager. As a decorated combat aviator during the war in the Middle East, I have demonstrated my ability to lead others and perform while remaining in control under pressure.

I hope you will welcome my call soon to arrange a brief meeting at your convenience to discuss your current and future needs and how I might serve them. Thank you in advance for your time.

Sincerely yours,

Robert James

Alternate last paragraph:
I hope you will call or write me soon to suggest a time convenient for us to meet and discuss your current and future needs and how I might serve them. Thank you in advance for your time.

ROBERT JAMES
1110½ Hay Street, Fayetteville, NC 28305   (910) 483-6611

OBJECTIVE

To apply my analytical skills and financial expertise to an organization that can use a talented, tenacious young professional offering a high level of interest in financial planning along with outstanding leadership and motivational skills refined as a military officer.

EDUCATION

B.S., Mechanical Engineering (Aerospace Engineering), **The United States Military Academy at West Point,** NY, 1989.
* Gained valuable lessons in persevering under stress and pressure as well as how to effectively apply my strong motivational, leadership, and analytical abilities.

TRAINING

Excelled in intensive and demanding programs including flight training leading to qualification as a helicopter pilot; jungle warfare training; and airborne training.
Completed an advanced program emphasizing technical writing and briefing skills.

EXPERIENCE

OPERATIONS MANAGER. U.S. Army, Korea (1994). Planned, coordinated, and managed a wide range of areas in a 300-person organization including preparing and writing action plans.

* Applied my strong analytical skills and ability to use written and verbal communication to prepare detailed and concise operational plans.
* Polished my effectiveness in presenting tightly constructed and easy to understand briefings to executives and large groups of people.
* Was cited for my expertise in teaching new employees the proper methods of writing thorough operational plans.
* Was honored with a Meritorious Service Medal in recognition of my exceptional abilities and accomplishments during five years of military service.

PERSONNEL ADMINISTRATION MANAGER. U.S. Army, Ft. Bragg, NC (1992-93). Applied my sound judgment and analytical skills while making decisions on where to assign new management personnel within a 1,300-person parent organization in order to maximize each person's strengths.

* Earned praise for my attention to detail displayed while coordinating the complex details of regularly scheduled and special meetings and briefings.
* Gained exposure to computer database management and the integration of automated systems into planning.
* Earned a Commendation Medal for my contributions in a managerial role.

PILOT and **OPERATIONS MANAGER.** U.S. Army, Ft. Bragg, NC (1991-92). Directed the training and performance of 16 people, half of whom were helicopter pilots and the others mechanics, as well as the maintenance and operation of $16 million worth of sophisticated aircraft and control of supporting equipment.

* Demonstrated the ability to provide a team of technical specialists with strong leadership and guidance through my natural leadership abilities.
* Was awarded the Kuwait Liberation Medal for my efforts which directly led to the liberation of Kuwait during the war in the Middle East.

**AREAS
of
SPECIAL
KNOWLEDGE**

Offer experience in troubleshooting computer problems and in using automated equipment for research.
Am knowledgeable of Excel, dBase, Lotus 1-2-3, Word, and WordPerfect software.
Familiar with key investment vehicles such as stocks, bonds, mutual funds, options, and other areas and can evaluate companies as prospective investments.
Have a working knowledge of German.

PERSONAL

Entrusted with a Secret security clearance. Enjoy reading financial publications and subscribe to the *Wall Street Journal, Fortune, Forbes, Business Week, Worth,* and *Smart Money.* For five years, have successfully maintained my own stock portfolio using my PC.

December 19, 1994

Tarrant County Job Opportunities
Tarrant County Personnel
100 E. Weatherford
Ft. Worth, TX 76196-0105

Dear Sir or Madam:

Can you use an articulate and innovative manager who offers a strong background in logistics, technical operations, and automated data processing management?

I am sending my resume in response to your Controller's position.

As a U.S. Army officer I became adept at developing plans, molding teams, and ensuring the success of organizational goals. I have managed logistics support for an organization with 500 employees, controlled multimillion-dollar inventories of sophisticated equipment, and developed cost-saving ideas for various companies.

As you will see from my resume, I have consistently been able to develop and implement innovative programs and cost-saving ideas in every position I have held. For example, in my most recent position as the Director of Logistics and Budgeting for a 500-person organization, I reduced the cost of an office automation project 29% by going outside the usual sources to find the best equipment for the money. On numerous occasions, I have taken over substandard operations and transformed them into models of efficiency.

I offer a background of adaptability and dedication to excellence which I am certain I could apply in a manner beneficial to your organization. I am especially proud of my reputation for unquestioned integrity and high moral standards.

I hope you will call or write me soon to suggest a time convenient for us to meet and discuss your current and future needs and how I might serve them. Thank you in advance for your time.

Sincerely yours,

Jonathan Kremer

JONATHAN KREMER
1110½ Hay Street, Fayetteville, NC 28305   (910) 483-6611

OBJECTIVE

To contribute my analytical, decision-making, and managerial skills to an organization that can benefit from my knowledge of logistics/budgeting and automated systems as well as my abilities in seeing plans through to completion and performing under pressure.

EXPERIENCE

DIRECTOR OF LOGISTICS AND BUDGETING. U.S. Army, Ft. Bragg, NC (1993-94). Was cited for providing sound advice, using informed judgment, and displaying strong decision-making skills while reducing costs and improving efficiency as the coordinator of logistics support for a 500-person organization with a $500,000 annual operating budget.
* Identified inventories of excess equipment and developed a program which reduced operating costs 10% through collecting these items at a central location.
* Located new open market sources for automated data processing systems which reduced the estimated purchase price by 29% of the price of using traditional sources.
* Established the standards for hazardous waste handling with a program accepted as the guideline for other companies within the parent organization to follow.
* Displayed managerial skills and versatility overseeing successful maintenance and facilities upkeep programs and food service support operations.

Established the following track record of accomplishments, U.S. Army, Germany:
TECHNICAL OPERATIONS MANAGER. (1991-93). Rebuilt and revitalized a struggling, substandard operation into six cohesive teams of specialists within only four months.
* Developed and implemented a personnel records section database of 70,000 critical items which was then copied by three "sister" companies for its usability and effectiveness.
* Advised a chief executive on technical and operational aspects of the strict employment and transport of nuclear weapons.
* Earned the distinction as the first company in the Army to pass stringent inspections of nuclear weapons site operations/procedures and earn a new type of certification.
* Earned an "Impact Award" for exceptional results achieved in this pilot test.

FIRST-LINE SUPERVISOR. (1990-91). Provided strong leadership during a period of turbulence caused by functional reorganizations and major changes during worldwide Congress-mandated personnel reductions and draw downs.
* Polished my ability to manage a staff and administrative functions in a 50-person company through my enthusiastic and energetic style of leadership.
* Ensured a quality maintenance program for 20 vehicles and other equipment required to support a sophisticated weapons system.

TECHNICAL OPERATIONS MANAGER. (1989-90). Was promoted to a more advanced level of management based on my outstanding results achieved in my first assignment as a military officer in charge of a five-person team with more than $305,000 worth of equipment.
* Accomplished the highest scores out of 72 teams in a test of training and strategy: received a 93% with the next highest team only earning 72%.

EDUCATION & TRAINING

B.A., Political Science, The University of Texas at Arlington, 1988.
* Displayed superior leadership and athletic abilities and was named as the football team captain in college and in high school and as an elected officer in high school FFA.
Excelled in training programs for military executives including Ranger School, the Army's "stress test" of physical and mental limits.

SPECIAL SKILLS & KNOWLEDGE

* Offer knowledge of DOD contracting process including contracting for and procurement of supplies and services as well as cost estimating, budget management, planning, analysis and factoring.
* Am highly familiar with the latest computer technology and experienced with software:

Lotus 1-2-3	Windows	Enable	WordPerfect
MultiMate	Harvard Graphics	ProWrite	DOS operating system

PERSONAL

Known for integrity and high ethical standards, was entrusted with a Top Secret security clearance. Earned one achievement and **three** commendation awards for accomplishments.

Date

Exact Name of Person
Title or Position
Name of Company
Address (no., street)
Address (city, state, zip)

Dear Exact Name of Person: (or Dear Sir or Madam if answering a blind ad.)

I would appreciate an opportunity to talk with you soon about how I could benefit your organization through my keen analytical skills as well as my financial management expertise gained as a military officer.

As a Captain in the U.S. Army with an M.B.A. in management, I have excelled in a wide range of financial management roles. Most recently I was selected to train and supervise 130 employees involved in maintaining over 24,600 payroll accounts which totaled $70 million monthly. Because of my management skills, I was able to reduce the number of overdue travel allowances and civilian debts. Previously as a budget manager for a large organization, I was credited with improving financial management while planning a $1.5 million operating budget.

In 1985, I saved the government $3 million yearly by streamlining payroll procedures in Europe. I have overseen the smooth implementation of new computer systems and I was selected because of my excellent speaking skills to brief top executives on financial programs. I offer extensive experience in foreign currency conversion.

You would find me to be a dedicated and motivated professional who excels in making ideals come to life. I love meeting a challenge!

I hope you will welcome my call soon to arrange a brief meeting at your convenience to discuss your current and future needs and how I might serve them. Thank you in advance for your time.

Sincerely yours,

Michael Zimmerman

Alternate last paragraph:
I hope you will call or write me soon to suggest a time convenient for us to meet and discuss your current and future needs and how I might serve them. Thank you in advance for your time.

MICHAEL ZIMMERMAN

1110½ Hay Street, Fayetteville, NC 28305   (910) 483-6611

OBJECTIVE

To benefit an organization that can use a dedicated financial executive who offers keen analytical skills, outstanding communication and decision-making abilities, as well as management experience gained as a military officer.

EDUCATION & TRAINING

M.B.A. degree in Management, Golden Gate University, 1989.
B.S. degree in Business Management, Rider College, Lawrenceville, NJ, 1980.
Completed Army training in budgeting, finance, and management.

EXPERIENCE

CHIEF, PAYROLL AND EXAMINATION DIVISION. U.S. Army, Korea (1989-present). As a captain in the U.S. Army, was specially chosen to train and supervise 130 employees involved in updating/maintaining over 24,600 payroll accounts totaling $70 million in monthly payments; oversee the administration of travel accounts.
* Manage all contracts with commercial vendors in dollar/foreign currency.
* Significantly reduced overdue travel allowances and civilian debts; achieved a one-to-three day turnaround time for travel vouchers.
* Planned and implemented the conversion to automated systems.
* Gained extensive knowledge of currency conversion.

PAYROLL DIVISION CHIEF. U.S. Army, Ft. Bragg, NC (1988-89). At the nation's largest military base, managed a staff of 76 military and civilian employees; supervised payroll administration for 21,000 personnel.
* Streamlined payroll processing for newly assigned employees.
* Through one-on-one and group conferences, improved communication between payroll department and organizational managers.
* Personally designed and conducted a training program for budget managers and non-financial managers.
* Praised for "foresight, perception, and outstanding analytical ability."
* Gained expertise in conducting audits.

BUDGET MANAGER. U.S. Army, Ft. Bragg, NC (1986-88). Restructured the budgeting process while preparing a $1.5 million annual operating budget for an organization of 2,000 people; briefed top executives.
* Established an advisory committee for management; improved fund control.
* Developed and implemented an automated budget system.
* Designed excellent training and cross-training programs.

DISBURSEMENT MANAGER. U.S. Army, Germany (1985). Saved the government $3 million yearly by increasing office efficiency while overseeing the distribution of $1.8 million monthly to 13 organizations in three locations throughout Europe.
* Developed "long distance" disbursing procedures which decreased expenses.

CHIEF OF PAYROLL AND TRAVEL. U.S. Army, Germany (1984-85). Excelled in providing payroll and financial services to 7,600 personnel in three dispersed locations; implemented a new computer system.
* Was specially chosen to implement a community internal control program.
* Was selected to brief generals and other executives on financial programs.
* Managed and trained a financial/administrative staff of 50.

PERSONAL

Hold Secret security clearance. Proficient with numerous software programs.

Date

Exact Name of Person
Title or Position
Name of Company
Address (no., street)
Address (city, state, zip)

Dear Exact Name of Person: (or Dear Sir or Madam if answering blind ad.)

I would appreciate an opportunity to talk with you soon about how I could contribute to your organization through my 30 years of experience in fire services.

I have national certification in the following areas: Fire Officer I, Training Officer I, Inspector I, and Fire Fighter III. During my years of service I have developed a working knowledge of all Air Force regulations pertaining to the fire protection career field as well as the 40 series which pertains to civilians.

Currently the Lead Fire Fighter and Station Chief with the 23rd Civil Engineers at Pope AFB, I also am the Training Chief for my reserve unit, the 915th CES. I am licensed as an Electrical Contractor and apply this knowledge as part of the Cumberland County Arson Squad.

I hope you will welcome my call soon to arrange a brief meeting at your convenience to discuss your current and future needs and how I might serve them. Thank you in advance for your time.

Sincerely yours,

Richard Sasser

Alternate paragraph:
I hope you will call or write soon to suggest a time convenient for us to meet and discuss your current and future needs and how I might serve them. Thank you in advance for your time.

RICHARD SASSER
1110½ Hay Street, Fayetteville, NC 28305   (910) 483-6611

OBJECTIVE   To contribute to the Air Force Reserves as a Fire Chief based on my experience in the fire service field, reputation as a leader, and knowledge of Air Force policies and procedures.

CERTIFICATIONS   Offer national certification as a **Fire Officer I, Training Officer I, Inspector I,** and **Fire Fighter III.** Certified by the State of NC as a **CPR Instructor** and **Self Aid and Buddy Care Instructor.** Hold an Electrical Contractor's License issued by the State of NC.

EXPERIENCE   **LEAD FIRE FIGHTER** and **STATION CHIEF.** U.S. Government, 23rd Civil Engineers, Pope AFB, NC (1985-present).
Provide leadership to a team of four fire fighters while remaining aware at all times of military aircraft, landing zones, and physical configurations of planes and their personnel so that my crews can be used most effectively.
* Controlled the activities of fire fighting equipment, vehicles, and personnel.
* Directed crew response so they can be used to attack the fire rapidly and thoroughly.
* Contributed to the success of the Pope Emergency Response Team and directed the Hazardous Materials Team when the leader was unavailable.

TRAINING CHIEF. U.S.A.F. Reserves, 915th Civil Engineers, Pope AFB (1987-present).
Schedule training and conduct classes for structural and crash drills in accordance with Air Force Reg. 92-1 and 93-3.
* Presented classes which prepared personnel to deal with any type of emergency.

Contributed professionalism and expertise to the 317th Civil Engineers, Pope AFB, NC
FIRE STATION CAPTAIN. (1990-91). Received a certificate and letter of appreciation for my contributions when called to active duty during the war in the Middle East.
* Directed 20 military fire fighters and oversaw the operation of vehicles and equipment when responding to fire emergencies on the base.

FIRE INSPECTOR. (1980-85). Inspected new construction for compliance with fire safety regulations, made recommendations on substandard findings, checked fixed fire suppression systems, and inspected potentially hazardous areas.
* Tested and performed minor maintenance on fixed systems.
* Learned fire codes and how they had to be integrated into buildings during construction.
* Became familiar with the physical layouts and locations of facilities by inspecting every building on base regularly.

FIRE FIGHTER and **DRIVER.** (1974-80). Gained knowledge of each of the P-series vehicles and their unique operating capabilities while driving and operating each.
* Became skilled in using manually operated and power extraction tools, emergency generators, axes, pike poles, ladders, winches, nozzles, and all other related tools.

EDUCATION & TRAINING   Have completed approximately 51 hours toward an associate's degree in **Fire Science,** Central Texas College, Pope AFB, NC.
Studied Business Management at Lafayette College, Fayetteville, NC.

EQUIPMENT EXPERTISE   Offer experience with fire department equipment, vehicles, and communications systems including the following:
Fire equipment: Jaws of Life, Porta-Power, skin penetrator, and SCBA.
Vehicles: all P-series vehicles — 2, 4, 8, 10, 12, 18, 19, 20, 22, and 26
Communications systems: shortwave radio and two-way radio
Electrical equipment: multimeters, ohmmeters, voltage testers, and drills
Computers: Wang computers, FAMS system, and Windows
Other equipment: gas detectors, heat gun, and safety winch for confined spaces

PERSONAL   Feel that I have developed strong rapport with the fire fighters at Pope AFB and that I would have their complete backing if selected as Fire Chief. Am familiar with Air Force regulations.

Date

Dear Sir or Madam:

I would appreciate an opportunity to talk with you soon about how I could benefit your organization through my proven "track record" in restaurant management and administration, coupled with my know-how in preparing virtually all kinds of international and classic American food.

Restaurant management skills

As a restaurant operations manager for a dining room and eating establishment, I have combined strengths from my extensive experience and specialized training to plan and direct quality catering services, banquets, and daily menus. Regarded as a cost-conscious manager, I have become expert in managing and training chefs as well as in administering inventory and operational expenses. I have reduced production costs by 15% through effective food waste control and selective food purchases.

Cooking/Gourmet Expertise

My excellence in food preparation has earned me many distinctions. For example, I was one of the first women "Executive Chefs" certified by the American Culinary Federation (ACF). I am also a member of the national and local chapters of the organization, and presently serve as president of the local chapter.

I feel certain you would find me to be an excellent manager who is skilled in planning and delivering popular menus at popular prices.

I hope you will welcome my call soon to arrange a brief meeting at your convenience to discuss your current and future needs and how I might serve them. Thank you in advance for your time.

Sincerely yours,

Martha McCoy

MARTHA MCCOY
1110 ½ Hay Street, Fayetteville, NC 28305   (910) 483-6611

OBJECTIVE

To offer my extensive experience in restaurant administration to a company needing a cost-conscious food service manager with expertise in catering, buffets, and menu planning related to both international and classic American cuisine.

DISTINCTION

* Became one of the first women "Executive Chefs" certified by the American Culinary Federation (ACF).
* Am a member of the national and local chapters of the American Culinary Federation, based on 20 years of excellence in food preparation; am president of the local chapter.

EXPERIENCE

RESTAURANT OPERATIONS MANAGER. U.S. Air Force, Pope Air Force Base, NC (1983-present). Plan, direct, and supervise food preparation and operations for special party catering, banquets, and daily menus for an officers' restaurant and dining room serving 7,000 people monthly.
* Supervise 35 employees; train and instruct cooks.
* Coordinate recipes and menus both standardized and special.
* Maintain adequate food supplies and stock.
* Reduced production costs 15% by purchasing quality products and controlling food waste and portioning.
* Demonstrated financial expertise in managing operating expenses such as food and labor costs.
* Became skilled in office administration related to effective food service.

KITCHEN MANAGER and **COOK FOREMAN.** Pope AFB, NC (1978-83). Oversaw food preparation and serving activities for a dining facility serving 6,000 people a day while planning a monthly calendar of menus.
* Established requirements for inventory and supplies.
* Refined my planning skills in providing popular, cost-effective menus.\

KITCHEN/INVENTORY MANAGER. Pope AFB, NC (1975-78). Purchased food supplies while simultaneously managing kitchen operations.
* Strengthened my inventory management abilities in controlling food costs.

CATERING/KITCHEN SUPERVISOR. Pope AFB, NC (1971-75). Learned to expertly use a cyclic menu and a production sheet while managing dining room menus and handling food preparation and catering for special functions.

TRAINING

Excelled in specialized on-the-job training and seminars in the following:
Administration/Management: food/labor/beverage cost control, inventory, purchasing, office procedures, and food operations.
Cooking: advanced culinary art in food preparation and sanitation.

EDUCATION

Bachelor of Science (B.S.) degree now pending approval from the federal government through the American Culinary Federation.
Earned a diploma in Food and Beverage Management, Educational Institute of the American Hotel and Motel Association.

PERSONAL

Am cost-conscious and popularity-oriented in preparing international and classic American cuisine. Know how to balance costs and quality.

Date

Exact Name of Person
Title or Position
Name of Company
Address (no., street)
Address (city, state, zip)

Dear Exact Name of Person: (or Dear Sir or Madam if answering a blind ad.)

I would appreciate an opportunity to talk with you soon about how I could contribute to your organization through my expertise in food service management, procurement, and budgeting, along with my abilities in training and motivating employees and in planning and organizing projects and operations.

Management experience
Currently I manage operations of an 1,800-person dining facility serving 2,500 meals daily while administering an annual budget of $2.5 million. This year the facility was recognized as the best out of 150 and was selected as one of the top eight facilities throughout the U.S. I have supervised operations and management of as many as 13 facilities at one time. In one job as a Food Service Consultant, I evaluated facilities and recommended improvements.

Procurement know-how
An integral part of my experience has been food, supplies, and technical equipment procurement. In one job I supervised procurement, receipt, and storage of $80,000 in food supplies daily which amounted to purchasing of $4.5 million yearly.

Budgeting skills
My expertise in budgeting has enabled me to keep costs down while increasing quality of services. Most recently, when local "fast food" establishments opened on Army installations, I developed and implemented a "fast food" concept that increased a facility's earnings $200 per day. The concept is currently being studied for implementation on Army bases worldwide.

I hope you will write or call me soon to suggest a time when we could meet in person to discuss your current and future needs and how I might serve them. Thank you in advance for your time.

Sincerely yours,

Jamie Nettleton

Alternate last paragraph:
I hope you will welcome my call soon to arrange a brief meeting at your convenience to discuss your current and future needs and how I might serve them. Thank you in advance for your time.

JAMIE NETTLETON

1110½ Hay Street, Fayetteville, NC 28305   (910) 483-6611

OBJECTIVE

I want to benefit an organization through my experience in food service management, procurement, and budgeting, along with my abilities in training and motivating others while expertly planning and organizing special projects.

EXPERIENCE

DINING FACILITY MANAGER. U.S. Army, Ft. Bragg, NC (1983-present). Manage operations of an 1,800-person capacity dining facility serving 2,500 meals daily while administering a budget of $2.5 million annually.
* Supervise, train, and motivate 190 civilian and military employees.
* Coordinate procurement of food, equipment, and supplies; plan menus.
* Developed and implemented a "fast food" concept which increased revenue by $200 daily; this concept is currently being studied for possible implementation at military bases worldwide.
* Managed the dining facility recognized as the best out of 150 for 1985 and which was selected as one of the best eight throughout the U.S. Army.

FOOD PROCUREMENT DIRECTOR. U.S. Army, Ft. Bragg, NC (1982-83). Supervised procurement, receipt, and storage of $80,000 in food supplies daily which amounted to $4.5 million annually.
* Transported food to 35 facilities, coordinating 10 delivery trucks.
* Monitored and reviewed 35 dining facility accounts for accuracy.
* Procured, received, stored, issued, and rotated 720,000 operational meals worth $2.7 million as part of an emergency plan.
* Created a training program that vastly improved rations accountability.

FOOD SERVICE CONSULTANT and **SUPERVISOR.** U.S. Army, Korea (1981-82). While determining and implementing food service policy, supervised operations of 13 dining facilities serving 10,000 meals daily.
* Evaluated facilities and recommended improvements and changes.
* Administered a $4 million annual budget; supervised 400 people.
* Implemented procedures that improved equipment procurement.
* Wrote and implemented standard operating procedures for dining facility operation.

Other experience: U.S. Army, various locations worldwide. Developed detailed knowledge of food preparation as well as managerial skills while working my way up in jobs as Cook, Baker, Instructor, and Manager.
* Was promoted to the highest position in the Army's Food Service field.
* Developed reporting procedures, now used worldwide, to identify 13 categories of diners and save the local facility $12,000.
* Received the highest peacetime award for managing the facility selected as the best.
* Renovated two dining facilities at a $1 million cost.
* Planned and coordinated a $30,000 project to improve a facility's drainage system and sanitation according to EPA waste disposal standards.

EDUCATION

Hold an Associate of Arts (A.A.) degree in Administration of Justice, Los Angeles Community College, Los Angeles, CA, 1979.
Excelled in numerous U.S. Army training programs, including 2,000 hours in food service training and 2,160 hours in management training.

PERSONAL

Have know-how in technical equipment and foodstuffs purchasing.

Date

Exact Name of Person
Title or Position
Name of Company
Address (no., street)
Address (city, state, zip)

Dear Exact Name of Person: (or Dear Sir or Madam if answering a blind ad.)

I would appreciate an opportunity to talk with you soon about how I could benefit your organization through my expertise in hazardous material management, my abilities as a communicator and motivator, and my outstanding problem-solving and decision-making skills.

As an officer in the U.S. Army, I currently oversee the transportation/ storage/disposal of hazardous waste while managing operations for a 126-person chemical company. I created a storage and transportation plan which was approved by the Environmental Protection Agency and wrote standard operating procedures for a wide range of chemical operations, equipment maintenance, and site/materials security.

Previously I was chosen to "turn around" a troubled 20-person operation and within five months had implemented training programs which made it the best in its parent organization. I have created training and operations programs which were rated "extremely successful" by top military planners.

You would find me to be a highly motivated professional who is known for outstanding judgement in a crisis.

I hope you will welcome my call soon to arrange a brief meeting at your convenience to discuss your current and future needs and how I might serve them. Thank you in advance for your time.

Sincerely yours,

Michael A. Cozza

Alternate last paragraph:
I hope you will call or write me soon to suggest a time convenient for us to meet and discuss your current and future needs and how I might serve them. Thank you in advance for your time.

MICHAEL A. COZZA
1110½ Hay Street, Fayetteville, NC 28305   (910) 483-6611

OBJECTIVE

I want to benefit an organization through my background in hazardous waste control management, my outstanding skills as a communicator and motivator, and my creative problem-solving and decision-making abilities.

EXPERIENCE

HAZARDOUS WASTE CONTROL MANAGER. U.S. Army, Ft. Bragg, NC (1989-present). Because of my waste management expertise, was handpicked to oversee the storage/disposal of hazardous waste while managing operations for a 126-person chemical company; control a $154,000 operating budget.
* Forecast transportation and storage needs for hazardous waste.
* Ensure security for dangerous materials; oversee maintenance operations.
* Supervise a 16-person executive office staff.
* Created and implemented a **hazardous material storage and disposal plan** which was approved by the Environmental Protection Agency.
* Wrote and published standard operating procedures for chemical operations, maintenance, and inspections.
* Was cited with dramatically increasing efficiency of operations; received unusually high scores on site and operational inspections.
* Assumed the role of acting general manager during the manager's absence.

OPERATIONS/NUCLEAR, BIOLOGICAL, AND CHEMICAL (NBC) MANAGER. U.S. Army, Ft. Bragg, NC (1988-89). Was selected to "turn around" this troubled operation, and implemented new training programs which made it the best in its parent organization within five months; supervised 20 people operating/maintaining $1.5 million of sophisticated equipment.
* Managed all nuclear, biological, and chemical operations and training.
* Raised the efficiency of maintenance operations to its highest level ever.
* Received a respected medal for my ability to manage operations and improve morale.

NUCLEAR, BIOLOGICAL, AND CHEMICAL (NBC) OPERATIONS MANAGER. U.S. Army, Ft. Bragg, NC (1987-88). Was commended during top-level inspections for integrating "train the trainers" training, personnel training, and inspections into an "extremely successful" NBC program for a 400-person organization; advised top military executives on NBC operations while supervising a staff of seven people.
* Acted as liaison with other Army, Air Force, and Marine NBC units.
* Coordinated "modernizations" for operations; forecasted long-range needs.

EDUCATION

Bachelor of Science in Chemistry, Florida Institute of Technology, Melbourne, FL, 1986.

TRAINING

Completed courses in Business, Fayetteville State University, NC.
Graduated from Army training courses in personnel management, hazardous waste transportation/storage/disposal, and NBC operations.
* Ranked **first** in my class, Chemical Officer Basic Course.

EQUIPMENT EXPERTISE

Operate chemical detection equipment: M8A1, alarm, chemical agent monitor.
Operate radiological detection equipment: IM-93, Dosimeter, IM 174, and AN/PDR-27 radiacmeters; use Zenith Laptop and IBM personal computers.

PERSONAL

Am skilled in NBC detection, reconnaissance, and decontamination. Hold Secret security clearance. Known for excellent judgement in a crisis.

Date

Exact Name of Person
Title or Position
Name of Company
Address (no., street)
Address (city, state, zip)

Dear Exact Name of Person: (or Dear Sir or Madam if answering a blind ad.)

I would appreciate an opportunity to talk with you soon about how I could contribute to your organization through my expertise in health care administration.

As you will see from my resume, I hold an undergraduate degree in Health Care Administration and a graduate degree in Human Resources Management. In addition, I have completed extensive training in Total Quality Leadership (TQL) and have applied that training in health care environments to streamline staffing requirements, improve equipment capability, and enhance the quality of services. I sincerely believe I have the ability to step into any nursing facility, outpatient practice, hospital, or health management organization and figure out new ways to enhance productivity and boost morale.

Not only do I have technical expertise in managing human resources and administering health care, but also I offer a reputation as a caring and compassionate person who believes that tact and diplomacy are essential tools for any supervisor. In every job I have held subordinates have come to rely on me for compassion, but they also trust my judgement and common sense in determining fair solutions for problems. I believe strongly in motivating and encouraging staff by recognizing their contributions and providing appropriate awards/recognition for people who "make things happen." I believe in leadership by example.

You would find me in person to be a congenial professional who has found that flexibility and adaptability are key ingredients for success in the health care field.

I hope you will welcome my call soon to arrange a brief meeting at your convenience to discuss your current and future needs and how I might serve them. Thank you in advance for your time.

Sincerely yours,

Carroll McKinney

Alternate last paragraph:
I hope you will call or write me soon to suggest a time convenient for us to meet and discuss your current and future needs and how I might best serve them. Thank you in advance for your time.

CARROLL MCKINNEY
1110 ½ Hay Street, Fayetteville, NC 28305   (910) 483-6611

OBJECTIVE   To offer my versatile experience in health care administration to a health services organization that can use a caring and compassionate manager known for a commitment to Total Quality Leadership (TQL) as well as for a tactful and diplomatic style of solving problems.

EDUCATION   **Master of Arts**, Human Resources Management, Pepperdine University, Malibu, CA, 1981.
Bachelor of Science, Health Care Administration, Southern Illinois University, Carbondale, IL, 1979.

EXPERIENCE   **HEALTH CARE ADMINISTRATOR.** Branch Medical Clinic, Silverdale, WA (1992-present). Supervise a 60-person staff of health care providers and support personnel providing primary care to 12,000 people, while also managing a $450,000 clinical budget.
* Creatively applied my expertise in Total Quality Leadership to streamline staffing requirements, improve equipment capability, and enhance quality assessment.
* Formulated, implemented, and coordinated new health services programs.
* Collected data related to patient care and staff performance; conducted performance reviews with employees to ensure that high standards of care are met or exceeded.

DEPARTMENT HEAD, PATIENT ADMINISTRATION. Naval Hospital, Long Beach, CA (1989-92). Coordinated administrative matters related to the treatment and disposition of 9,000 patients annually.
* Transformed a disorganized operation into a hub of efficiency which became respected for excellent records management, statistical data collection, and decedent affairs administration.
* Was commended for using my tactful professional style of dealing with people to enhance employee morale and improve coordination among all staff.

ADMINISTRATIVE OFFICER. Naval Hospital Ship Mercy, Oakland, CA (1986-89). Managed all support services and administration for a staff of 450 people involved in medical and non-medical activities ranging from patient administration to housekeeping and security.
* Became comfortable managing people performing jobs which I knew nothing about.

ADMINISTRATIVE OFFICER. Dental Technician School, San Diego, CA (1984-86). At this prestigious dental academy graduating 600 dental technicians annually, coordinated all support and administrative services for a staff of 40 people serving a 180-person student body.
* Oversaw administration of personnel records, documented training progress, ordered supplies/equipment, oversaw equipment calibration and preventive maintenance, and assured the high quality delivery of services ranging from clerical support to facility maintenance.
* Became known for my deep commitment to enhancing staff morale and advancing the careers of future leaders through targeting training needs and promotion opportunities.

MEDICAL DEPARTMENT CHIEF. U.S.S. Peleliu, Long Beach, CA (1982-84). Led this department to earn two consecutive "outstanding" ratings during rigorous annual inspections of the primary and emergency health care provided by a 40-person staff to a crew of 2,000 people.
* Used my management skills to improve all areas of operations including quality assurance, financial control, equipment operation, medical supply, occupational safety, patient administration, and decedent affairs.

DATA PROCESSING DIRECTOR. Naval Hospital, Camp Pendleton, CA (1979-82). Took over the management of an outmoded information system in an antiquated facility, and eventually developed the concept for and obtained approval for funding a modern ADP operation.
* Supervised a staff of seven people involved in providing data processing services for a 200-bed hospital; oversaw data processing of admissions data, financial and personnel information, as well as workload and staffing statistics.

PERSONAL   Speak and read German. Am known for keeping one eye on the bottom line and the other eye on operations in order to continuously improve services and results.

Date

Exact Name of Person
Title or Position
Company Name
Address (number and street)
Address (city, state, ZIP)

Dear Exact Name of Person: (or Dear Sir or Madam if answering a blind ad.)

I would appreciate an opportunity to talk with you soon about how I could contribute to your organization through my administrative management experience, strong interpersonal skills, and reputation for high personal standards and ethics.

As you will see from my enclosed resume, I have refined my knowledge in areas ranging from budgeting, to human resource management, to purchasing and inventory control, to customer relations. I also have gained experience in ensuring compliance with OSHA and other governmental standards, overseeing quality assurance activities, and supervising risk management and safety programs.

Although my experience is in the many aspects of the health care management field and my B.S. degree is in Health Care Management, I offer personal qualities, management skills, and technical knowledge that would easily transfer to any activity which requires attention to detail, communication skills, and an ability to deliver the highest quality results.

I hope you will welcome my call soon to arrange a brief meeting at your convenience to discuss your current and future needs and how I might serve them. Thank you in advance for your time.

Sincerely yours,

Howard Kubinski

Alternate last paragraph:
I hope you will call or write me soon to suggest a time convenient for us to meet and discuss your current and future needs and how I might serve them. Thank you in advance for your time.

HOWARD KUBINSKI

1110½ Hay Street, Fayetteville, NC 28305   (910) 483-6611

OBJECTIVE

To apply a broad base of experience to an organization that can benefit from my skills in office administration, records management, inventory control, and budgeting as well as my specialized education and knowledge of the health care industry.

EDUCATION & TRAINING

Earned a B.S. degree in **Health Care Management,** Park College, Parkville, MO, 1995.
* Graduated *cum laude*; excelled in specialized course work including the following:

organizational behavior	labor relations	public health issues
micro- and macroeconomics	social problems	health insurance
managerial communication	social psychology	accounting I and II
production and operations management		financial management
laws of hospital administration and medical care		statistics and business math
senior thesis/seminar in health care management		the hospital and the community

Completed extensive training including a 400-hour health care professional training program and a leadership development course.

SPECIAL SKILLS

Office administration and operations: human resource management, budgeting, records, quality control, purchasing and receiving, inventory control, scheduling, safety, and risk management
Computers and office machines: DOS 6.0, Microsoft Word, PowerPoint, Excel, WordPerfect, Harvard Graphics, and Windows
use standard office equipment: typewriters, copiers, multiline phones, and fax machines
Medical procedures: am certified in CPR and familiar with operating room protocol and procedures as well as infection control procedures

EXPERIENCE

MEDICAL CLINIC ASSOCIATE MANAGER. U.S. Air Force, San Antonio, TX (1994-95). Selected for a position usually reserved for more senior personnel, provided strong leadership despite severe manpower shortages as manager of the nonmedical staff of a clinic with nine resident surgeons and five staff surgeons.
* Ensured that the clinic operated smoothly by determining work assignments and training new employees in safety and operational procedures for even-better patient care.
* Established a thorough infection control inspection routine which resulted in improved conditions and reduced the chances of passing infections.
* Became familiar and ensured compliance with requirements and regulations set up by OSHA, the medical center administrator, and the department chairman.
* Screened potential patients and made decisions on accepting them into the clinic; handled complaints.

MEDICAL RECORDS MANAGER and **QUALITY ASSURANCE COORDINATOR.** USAF, San Antonio, TX (1992-94). In a department with an average of 385 patients a day, controlled an inventory of 8,000 medical records including making patient appointments, conducting third-party billings, and screening records to ensure quality and risk management avoidance.
* Collected daily figures on numbers of patients seen and used this information to prepare monthly production requirements.
* Encouraged a sense of team work in a reception staff with diverse backgrounds and work experience and prepared updated job descriptions to help pinpoint responsibilities.
* Became especially skilled in filling canceled appointments by maintaining a 98% fill rate.

MEDICAL SUPPLY MANAGER. USAF, Grand Forks, ND (1990-92). Controlled a $180,000 medical equipment inventory, receivables, and expenditures averaging approximately $94,000 for a medical clinic with from 12 to 15 care providers.
* Was cited for my ability to ensure supply activities were completed on time while maintaining quarterly budgets and reporting figures to the hospital board on a regular basis.
* Justified purchase requests and weighed them against those from other departments.
* Located a source and procured $14,000 worth of badly needed equipment.
* Developed a successful competitive bidding system for large equipment purchases.
* Volunteered as a medic for the state Special Olympics two years running.

SAFETY DIRECTOR. USAF, Grand Forks, ND (1988-90). Coordinated safety training for 12 professional staff members and 32 auxiliary personnel; practiced health care according to OSHA and clinical safety guidelines.

PERSONAL

Known for my integrity and personal values, was entrusted with a Secret security clearance. Offer strong communication and customer service skills. Am very creative.

Date

Exact Name of Person
Title or Position
Name of Company
Address (no., street)
Address (city, state, zip)

Dear Exact Name of Person: (or Dear Sir or Madam if answering a blind ad.)

I would appreciate an opportunity to talk with you soon about how I could contribute to your organization through my extensive management experience as a junior military officer.

After graduating with my B.S. degree in History and Sociology, I was commissioned as an officer in the U.S. Army specializing in the medical field. Evaluated in writing as "a gifted young officer with incredible potential for achieving great things," I have proudly managed the provision of services including emergency evacuation by helicopter and ambulance, frontline medical and surgical treatment, dental care, and hospitalization. In my most recent job as manager of a 29-person medical unit which included a physician's assistant and a surgeon serving an 800-employee organization, I proudly trained and led some of the world's finest airborne medics.

In all my jobs as a military officer, I was placed in "hot-seat" positions in charge of making decisions in situations where there was no room for error because a wrong choice could lead to loss of life and property. I have learned how to make prudent decisions under the pressure of tight deadlines and under the stress of combat-like conditions, and I am certain the problem-solving and decision-making skills I have refined in "life-or-death" situations would be transferable to any type of organization. I offer a proven ability to train others; recently I have trained nonmedical personnel to achieve certifications in life saving, and in my previous job I initiated an employee-taught medical training program related to ambulance services. I am skilled at inventory control and have been extensively involved in the purchasing of equipment and supplies.

You would find me in person to be a self-motivated, goal-oriented individual who prides myself on producing top-quality results at all times.

I hope you will call or write me soon to suggest a time convenient for us to meet and discuss your current and future needs and how I might serve them. Thank you in advance for you time.

Sincerely yours,

Richard B. Smothers

Alternate last paragraph:
I hope you will welcome my call soon to arrange a brief meeting at your convenience to discuss your current and future needs and how I might serve them. Thank you in advance for your time.

RICHARD B. SMOTHERS
1110½ Hay Street, Fayetteville, NC 28305   (910) 483-6611

OBJECTIVE

To benefit an organization that can use a dedicated young professional who offers extensive experience in planning and directing the provision of medical services including coordinating field hospital activities and managing medical evacuations by ground, sea, and air.

EDUCATION & SPECIALIZED TRAINING

Completed B.S. degree in History with a minor Sociology, Jacksonville University, FL, 1992; 3.1 GPA.
* Held numerous leadership positions: elected president and vice-president of fraternity, appointed member of university curriculum committee, and selected as ROTC executive officer and training officer.
* As a military officer, specialized in the medical field and completed the Officer's Course in the Medical Service Corps.
* Completed rigorous training programs including Air Assault School (learned to set up helicopter landing zones); Airborne School (became a skilled parachutist); Air Movement Operations Course (learned to survey/inspect hazardous materials for air transport); Airborne Leaders Course (learned management techniques for hostile environments); and Small Unit Leader's Protection Course (was trained in safety management and OSHA).

EXPERIENCE

MEDICAL UNIT MANAGER. U.S. Army, Ft. Bragg, NC (1994-Jan 96). In charge of a 29-person platoon which included a surgeon and physician's assistant, have become skilled in coordinating frontline medical treatment, emergency resuscitation, and evacuation by helicopter or ambulance for an 800-person airborne organization involved in hazardous missions worldwide.
* Have proudly trained, led, and managed some of the world's finest airborne medics.
* Have provided medical services during parachute assaults, offensive and defensive operations, and in a wide range of hazardous environments.
* Personally accounted for $500,000 in equipment and managed a $15,000 annual budget.
* Trained nonmedical personnel to achieve their Combat Life Saver Certification.
* Trained and evaluated Puerto Rican National Guardsmen; prepared my medical unit for the parachute assault mission into Haiti which President Clinton canceled at the last minute.
* On my own initiative, revitalized the organization's sports program.
* Was evaluated in writing as "a gifted young officer with incredible potential for achieving great things."

TREATMENT UNIT MANAGER. U.S. Army, Ft. Bragg, NC (1993-94). At the world's largest U.S. military base, was in charge of 29 people who were responsible for providing all medical care for a 3,000-person airborne organization which had to remain continuously ready to relocate worldwide.
* Maintained employee skills in a combat-ready, emergency-ready condition.
* Established and managed a field hospital with major surgical capabilities, the capacity for hospitalizing people up to 72 hours, and the ability to provide full dental care.
* Controlled more than $1.5 million in equipment.
* Initiated an employee-taught medical training program related to ambulance services.
* During numerous projects, flawlessly managed the ordering and logistics of medical equipment and supplies.

AMBULANCE UNIT MANAGER. U.S. Army, Ft. Bragg, NC (1993). Managed 16 soldiers and $1 million in equipment while managing a fleet of ambulances providing emergency evacuation services for a 3,000-person airborne organization; also coordinated air evacuation services by helicopter.
* Became skilled in coordinating with social services organizations, hospitals, airports, private transportation companies, and others involved in providing emergency transport.
* Rewrote standard operating procedures for emergency evacuations after serving in this position; those SOPs are still in use.

AWARDS

Received three separate Army Achievement Medals and one Humanitarian Service Medal.

PERSONAL

Am single and will relocate according to employer needs.

Date

Exact Name of Person
Title or Position
Name of Company
Address (no., street)
Address (city, state, zip)

Dear Exact Name of Person: (or Dear Sir or Madam if answering a blind ad.)

Can you use a hard-working young professional who has earned a reputation for knowledge, skills, and abilities gained working in the medical field in direct patient care settings as well as in the areas of medical office procedures and records management?

During approximately seven years of experience while serving my country in the U.S. Army, I earned numerous medals and awards in recognition of my professionalism and accomplishments. As a medical specialist I was an important contributor to the success of a unit which was often called on to respond to emergencies in locations throughout the world. I was honored for my professionalism under austere conditions and in crisis situations in Haiti and Somalia as well as during Hurricane Andrew relief efforts in Florida.

As you will see from my enclosed resume, I completed extensive training which led to certification in the areas of nursing procedures and preventive medicine along with medical and dental office administration. I would like to point out some of the highlights of my special skills and areas of knowledge which are explained in detail on my resume: I am familiar with most standard office equipment, medical office administration/record keeping, common medical terminology, and activities ranging from triage, to CPR/first aid/resuscitation, to preparing patients for evacuation, to charting and collecting vital signs.

I hope you will welcome my call soon to arrange a brief meeting at your convenience to discuss your current and future needs and how I might serve them. Thank you in advance for your time.

Sincerely yours,

Kathryn Anne Chandler

Alternate last paragraph:
I hope you will call or write me soon to suggest a time convenient for us to meet and discuss your current and future needs and how I might serve them. Thank you in advance for your time.

KATHRYN ANNE CHANDLER
1110½ Hay Street, Fayetteville, NC 28305   (910) 483-6611

OBJECTIVE

To offer knowledge and skills in the medical field to an organization that can use a dedicated young professional who offers practical experience in the areas of providing primary medical care, maintaining medical equipment, and conducting administrative operations.

EDUCATION

Completed course work by correspondence which led to certifications in nursing, preventive medicine, and medical and dental office administration.

TRAINING

Excelled in more than 440 hours of medical proficiency training courses which emphasized such subjects as the following:

collecting specimens	drawing blood
preparing nursing notes	processing EKGs
responding to medical emergencies	logging lab results
supervising and scheduling personnel	setting up IV infusions
overseeing equal opportunity programs and responding to complaints	

* Maintained a high academic average and displayed leadership which led to my recognition as Honor Graduate of my three-month medical proficiency class.

EXPERIENCE

SENIOR MEDIC and **MEDICAL EQUIPMENT SPECIALIST.** U.S. Army, Ft. Drum, NY (1990-95). Won several awards and medals for my accomplishments during crisis situations and international operations as a Medic with an organization frequently called on to respond to real-world emergencies.
* Became highly skilled in preparing for and handling mass casualties and served in Somalia and Haiti as well as in Florida during Hurricane Andrew relief efforts.
* Learned to maintain critical medical equipment and was selected to train new personnel in this important area.
* Was cited as an important contributor to efforts which resulted in my unit receiving a prestigious Joint Meritorious Unit Award for our part in "Operation Restore Hope" in Somalia.
* Received the National Defense Service Medal for my professionalism and skills applied as a Combat Medic during the war in the Middle East and an Armed Forces Expeditionary Medal for my contributions during actions in Haiti.
* Following Hurricane Andrew relief efforts in Florida, was honored with a Humanitarian Service Medal for my professionalism and ability to handle the pressure and stress of dealing with severely injured patients after a devastating natural disaster.
* Received the second of two Army Achievement Medals in 1991.

MEDICAL RECORDS SPECIALIST. U.S. Army, Germany (1988-90).
Maintained the medical records for approximately 100 people while handling routine medical screening and care including immunizations, sutures, collecting patient information for doctors, and taking blood pressure, temperature, and other vital signs.
* Used my training and knowledge to make diagnoses of simple medical problems so that this information could be given to the doctor who would be seeing the patient.
* In recognition of my willingness to take on new responsibilities and quickly master new procedures, was trained in casting and basic lab procedures such as urinalysis.
* Contributed skills in settings including the intensive care unit and while charting patient vital signs on a ward in the Wurzburg evacuation hospital.
* Became familiar with various types of medical equipment, their use, and maintenance.
* Was honored with my first achievement medal for contributions to the quality of medical care and professional handling of important medical records.

SPECIAL SKILLS

Through training and experience, have become skilled in procedures including:

CPR/first aid	resuscitation	triage
passing medications	aeromedical evacuation	starting IVs
collecting, monitoring, and recording vital signs		

Am knowledgeable of most common medical terminology.

PERSONAL

Am highly motivated and can be counted on to handle the pressures of a heavy work load without sacrificing quality. Have a reputation for adaptability and flexibility.

129

Date

Exact Name of Person
Title or Position
Name of Company
Address (no., street)
Address (city, state, zip)

Dear Exact Name of Person: (or Dear Sir or Madam if answering a blind ad.)

I would appreciate an opportunity to talk with you soon about how I could contribute to your organization through my experience in medical office management and health care administration.

While serving my country in the U.S. Air Force, I completed extensive training in many different areas of health care administration. I am experienced in utilizing medical terminology, and I have supervised up to 10 employees. In one job as a Supervisor of Outpatient Records I devised a systematic method of filing outpatient embossed cards which eliminated a time-consuming and expensive process of handwriting information on medical files. I am known for my creativity in finding new yet simple ways to make any operation run more efficiently. In a job as a Medical Readiness Clerk I improved a highly deficient clinic security program. In another job as a Biostatistics Supervisor, I was known for my ability to tactfully defuse public relations problems while negotiating with civilian hospitals and agencies to handle debt/collections matters.

You would find me to be a gracious individual who prides myself on performing any task to the best of my ability. I have been praised in writing as exceptionally skilled in all areas of health management and as highly self motivated and hard working. I was placed in positions of trust and responsibility while serving in the Air Force and was entrusted with a Top Secret SCI security clearance.

A member of the American College of Healthcare Executives, I am knowledgeable of software including WordPerfect, Lotus 1-2-3, WordStar, dBase, and Professional Write.

I hope you will call or write me soon to suggest a time convenient for us to meet and discuss your current and future needs and how I might serve them. Thank you in advance for you time.

Sincerely yours,

Jane Doe

Alternate last paragraph:
I hope you will welcome my call soon to arrange a brief meeting at your convenience to discuss your current and future needs and how I might serve them. Thank you in advance for your time.

JANE DOE

1110½ Hay Street, Fayetteville, NC 28305   (910) 483-6611

OBJECTIVE   To contribute to an organization that can use a medical administration specialist who offers excellent computer operations skills along with experience in performing nearly every kind of office activity related to medical operations administration.

AFFILIATIONS   Member, American College of Healthcare Executives

COMPUTERS   Trained to use computer software and operating systems including Windows, Enable, Lotus 1-2-3, WordPerfect, WordStar, dBase, and Professional Write; have used computer systems manufactured by IBM, Zenith, Packard Bell, and Zeos; experienced in using E-Mail.
* Have utilized the **Stand Alone Scheduling System (SASS)** to make patient appointments and the **DEERS System** to verify DEERS enrollment.

MEDICAL TERMINOLOGY
* Have utilized medical terminology as a Health Services Management Journeyman.
* Utilized medical terminology to read records and physician diagnoses/procedures.
* Excelled in formal classroom training focused on identifying medical prefixes, suffixes, root words, and their definitions; then received extensive on-the-job training while using medical terminology for correspondence and day-to-day oral communication.

EXPERIENCE   **BIOSTATISTICS SUPERVISOR.** U.S. Air Force, Pope AFB, NC (1993-94). Processed medical claims, paid active duty members' emergency medical bills from civilian facilities, and processed cash collection vouchers for fees collected for researching medical records for insurance companies.
* Was evaluated in writing as "exceptionally skilled in all areas of health management" and as "highly self motivated and hard working."
* Used the ICD-9-CM book to verify civilian physician diagnosis and procedures prior to paying hospital bills; utilized ICD-9-CM to audit medical records and to verify final diagnoses and procedures from patients' records.
* Maintained publications library; acted as Assistant Alternative Care Program Manager.
* Routinely conducted briefings, wrote training reports, authored Operations Instructions and standard operating procedures, and prepared employee performance reports.
* Tactfully resolved outstanding debt problems with civilian hospitals.

SUPERVISOR OF OUTPATIENT RECORDS. U.S.A.F., Germany (1992-93). Supervised five employees and maintained 9,000 medical records while assisting with Quality Service (QS) Audits and Patient Administration Measurement and Evaluations (M&E) Studies.
* Devised a systematic method of filing outpatient embossed cards, thus eliminating the need to handwrite information in medical records; played a key role in the management of the Personnel Reliability Program and the Tumor Registry.
* Established standard operating procedures for mailing/processing medical records.
* Stepped in as manager of Ambulatory Care for two months and excelled in the job.

MEDICAL READINESS CLERK. U.S. Air Force, Germany (1991-92). Was promoted rapidly after excelling in performing a variety of office tasks related to filing medical documents, managing Self-Aid Buddy Care Program which included training instructors, maintaining office publications, and overseeing mobility disaster preparedness programs.
* Researched, revised, and improved a highly deficient clinic security program.

ADMINISTRATIVE PERSONNEL CLERK. U.S. Air Force, Germany (1991). Received a quick promotion based on my performance in managing the clinic's publications library/filing system.

EDUCATION   Completing B.S. degree in Business Administration with a concentration in Health Care, Methodist College, Fayetteville, NC.
While serving in the Air Force, completed nearly three years of college-level training in the Health Service Management field in areas including medical records management, hospital admissions administration, outpatient administration, and medical office management.

PERSONAL   Am a quality-conscious individual known for my grace and tact in handling people. Am known for unquestioned integrity; held a Top Secret SCI security clearance.

Date

Exact Name of Person
Title or Position
Name of Company
Address (no., street)
Address (city, state, zip)

Dear Exact Name of Person: (or Dear Sir or Madam if answering a blind ad.)

I would appreciate an opportunity to talk with you soon about how I could contribute to your organization through my expertise as a medical laboratory technician/technologist along with my proven ability to train, motivate, supervise, and develop others. As a Michigan native, I shall be relocating back home upon completing my military service.

As you will see from my resume, most recently I have excelled in working at two jobs simultaneously while also going to school at night to earn a second bachelor's degree — a Bachelor of Science degree in Medical Lab Technology. As a Medical Lab Technician with a civilian major medical center, I perform quantitative and qualitative tests on blood and body fluids while working in all lab sections. In my other job, I am excelling as an Instructor/Writer while developing lesson plans and instructing more than 300 students annually in laboratory procedures. I take great pride in the fact that I have trained some of the world's finest medics, and I have redesigned lesson plans for teaching bacteriology, blood bank, parasitology, and mycology.

Previously I worked as a Medical Lab Technician at a forensic toxicology drug testing laboratory, where I also acted as supervisor of 10 people performing specimen testing.

I can provide outstanding personal and professional references, and I offer a reputation for unquestioned integrity. While serving my country in the U.S. Army, I received a medal for my role in a covert operation with the C.I.D., during which I was offered a bribe for "fixing" a specimen of a cocaine user. I am known for attention to detail, honesty, and reliability.

I hope you will welcome my call soon to arrange a brief meeting at your convenience to discuss your current and future needs and how I might serve them. Thank you in advance for your time.

Sincerely yours,

Larry Bruce Cook

Alternate last paragraph:
I hope you will call or write me soon to suggest a time convenient for us to meet and discuss your current and future needs and how I might serve them. Thank you in advance for your time.

LARRY BRUCE COOK
1110½ Hay Street, Fayetteville, NC 28305   (910) 483-6611

OBJECTIVE

To benefit an organization that can use an experienced medical lab technician/technologist with skills related to chemical pathology, forensic toxicology, and other areas along with proven supervisory, communication, instructional, research, and problem-solving abilities.

LICENSES & CERTIFICATIONS

Medical Laboratory Technician, American Society of Clinical Pathologists
Medical Laboratory Technician, American Medical Technologists
Eligible for ASCP Certification as a Medical Technologist

EDUCATION

Bachelor of Science, Biology and Psychology, University of the State of New York, 1995.
Bachelor of Health Science in Medical Lab Technology, Campbell University, Buies Creek, NC, 1995.
More than one year of training at Academy of Health Sciences in advanced laboratory skills.
Completed training sponsored by Society of Armed Forces Medical Lab Scientists.

EXPERIENCE

For the past two years, have been working at two jobs — one military, one civilian — while also going to college full time in the evenings; offer strong time management skills:
INSTRUCTOR/WRITER. U.S. Army Special Warfare Center, Ft. Bragg, NC (1992-present). Have earned a reputation as an outstanding communicator while instructing more than 300 students annually in laboratory procedures and in techniques for maintaining medical standards established by physicians and veterinarians.
* Developed and refined lesson plans; redesigned and rewrote bacteriology, blood bank, parasitology, and mycology lessons in a new, more user-friendly format.
* Taught laboratory subjects including hematology, urinalysis, bacteriology, blood bank, parasitology, mycology, and serology.
* Accounted for $150,000 in equipment and materials.
* Incorporated into lesson plans my formal training related to hazardous waste handling and disposal and my knowledge of incinerator operations and environmental laws.

MEDICAL LAB TECHNICIAN. Cape Fear Valley Medical Center, Fayetteville, NC (1992-present). At one of the largest medical centers in the southeast, performed quantitative and qualitative tests on blood and body fluids in the stat lab and in these other lab sections:
microbiology   hematology   urinalysis   coagulation   blood bank   chemistry

MEDICAL LAB TECHNICIAN and **SUPERVISOR.** Forensic Toxicology Drug Testing Laboratory, Ft. Meade, MD (1988-91). While excelling as a Medical Lab Technician, acted as supervisor of 10 military and civilian personnel involved in specimen processing, and was responsible for the legal chain of custody on all specimens as well as the processing of specimens for further testing.
* Also functioned as a *Radio Immuno Assay Technician*, monitoring quality control and assurance; produced controls and standards, performed calibration of pipettes, and prepared statistical calculations.
* Developed expertise in performing *extractions*, including chemical extractions of specimens for final analysis in GC/MS.
* Played a key role in rewriting the Standard Operating Procedures Manual.
* Received an Army Achievement Medal for a covert operation I performed with the C.I.D.; refused to accept a bribe for "fixing" a specimen for a cocaine user.
* Received two other medals during this time period, one for being named *Soldier of the Quarter* and the other for exceptionally meritorious service.

SECURITY SQUAD LEADER. Pine Knob Music Theatre, Clarkston, MI (1987). Refined my ability to stay calm during crises while supervising security patrols during concerts.

EQUIPMENT EXPERTISE

Proficient in the operation and general maintenance of the following:
Kodak Ektachem 700 & 850, DT 60   **Abbott** TDX, FLX, ADX, IMX
Coulter STKR, STKS, MAXM   **MLA** 1000, 800; **Rapimat** Auto UA Machine
BACTEC Bacti-Alert for Blood Culture   **Baxter** microscan

PERSONAL

Can provide exceptionally strong personal and professional references upon request. Take pride that I have trained some of the best medics in the world. Have held a **Top Secret security clearance with SBI.** Proficient with software including WordPerfect, Enable, Lotus 1-2-3, and dBase and am proficient with the DOS and Windows operating systems.

Date

Exact Name of Person
Title or Position
Name of Company
Address (no., street)
Address (city, state, zip)

Dear Exact Name of Person: (or Dear Sir or Madam if answering a blind ad.)

I would appreciate an opportunity to talk with you soon about how I could contribute to your organization through my experience in logistics and inventory management, my ability to motivate personnel, and my knowledge of computer systems operation.

Medical logistics management
While serving my country in the U.S. Air Force, I was recently selected to manage a multi-million-dollar hospital logistics account which earned top ratings among its 25 sister hospitals. During an intensive 20-day inspection, I received perfect scores on all areas for which I was accountable. In a previous job I created logistics policies which provided excellent customer service, and I also designed employee training and customer education "packages."

Aviation logistics management
While meeting the special logistics needs of Air Force aviation organizations worldwide, I rose to "top-level" management and earned a reputation for finding creative solutions to logistics problems. During the implementation of a new computer system, I studied workload trends and increased efficiency by reorganizing operations. By resolving a variety of purchasing problems, I eliminated unnecessary purchases and saved thousands of dollars yearly.

You would find me to be a dedicated and hard-working manager who excels in setting goals and motivating personnel to achieve them. I am sure you will find in me the knowledge you need to make your ideals "come to life."

I hope you will welcome my call soon to arrange a brief meeting at your convenience to discuss your current and future needs and how I might serve them. Thank you in advance for your time.

Sincerely yours,

Richard Shulman

Alternate last paragraph:
I hope you will call or write me soon to suggest a time convenient for us to meet and discuss your current and future needs and how I might serve them. Thank you in advance for your time.

RICHARD SHULMAN
1110½ Hay Street, Fayetteville, NC 28305   (910) 483-6611

OBJECTIVE

To benefit an organization through my management and logistics systems "know-how," my ability to motivate personnel, my skill in planning and organizing projects, and my knowledge of computer operations.

CLEARANCE & SPECIAL SKILLS

* Hold Secret Security Clearance 2-NAC.
* Excel in meeting the logistics needs of medical and aviation organizations.
* Am very knowledgeable of U.S. Government and Department of Defense contracting and logistics systems.
* Operate WANG office automation systems and UNIVAC 1050 II systems.

EXPERIENCE

HOSPITAL LOGISTICS MANAGER. U.S. Air Force, Carswell AFB, TX (1987-90). Managed a hospital logistics account consistently described as "the best" compared to 25 sister hospitals: while managing 17 people, supervised the purchasing of $10 million in medical/dental supplies yearly and controlled a supply inventory of $1.5 million and an $8 million equipment account.
* Received perfect scores on **all** areas for which I was accountable after a grueling 20-day audit/inspection.

20 Years of Expertise in Managing Aviation and Medical Logistics

MEDICAL LOGISTICS CONSULTANT. U.S.A.F., Carswell AFB, TX (1985-86). Created, published, and implemented logistics policies related to customer service and employee training/customer education.
* Developed a method to track the inventory of Schedule III, IV, and V narcotics which resolved all discrepancies.
* Increased efficiency/accuracy by reorganizing the purchasing department.
* Organized one of the U.S.A.F.'s first medical logistics conferences; after its success, as was asked to host a second conference.
* Purchased $450,000 of equipment for a hospital construction project.

SUPPLY/QUALITY CONTROL ADMINISTRATOR. U.S.A.F., Offutt AFB, NE (1980-84). Was selected for this job determining the priorities to be used in ordering material; ordered and distributed medical supplies while performing quality control checks on materials which had become unsuitable/hazardous.

Highlights of Aviation Logistics Management: Rose to top levels of management while overseeing logistics systems for U.S.A.F. aviation organizations worldwide.
* Increased the efficiency and accuracy of computer operations by studying workload trends and "restructuring" the system for maximum flexibility.
* Created automated data processing procedures which reduced the manpower and cost needed to produce timely, accurate reports.
* Saved thousands of dollars yearly by resolving purchasing problems.
* Named "Supply Technician of the Year" for obtaining/distributing repair supplies.

EDUCATION & TRAINING

B.S. in **Occupational Education**, Southern Illinois University, 1979.
A.A. in **Information Systems Management**, Community College of the A.F., 1990.
Excelled in college-level U.S.A.F. training in management, inventory control, supply systems, purchasing, and computer operations.
* Was named **Honor Graduate** from Medical Material School.

PERSONAL

Have always earned "excellent" ratings on high-level inspections.

Date

Exact Name of Person
Title or Position
Name of Company
Address (no., street)
Address (city, state, zip)

Dear Exact Name of Person:` (or Dear Sir or Madam if answering a blind ad.)

I would appreciate an opportunity to talk with you soon about how I could benefit your organization through my experience and education in Psychology as well as my abilities as a communicator and administrator.

With a Ph.D. in Clinical Psychology, I have acquired extensive clinical experience as a Staff Psychologist in the U.S. Army.` While earning my doctorate, I excelled in clinical and administrative roles at the Army's busiest hospital.` Known as a charismatic leader, I often acted as the Chief of Psychological Services while providing a full range of psychotherapeutic and consultation/evaluation services.`

With a reputation as a caring professional and articulate communicator, I am skilled in using a wide range of standardized psychological tests and psychodiagnostic assessment tools.` An outstanding project coordinator and teacher, I have excelled in developing training for staff and conducting workshops in areas such as patient/staff relations, teen pregnancy, and suicide prevention.

You would find me to be a dedicated professional who offers the experience and knowledge needed to help achieve the realization of your organizational objectives.

I hope you will welcome my call soon to arrange a brief meeting at your convenience to discuss your current and future needs and how I might serve them.` Thank you in advance for your time.

Sincerely yours,

Susan Rhodes

Alternate last paragraph:
I hope you will call or write me soon to suggest a time convenient for us to meet and discuss your current and future needs and how I might serve them.` Thank you in advance for your time.`

SUSAN RHODES
1110½ Hay Street, Fayetteville, NC 28305   (910) 483-6611

OBJECTIVE   To benefit an organization that can use an experienced psychologist who offers extensive clinical experience and the ability to manage resources and administrative activities.

EDUCATION & TRAINING

Ph.D. in **Clinical Psychology**, University of Tennessee at Knoxville, 1989.
* While working as a clinical psychologist for the U.S. Army, collected data for and completed a doctoral dissertation entitled "Sex-Role Attitude-Behavior Congruence and Life Stress as Predictors of Dyadic Adjustment Among Black Couples."
* Was awarded a highly competitive Army Health Professions Scholarship, 1980.

B.A. in Psychology, University of Detroit, MI, 1978.
* Member, Psi Chi National Psychology Honor Society.

Excelled in numerous Army and civilian training programs in Psychology; continued my education by attending various workshops and seminars.

EXPERIENCE

STAFF PSYCHOLOGIST. U.S. Army, Ft. Bragg, NC (1986-90). Earned a reputation as a caring professional, outstanding communicator, and charismatic leader while providing individual, family, and group psychotherapy, crisis intervention services, and medical consultations for patients in the Army's busiest hospital.
* Conducted psychometric evaluations: neuropsychological, forensic, and psychotherapeutic; participated in daily case conferences.
* Supervised up to five paraprofessional behavioral science technicians.
* Excelled in handling a wide range of administrative duties.
* Oversaw inpatient psychiatric group therapy sessions.
* Often acted as Chief of Psychological Services, overseeing administrative and clinical services; during an eight week period, maintained the quality of care during a severe staffing shortage.
* Earned a respected commendation while serving on Adolescent Pregnancy and Family Advocacy Case Management Teams.
* In 1988 and 1989, managed teams of 20 staff members conducting psychiatric and neurological examinations on 3,400 officer trainees; augmented the tests by implementing a reading/comprehension test.
* Combined computerized assessment techniques and hand-scored methods to determine psychotherapeutic needs and psychiatric diagnoses.
* Excelled in using a wide range of psychological tests and assessment tools.
* Coordinated and led training and classes for staff in areas related to patient/staff relations, inpatient group therapy, teen suicide, and human behavior/psychopathology.

PSYCHOLOGY INTERN. U.S. Army, Ft. Gordon, GA (1984-85). Supervised five paraprofessionals while completing on-the-job training in child/family experience, adult medical/psychiatric, and community mental health; provided long- and short-term treatment and crisis intervention; developed and conducted assertiveness training programs.

PSYCHOLOGY ASSOCIATE. University of Tennessee, Knoxville, TN (1980-84). During four one-year training practicums, provided in- and outpatient psychotherapeutic services to patients of all ages; completed complex evaluations for agencies including public courts, the Department of Social Services, and schools.

AFFILIATION   Member, American Psychological Association

PERSONAL   Hold Secret security clearance. Excel in setting and achieving high goals.

Date

Exact Name of Person
Title or Position
Name of Company
Address (no., street)
Address (city, state, zip)

Dear Exact Name of Person: (or Dear Sir or Madam if answering a blind ad.)

I would appreciate an opportunity to talk with you soon about how I could contribute to your company through my proven expertise in personnel recruitment as well as my outstanding communication and sales abilities.

While serving my country in the U.S. Air Force, I have excelled in one of the toughest recruiting fields: the medical profession. Most recently, I "turned around" a troubled medical recruiting operation into one of the best in the country. I led the office to achieve 200% of its goals within six months in 1989 and had achieved 266% of my quota within the first six months of 1990. Known for my excellent management and "sales" skills, I have been selected for numerous honors.

In previous jobs, I earned a reputation as an outstanding achiever while managing administrative services. With a reputation as an astute problem solver, I once reduced the rate of late correspondence in one office from 90% to below 6% while dramatically improving accuracy. I offer a knowledge of several computer systems.

You would find me to be a dedicated professional who "gives his all" in every job. A "born motivator and leader," I have coached several high school and youth teams to victory.

I hope you will welcome my call soon to arrange a brief meeting at your convenience to discuss your current and future needs and how I might serve them. Thank you in advance for your time.

Sincerely yours,

Wayne Batten

Alternate last paragraph:
I hope you will call or write me soon to suggest a time convenient for us to meet and discuss your current and future needs and how I might serve them. Thank you in advance for your time.

WAYNE BATTEN

1110½ Hay Street, Fayetteville, NC 28305   (910) 483-6611

OBJECTIVE

To benefit an organization that can use an enthusiastic personality who offers proven personnel recruiting expertise as well as outstanding communication, motivational, and sales abilities.

EXPERIENCE

HEALTH CARE/MEDICAL INDUSTRIES RECRUITER. U.S. Air Force, Iowa City, IA (1989-90). As a personnel recruiter and "head hunter" in the health care/medical field, transformed a "troubled" recruiting office covering over 50,000 square miles into one of the top medical recruiting offices in the nation; achieved 200% of the 1989 annual health professions recruiting goal within six months.
* Designed and managed effective marketing campaigns and sales plans; made presentations on military careers to health care professionals.
* Controlled a $100,000 budget; supervised a staff of two.
* Was "Top Medical Recruiter" in the northern midwest, 1989; was named to the "Commander's Club" reserved for the best recruiters nationwide.
* Named "Manager of the Year," 1989.
* Achieved 266% of my assigned yearly goal in the first six months of 1990.
* Maintained a 92.5% sales success rate and an 85% referral rate.
* Created marketing campaigns which reached over 10,000 people.

PERSONNEL RECRUITER. U.S.A.F., Iowa City, IA (1987-89). Earned honors in 1988 including "Rookie Recruiter of the Year," "Recruiter of the Year," and "Top Regional Recruiter" while turning an average office into a "top seller" achieving double its sales goals.
* Produced market and production analyses; conducted vocational tests.
* Exceeded my sales quotas by 40% in 1987 and 123% in 1988; achieved 333% of my goal for executive trainee applicants in 1988.

ADMINISTRATIVE SERVICES MANAGER. U.S.A.F., Germany (1984-87). Was named "Administrator of the Year," 1985 and 1986 while managing an eight-person team providing administrative services for a 140-person organization.
* Reduced the rate of late correspondence from 90% to below 6% while maintaining a 98% accuracy rate.
* Learned to operate, and wrote standard operating procedures for, three state-of-the-art computer systems.
* Received the "Manager of the Year" award, 1986.

ADMINISTRATOR. U.S.A.F., Germany (1983-84). Was handpicked to manage an 18-person administrative office supporting a research and development project.

ADMINISTRATIVE AIDE. U.S.A.F., Little Rock, AR (1981-83). Earned rapid promotion to "middle management" while learning computer skills.

EDUCATION

A.A. degree in Information Systems Management, Community College of the Air Force, will be awarded 1991.
Excelled in college-level U.S.A.F. training related to marketing/recruitment, administration/management, and computer operations.

PERSONAL

Operate IBM PC, Wang, and Honeywell computers. An excellent coach, have led many high school/youth teams to victory. Am a "born motivator." Hold Top Secret security clearance with SBI and SCI.

Date

Exact Name of Person
Title or Position
Name of Company
Address (no., street)
Address (city, state, zip)

Dear Exact Name of Person: (or Dear Sir or Madam if answering a blind ad.)

I would appreciate an opportunity to talk with you soon about how I could contribute to your organization through my unusually strong combination of both nursing and consulting experience.

Since earning my Masters of Nursing (M.N.) degree with a 4.0 GPA, I have excelled in jobs which placed me in top-level consulting positions with decision-making authority regarding the medical products purchased and surgical services offered at major Army hospitals and medical centers. While being promoted to the rank of lieutenant colonel in the U.S. Army, I have earned a reputation as a persuasive communicator with vast knowledge of virtually every product utilized in medical environments.

In my current job as a Registered Nurse, I am also the Chief, Department of Nursing (Evenings/Nights) at Womack Army Hospital, and I have played a key role in the dramatic upgrading of what was a community hospital operating room into what is now a state-of-the-art major medical center. I am widely respected for my ability to apply my vast knowledge in creative ways. For example, in consultation with my colleagues, I conceived of and have implemented an idea for a pre-operative admission unit which has centralized all pre-operative activities into a "one-place, one-stop set up" for patients. I also have been a major contributor to decisions on equipment upgrades for general surgery, orthopedic, OB-GYN, GU, and ENT services. Recently I played a major role in purchasing vaporized hydrogen peroxide sterilization equipment which will shortly be replacing ethylene oxide sterilizers.

I believe I offer a unique ability to provide in-depth user-based technical knowledge and experience about the products your company is marketing to the medical community. I have excelled in jobs as a Director of Surgical Services, Operating Room Supervisor, Head Nurse, and Staff Development Coordinator so I have been the customer of the products which I would now like to assist in selling. With my strong background in administration and training, I am certain I could offer myself to hospitals for administrative posts when I leave the service this year, but what interests me most is the possibility of representing your company's very fine product line.

You would find me to be friendly professional and I am certain I could become a most valuable asset for your sales team. I can provide outstanding personal and professional references.

I hope you will call or write me soon to suggest a time convenient for us to meet and discuss your current and future needs and how I might serve them. Thank you in advance for you time.

Sincerely yours,

Larry Allan Caldwell

LARRY ALLAN CALDWELL

1110½ Hay Street, Fayetteville, NC 28305   (910) 483-6611

OBJECTIVE

To add value to an organization that can use a Registered Nurse who has risen to the rank of lieutenant colonel in the U.S. Army while acquiring expert knowledge of operating room equipment and medical supplies/products, earning a reputation as an extraordinary nursing administrator, and becoming known for exceptional consulting and decision-making skills.

EDUCATION

Masters of Nursing (M.N.) degree, LSU Medical Center, New Orleans, LA, 1984.
* Graduated with a 4.0 GPA and was selected for *Who's Who Among Students in American Colleges and Universities.*

Bachelor of Science in Nursing (B.S.N.) degree, Northwestern State University, Natchitoches, LA, 1974.

As a military officer, excelled in rigorous management and technical training programs and schools including Command & General Staff College.

EXPERIENCE

REGISTERED NURSE and **CHIEF, DEPARTMENT OF NURSING (Evenings/Nights).** Womack Army Medical Center, Ft. Bragg, NC (1994-present).

Manage Department of Nursing assets which include up to 75 professionals and paraprofessionals per shift while supervising all clinical practice and handling all staffing issues.
* Played a key role in the dramatic upgrading of a community hospital operating room into a state-of-the-art medical center OR; managed nursing assets while the center increased the number of elective surgery rooms from six rooms/day to 10 rooms/day as its surgical operational budget grew from $0.9 million to $2.5 million.
* Conceived of and implemented an idea, in consultation with my colleagues, for a pre-operative admission unit which has centralized all pre-operative activities including assessments, labs, EKGs, X-rays, and administrative services into a "one-place, one-stop set up" for patients; this has reduced costs and improved customer satisfaction.
* Am considered the medical center's "internal expert" on operating room equipment and sterile products.
* Was a major contributor to decisions on equipment upgrades for general surgery, orthopedic, OB-GYN, GU, ENT services; an example is vaporized hydrogen peroxide sterilization equipment which will shortly be replacing ethylene oxide sterilizers.
* Served briefly as **DIRECTOR OF SURGICAL SERVICES** in 1994 before getting promoted to my current job; oversaw a $2.7 million supply budget and a $7 million property book while managing a staff of 150 professionals and paraprofessionals providing support for more than 40 surgeons and 10 surgical specialties.
* Have been nominated for a prestigious Army award, along with three other individuals, for my work in saving $5.7 million through our expert team planning and establishment in 1994 of a field operating room performing 400 surgical procedures.

OPERATING ROOM SUPERVISOR. Womack Army Medical Center, Ft. Bragg, NC (1992-94).

Oversaw daily operations of an eight-room surgical suite with 10 surgical specialties performing more than 500 procedures monthly; managed a budget of $2 million while supervising up to 85 staff nurses and technicians.
* Purchased major safety monitoring equipment and sterilization equipment.

HEAD NURSE, OPERATING ROOM/CMS. Eisenhower Medical Center, Ft. Gordon, GA (1988-92).

Was first-line supervisor of an operating room/CMS staff of up to 75 individuals performing 13 surgical specialties in eight operating rooms handling total joints, major neurosurgical, open heart, major spinal procedures, and surgical care activities; oversaw medical residency programs.
* Served as the Operating Room Project Coordinator for the development of a multimillion-dollar cardio-thoracic surgical program.

141

- While playing a key role in implementing the cardio-thoracic surgical program, provided all assets needed to perform Percutaneous Transfemoral Coronary Angioplasty (PTCA) and Coronary Artery Bypass Graft (CABG) procedures; started the project in 1988 and approximately 50 procedures were performed in 1989.

HEAD NURSE, OPERATING ROOM/CMS. Kingdom of Saudi Arabia (1990-91).
Volunteered to go to the war zone during the Iraq-U.S. conflict; set up the operating room used during the war and directed daily activities of eight RNs and 30 operating room technicians.
- Created a catalogued warehousing system for all surgical supplies out of unused 40 ft. milvan for routine and emergency contingency supplies.
- Taught emergency thoracic and neurosurgical procedures for junior operating room staff members preparing them for the coming life-threatening combat casualties.

OPERATING ROOM/CMS SUPERVISOR. Republic of Korea (1987-88).
Managed a four-room operating room suite providing surgical support for all U.S. forces and their families.
- Played a key role in coordinating an exchange instructional program for Korean Army Nurse Corps operating room nurses.
- Was operationally in charge of the 121st Evacuation Hospital's OR/CMS Section.

STAFF DEVELOPMENT COORDINATOR. Walter Reed Army Medical Center, Washington, DC (1984-87).
Acted as Educational Coordinator for 120 operating room staff members, operating room nursing students, and operating room technician students while also serving as an Adjunct Faculty member for operating room nursing with James Madison School of Nursing and the University of Maryland School of Nursing.
- Administered an inservice education program, a quality improvement program, an operating room nursing program, and an operating room technician program.
- Served as a project officer on numerous interdisciplinary hospital committees.

STAFF NURSE, OPERATING ROOM/CMS. Keller Army Community Hospital, West Point, NY (1980-83).
Scrubbed and circulated on surgical procedure while serving as inservice coordinator for the unit.
- As Officer in Charge of the Central Material Section, oversaw all sterilization activities for the facility.
- Provided instruction for the operating room technician course.
- At a local school of nursing, served as a CPR instructor.
- Became accomplished in arthroscopic orthopedic surgical techniques.

Other experience: Served as a Staff Nurse at hospitals in the U.S. and West Germany.

LICENSE

Registered Nurse Louisiana License #32654, expires 31 December annually.
Registered Nurse North Carolina License currently being applied for.

AFFILIATIONS

Active member, Association of Operating Room Nurses.
- Presented numerous programs at local chapter meetings.

AWARDS

Have received numerous awards and honors for my consulting expertise, administrative excellence, and my ability to creatively apply my technical nursing knowledge.

PERSONAL

Enjoy the challenge of managing and adapting to change. Am a highly flexible and creative individual who offers excellent mechanical aptitude with common sense and highly refined decision-making skills. Believe in leadership by example; enjoy developing others. Can provide outstanding references.

Date

Exact Name of Person
Title or Position
Name of Company
Address (no., street)
Address (city, state, zip)

Dear Exact Name of Person: (or Dear Sir or Madam if answering a blind ad.)

I would appreciate an opportunity to talk with you soon about how I could contribute to your organization through my extensive experience in health care administration.

Most recently I have managed a hospital providing medical care for 52,000 people, including 42,000 migrant Cubans and Haitians. While administering a $15 million budget and directing a chain of command that includes 500 people, I have developed an exciting new "wellness program" while significantly improving procedures and systems for delivering health care. In my previous job I managed health care delivery for a 25,000-person community.

In a prior job I managed medical facilities and hospital construction programs in a nine-state area while managing $3.5 million in contracts for medical professionals. In that job I coordinated facility renovations, developed property management procedures, instituted Total Quality Management concepts, and became very knowledgeable of defense contracting while overseeing procurement of equipment and supplies.

As you will see from my resume, I offer a background that is probably unique in that I have also had extensive clinical experience. While being promoted from Seaman to Captain in the U.S. Navy, I gained experience as a primary care provider, laboratory technician, orthopedic cast room technician, and emergency room technician. Those early clinical experiences have been extremely valuable to me in my most recent administrative positions.

As a Diplomat in the American College of Healthcare Executives, I offer a "track record" of accomplishment and can provide outstanding personal and professional references. You would find me to be a congenial colleague with a total commitment to quality results and with a management style that others find "user friendly."

I hope you will welcome my call soon to arrange a brief meeting at your convenience to discuss your current and future needs and how I might serve them. Thank you in advance for your time.

Sincerely yours,

Adam H. Adcox

Alternate last paragraph:
I hope you will call or write me soon to suggest a time convenient for us to meet and discuss your current and future needs and how I might serve them. Thank you in advance for your time.

ADAM H. ADCOX
1110½ Hay Street, Fayetteville, NC 28305   (910) 483-6611

OBJECTIVE   To contribute to an organization that can use a health care executive who offers extensive knowledge of all clinical areas, dynamic leadership skills and administrative expertise, a strong commitment to total quality results, as well as a creative problem-solving style.

EDUCATION   **M.A. in Administration**, Pepperdine University, Los Angeles, CA, 1977.
B.S. in Health Care Administration, George Washington University, D.C., 1975.
Completed extensive executive education courses sponsored by the U.S. Navy related to legal aspects of medicine, health care management issues, and service delivery concepts.

AFFILIATIONS
* Diplomat, American College of Healthcare Executives
* Member, American College of Military Surgeons

COMPUTERS   Knowledgeable of WordPerfect, Harvard Graphics, dBase IV, and Lotus 1-2-3.

EXPERIENCE   **HOSPITAL ADMINISTRATOR.** U.S. Naval Hospital, Guantanamo Bay, Cuba (1993-present).
Manage a hospital that provides total health care support for 10,000 military and civilian personnel as well as 42,000 Cuban and Haitian migrants; oversee a system which includes:

> 55-bed acute care hospital   two 50-bed field hospitals
> freestanding outpatient clinic with 100,000 patient visits a year
> 24-hour advance cardiac life support emergency ambulance service
> occupational, preventive medicine, and emergency care for U.S. ships in Caribbean

* Administer a $15 million budget and oversee supervision of 500 people who include physicians, nurses, and other health care professionals.
* Planned and implemented procedures for providing health care support to Cuban and Haitian migrants in camps at Naval Base, Guantanamo Bay, Cuba.
* Developed a "wellness program" in this community; conceived of and implemented a computerized appointment system.
* Dramatically improved facilities by upgrading hospital electrical systems, renovating the freestanding clinic and emergency room, constructing a nursing home facility for aging Cubans, overseeing a 15,000-square-foot hospital addition, and planning/budgeting for a new hospital to be constructed in 1999.

CLINIC ADMINISTRATOR. Naval Medical Clinic, Kings Bay, GA (1990-93).
At a naval submarine base, oversaw the delivery of health care services for a 25,000-person community; oversaw a system which included:

> comprehensive outpatient services
> a 1,200-line-item pharmacy filling 10,000 prescriptions a month
> advanced cardiac life support emergency ambulance services
> complete radiology and laboratory services
> nuclear mass casualty management readiness and emergency department care

* Planned and vigorously promoted health maintenance and "wellness teaching" programs that made great progress in areas including weight control, stress management, exercise programs, and smoking cessation.
* Developed and implemented "managed care" initiatives that resulted in savings of more than $100,000 annually.
* Instilled a Total Quality Management philosophy which resulted in many improvements.
* Managed the development of highly effective contracts for medical waste disposal, reference laboratory service, and radiologist services.
* Was the only individual in the history of this command to attain a perfect score on the Navy Physical Readiness Test!

ASSISTANT CHIEF OF STAFF. Naval Medical Command Southeast, Jacksonville, FL (1987-90). Managed medical facilities and hospital construction programs in a nine-state area while also managing $3.5 million in contracts for health care professionals.
* Became extremely knowledgeable of defense contracting procedures, and provided technical advice in equipment procurement and material management.
* Developed and implemented a property management program which included Navy medicine's first bar code system for property identification.
* Coordinated the planning, design, and construction of a $53 million hospital renovation program.
* Developed a Quality Improvement Program for ensuring appropriate supplies and equipment support at hospitals and clinics.
* Coordinated procurement /installation of 14 X-Ray systems for naval hospitals in the southeast.

DIRECTOR OF ADMINISTRATION. U.S. Naval Hospital, Guantanamo Bay, Cuba (1986-87). Significantly improved nearly every aspect of the hospital's management information system while coordinating these and other functional areas:

		material management operation
education and training	comptroller functions	patient and personnel administration
food service	facilities management	bachelor housing/security/housekeeping

OUTPATIENT CLINIC ADMINISTRATOR. Branch Medical Clinic, Albany, GA (1983-86). Managed a main clinic and a satellite facility supporting 10,000 patient visits monthly; managed a 75-member staff which provided services including radiology, occupational health, laboratory, and a pharmacy filling 7,000 prescriptions monthly.
* Developed an extraordinarily efficient patient appointment system.
* Fostered excellent working relationships with patients and the community.

PHYSICIAN RECRUITER. Navy Recruiting Area Three, Macon, GA (1980-83). Excelled in recruiting physicians, nurses, dentists, and other health care professionals for service in the U.S. Navy; was named "Most Productive Physician Recruiter in the Navy in 1982."

MATERIAL MANAGEMENT DIRECTOR. U.S. Naval Hospital, Beaufort, SC (1978-80). Developed extremely successful and popular programs which were adopted for use in other medical facilities; designed and implemented programs that expedited the delivery of medical supplies while providing outstanding customer service professionals.
* Oversaw the procurement, receipt, safeguarding, and distribution of supplies, equipment, and services for a 150-bed hospital.

PERSONNEL DIRECTOR. U.S. Naval Hospital, Beaufort, SC (1975-78). Ensured the availability of staff to support a 150-bed acute care hospital.

Highlights of other experience:
PRIMARY CARE PROVIDER. Was responsible for the examination, diagnosis, and treatment of patients with general medical conditions.
CLINICAL LABORATORY TECHNICIAN. Performed clinical laboratory analysis.

CLEARANCE   Top Secret security clearance

SUMMARY OF EXPERIENCE

Hospital administration :	medical material management	patient records and administration
fiscal management	ambulatory care management	general hospital administration
facilities management	housekeeping/food service	education JCAHO

Clinical :	orthopedic cast room technician	emergency room/ambulance service
	ward management clinical laboratory	primary care as a provider

PERSONAL   Was promoted from Seaman Recruit to the officer rank of Captain (O-6), a rare accomplishment. Hobbies include running, cycling, weight lifting, operating my computer, gardening, scuba diving, and working with youth. Earned numerous prestigious medals and awards.

Date

Exact Name of Person
Title or Position
Name of Company
Address (no., street)
Address (city, state, zip)

Dear Exact Name of Person: (or Dear Sir or Madam if answering a blind ad.)

I would appreciate an opportunity to speak with you soon about how I could contribute to your organization through my education and experience in computer systems management and my skills in all phases of PC operations.

While working full time, I have recently been completing my B.S.degree in Information Systems Management. Over the course of the past eight years in the U.S. Army, I have excelled in jobs as a Systems Analyst. I am experienced in designing, configuring, and setting up systems, maintaining and repairing them, as well as in training others in computer applications. In every job I have held, I have increased organizational efficiency and employee productivity through my ability to train others and "translate" complex technical concepts into understandable language.

My software expertise is vast. I am familiar with virtually every popular software program on the market including Harvard Graphics, Lotus 1-2-3, DOS and Windows, WordPerfect, DBase, Procomm and Procomm Plus, Corel Draw, multimedia packages on CD ROM, and many others. Within a very short amount of time, I can rapidly master any new program or application, and I am highly proficient in working in the Windows environment. I offer detailed knowledge of computer databases, operating systems, and programming in BASIC and COBOL as well as extensive experience in systems security.

I offer a proven track record of exceptional performance backed by the maturity, natural leadership skills, and intelligence that can make me a valuable asset to your organization. You would find me in person to be a congenial individual who prides myself on my ability to develop rapport with people at all levels. I can provide outstanding personal and professional references at your request.

I hope you will welcome my call soon to arrange a brief meeting at your convenience to discuss your current and future needs and how I might serve them. Thank you in advance for your time.

Sincerely yours,

Albert Taylor

Alternate last paragraph:
I hope you will call or write me soon to suggest a time convenient for us to meet and discuss your current and future needs and how I might serve them. Thank you in advance for your time.

ALBERT TAYLOR
1110½ Hay Street, Fayetteville, NC 28305   (910) 483-6611

OBJECTIVE

To offer my self-motivation, initiative, creativity, intelligence, and highly refined analytical skills to an organization that can benefit from my expert software knowledge and experience as a systems analyst as well as my background in counterintelligence and security.

CLEARANCE & AREAS OF EXPERTISE

Top Secret security clearance with SCI (Sensitive Compartmented Information) access. Through training and experience, have become highly knowledgeable in areas such as:
Intelligence operations: intelligence collection and analysis   Special Operations
     surveillance/reconnaissance   investigations   interrogation
Computer operations: all facets of PC operations: building and setting up, maintaining, upgrading, and repairing as well as training others in systems operations
     programming in COBOL and BASIC   computer security   office automation
* Proficient with most popular software on the market including Harvard Graphics, Lotus 1-2-3, DOS and Windows, WordPerfect, DBase III & IV (can program in DBase), Corel Draw, multimedia packages on CD ROM, communications packages including Procomm and Procomm Plus, and many others.

EXPERIENCE

COUNTERINTELLIGENCE AGENT/ADP MANAGER. U.S. Army, Ft. Bragg, NC (1993-95). Consistently promoted ahead of my peers, supervise four team members and conduct investigations while ensuring the security of automated assets.
* Earned promotion to my current rank in under eight years, which usually 12 years.
* Chosen for a special assignment to Haiti, conducted operations including weapons raids, identification of possible hostile personnel, and Joint Special Operations.

SYSTEMS ANALYST/COUNTERINTELLIGENCE AGENT. U.S. Army, Germany (1989-93). Officially cited for my "honesty, integrity, and courage," excelled in a position which required me to wear "two hats": as a Systems Analyst, managed communications systems and, as a Counterintelligence Agent, conducted personnel security, counterespionage, and counterterrorism investigations.
* Set up and maintained 19 PCs and developed all the communications packages; initiated and implemented a new computer database system for tracking investigations and trained other personnel to use computer systems.
* Used my technical computer knowledge to upgrade ADP support by obtaining 11 additional operational systems; increased productivity through training.
* Was placed in charge of security for computer hardware, secure communications, and NBC (nuclear/biological/chemical) equipment worth in excess of $230,000.
* Orchestrated the "flawless apprehension" and debriefing of a foreign agent; completed 480 personnel security investigations and 25 defensive counterespionage cases; neutralized four foreign intelligence agents.
* Selected to attend two highly competitive advanced counterintelligence training courses.
* Developed and taught special NBC defense courses to prepare personnel for possible assignments to the Middle East in advance of the war in that area.
* Was officially cited for my thorough, high-caliber investigations with no deficiencies.
* Coached a subordinate to "expert" status with the .45-cal. pistol .

AUTOMATED DATA PROCESSING (ADP) SECURITY MANAGER. U.S. Army, Ft. Carson, CO (1988-89). Managed a team of specialists conducting risk analysis investigations on computer and communications systems used at a 24,000-person military community.
* Conducted successful investigations into several computer fraud cases.
* Excelled in providing support for state-of-the-art computer systems.
* Improved ADP security procedures through my skills in training and my example.

EDUCATION & TRAINING

B.S., Information Systems Management, University of Maryland, 1995.
Am studying Business Administration, Campbell University, Ft. Bragg, NC, campus.
Excelled in more than 2,940 hours of advanced training for counterintelligence agents including the FBI's Hostage Negotiation Course and a course in ADP security.

PERSONAL

Have been honored with a Meritorious Service and three Army Achievement Medals.

Date

Exact Name of Person
Title or Position
Name of Company
Address (no., street)
Address (city, state, zip)

Dear Exact Name of Person: (or Dear Sir or Madam if answering a blind ad.)

I would appreciate an opportunity to talk with you soon about how I could benefit your organization through my skills in operating and troubleshooting nearly every kind of telecommunications equipment, my familiarity with most systems used in intelligence operations, and my experience in supervising and motivating others.

While serving my country in the U.S. Navy, I operate and troubleshoot state-of-the-art satellite, microwave, and land cable telecommunications equipment used in the preparation, sending, and review of vital intelligence messages. I have played a key role in restoring communications during equipment failures and in updating equipment during a major ship overhaul.

With a Top Secret security clearance, I offer a working knowledge of Japanese. I have a "knack" for rapidly learning new skills. Before entering the military, I was promoted into critical jobs in the oil industry. With a reputation as an outstanding leader and motivator, I have been chosen for U.S. Navy leadership training and placed in supervisory roles.

You would find me to be a dedicated hard worker who offers outstanding troubleshooting and problem-solving skills.

I hope you will welcome my call soon to arrange a brief meeting at your convenience to discuss your current and future needs and how I might serve them. Thank you in advance for your time.

Sincerely yours,

Roger Salter

Alternate last paragraph:
I hope you will call or write me soon to suggest a time convenient for us to meet and discuss your current and future needs and how I might serve them. Thank you in advance for your time.

ROGER SALTER

1110½ Hay Street, Fayetteville, NC 28305   (910) 483-6611

OBJECTIVE	To benefit an organization through my technical telecommunications expertise, my knowledge of intelligence communications systems, as well as my experience as a supervisor and motivator.
CLEARANCE	Hold TOP SECRET security clearance.
EXPERIENCE	**COMMUNICATIONS SUPERVISOR.** U.S. Navy, Japan (1986-present). Supervise up to four people operating and troubleshooting state-of-the-art communications equipment used to prepare, send, and review vital incoming and outgoing intelligence messages.

* Have earned rapid promotion into "mid-management" because of my leadership ability and vast technical knowledge.
* Use satellite, microwave, and land cable communications equipment.
* Work closely with military and civilian organizations to troubleshoot and restore communications during equipment failures.
* Played a key role in implementing a highly sophisticated computer system; trained personnel in the use of new equipment.

COMMUNICATIONS EQUIPMENT OPERATOR. U.S. Navy, USS Midway (1984-86). Prepared, sent, and reviewed incoming and outgoing messages while troubleshooting communications equipment; updated and replaced equipment during a major systems overhaul.
* Gained practical experience in the use of TACINTEL equipment.

TACTICAL INTELLIGENCE (TACINTEL) EQUIPMENT SPECIALIST. U.S. Navy, Pensacola, FL (1983-84). Was selected for a year of college-level technical U.S. Navy training in the operation and troubleshooting of TACINTEL communications equipment.

EMPLOYMENT COUNSELOR. Employment Agency, Jackson, MS (1982-83). Refined my skills in communicating with people while placing them in jobs.

INSTALLER/SERVICE TECHNICIAN. Geolograph Pioneer, Inc., Houma, LA (1981). Installed and serviced state-of-the-art equipment on oil-drilling platforms to determine the depth of oil wells.

WIRELINE TECHNICIAN and **DRILLING FLUID ENGINEER.** NL Bariod/McCollugh, Houma, LA (1978-80). Mixed/serviced drilling fluid in oil wells; serviced drilling wireline units; was known for sound judgement in stressful and dangerous situations.

EQUIPMENT EXPERTISE	Operate/troubleshoot most kinds of telecommunications equipment/devices; familiar with almost all systems used in intelligence operations.

* Qualified on ST2D computer terminal, MUSIC system, technical control facility.
* Earned NEC-9185 (TACINTEL).

EDUCATION & TRAINING	Completed college-level U.S. Navy leadership training as well as training in operating and troubleshooting communications equipment including:

    TADIX/TRE   TACINTEL/NEC-9185 Technical Control Facilities   MUSIC
Science and General Studies, University of Colorado, Colorado Springs, CO.

PERSONAL	Have working knowledge of Japanese. Am knowledgeable of Japanese culture.

Date

Exact Name of Person
Title or Position
Name of Company
Address (no., street)
Address (city, state, zip)

Dear Exact Name of Person: (or Dear Sir or Madam if answering a blind ad.)

I would appreciate an opportunity to talk with you soon about how I could contribute to your organization through my exceptionally strong analytical, problem-solving, communication, and management skills.

As you will see from my resume, I have most recently been promoted ahead of my peers to manage a busy data processing office. I was selected for that position because of my previous performance as an intelligence analyst with the U.S. Army. While working with some of the world's most sophisticated (and usually classified) software programs, I excelled in performing international market research. I was specially selected to work with psychological operations experts on a research project about Haiti, and the study I produced has been widely praised and integrated into our nation's database of country research. I am skilled in conducting research, analyzing large volumes of data, and creating insightful reports that pinpoint problems and identify opportunities. In addition to pursuing a degree in market research, I have excelled in some of the military's most advanced training programs designed to refine analytical, problem-solving, and communication skills.

You would find me in person to be an enthusiastic individual with excellent written and oral communication skills. I pride myself on my high personal and professional standards of loyalty, reliability, and dedication, and I can provide strong references which will attest to those and other qualities. While serving my country, I was entrusted with one of the nation's highest security clearances — Top Secret with SBI.

I hope you will welcome my call when I try to arrange a brief meeting with you to discuss your current and future needs and how I might serve them. Thank you in advance for you time.

Sincerely yours,

Marvin Terry

Alternate last paragraph:
I hope you will welcome my call soon to arrange a brief meeting at your convenience to discuss your current and future needs and how I might serve them. Thank you in advance for your time.

MARVIN TERRY
1110½ Hay Street, Fayetteville, NC 28305   (910) 483-6611

OBJECTIVE

To benefit an organization that can use a dedicated young professional with extensive experience in market analysis and research, strong skills in office administration and computer system operation, as well as a proven ability to translate complex technical information into language that can be used in strategic decision making and operations planning.

CLEARANCE

Based on an exhaustive background investigation, was granted one of our nation's highest security clearances — Top Secret with SBI.

EXPERIENCE

SUPERVISING INTELLIGENCE ANALYST, SECURITY MANAGER, and **OFFICE ADMINISTRATOR.** U.S. Army, Ft. Bragg, NC (1993-96).
Was selected for a job normally held by someone higher in rank; manage a busy office and oversee the accurate and timely completion of correspondence and classified reports which usually must be prepared under extremely tight deadlines.
* Was specially selected as the main intelligence analyst working with high-level psychological operations experts on Uphold Democracy Haiti; undertook an exhaustive country research project and authored a highly praised report which is now part of the National Network of Intelligence Reports which provides the latest in country market research/information.
* Trained, motivated, and supervised two other intelligence analysts and monitored their work in a highly classified environment.
* Prepared and conducted briefings/debriefings for personnel assigned to terrorist and hostile intelligence service activities; coordinated with other agencies to disseminate information and analyze intelligence pertaining to religion, economics, demographics, politics, and other matters.
* Recently undertook a project during which I wrote the standard operating procedures (SOPs) for an 800-person organization; the SOPs I authored are used to safeguard classified material, computer systems, and other equipment valued at $4 million.
* Have received outstanding evaluations on all inspections of my work.
* Authored acclaimed reports on Somalia, Rwanda, and other countries.
* Am involved in a wide range of security-related matters; am the internal expert in completing paperwork for security clearances.
* Have become skilled in analyzing large volumes of data in order to pinpoint opportunities and identify problems.

INTELLIGENCE ANALYST. U.S. Army, Ft. Bragg, NC (1991-93).
Worked extensively on classified computer systems and prepared a wide range of classified reports and documents used in strategic decision making.

Other experience: **CREW CHIEF/CARPENTER.** Hackensack, NJ (1986-91). Learned to motivate construction workers to take pride in their work managing residential and commercial jobs.

EDUCATION

Am pursuing an associate's degree in International Marketing, Dominican College, Blauvelt, NY; degree expected in 1996.

TECHNICAL TRAINING

Completed some of the world's most sophisticated training programs related to intelligence operations; completed the Joint Operations Intelligence Course, the National Intelligence Course, and Intelligence Analysts Training.
Received extensive training in computer areas: completed POADS training on a DOS-based mainframe and Socrates training on the intelligence-gathering process.

COMPUTERS

Offer an ability to quickly master new software and hardware; have worked on some of the world's most sophisticated UNIX- and DOS-based systems.

PERSONAL

Can provide outstanding references. Am known for character and loyalty. Received several awards and medals for exceptional performance.

Date

Exact Name of Person
Title or Position
Name of Company
Address (no., street)
Address (city, state, zip)

Dear Exact Name of Person: (or Dear Sir or Madam if answering a blind ad.)

I would appreciate an opportunity to talk with you soon about how I could contribute to your organization through my experience in counterintelligence operations and security management as well as my skills as a communicator and motivator.

While serving my country in the U.S. Army as a Special Agent, I have acquired management experience related to intelligence, counterintelligence, and security operations. Currently I train and supervise personnel overseeing counterintelligence and security for special access programs located in six Army and four Department of Defense facilities. I am highly skilled in planning and conducting counterintelligence operations and in collecting, analyzing, and reporting information. I hold a Top Secret security clearance with SBI and am skilled in operating a wide range of firearms as well as COMSEC, HEXJAM, and other equipment.

As a security expert, I have often been selected to advise military leaders on personnel, information, and physical security programs. An outstanding manager, I have increased the efficiency of every organization I have worked with.

You would find me to be an adaptable and dynamic professional known for outstanding decision-making and problem-solving skills. Many people who know me consider my chief strength to be my ability to work with people and gain their confidence quickly.

I hope you will welcome my call soon to arrange a brief meeting at your convenience to discuss your current and future needs and how I might serve them. Thank you in advance for your time.

Sincerely yours,

Eugene Phipps

Alternate last paragraph:
I hope you will call or write me soon to suggest a time convenient for us to meet and discuss your current and future needs and how I might serve them. Thank you in advance for your time.

EUGENE PHIPPS

1110½ Hay Street, Fayetteville, NC 28305   (910) 483-6611

OBJECTIVE	To benefit an organization that can use an experienced counterintelligence and security professional who offers excellent communication and management skills as well as outstanding problem-solving ability.
CLEARANCE & SPECIAL SKILLS	Hold TOP SECRET security clearance with SBI dated February 1989. Operate COMSEC equipment including: KL-43, KY-57, MSQ-103, AN/PRD-10 and 11, MLKY-24, RACAL, and HEXJAM equipment. Am familiar with 9mm, .38 cal., and M16 firearms. Operate WANG computers with MultiMate, Office Writer, and dBase software.

EXPERIENCE

COUNTERINTELLIGENCE/SECURITY MANAGER. U.S. Army, Ft. Monroe, VA (1987-90). As a "Special Agent," was handpicked to train and supervise personnel overseeing counterintelligence and operational security for special access programs on six Army posts and four Department of Defense facilities.
* Planned, organized, and conducted counterintelligence investigations.
* Advised executives on security programs; prepared and reviewed reports.
* Was selected to train other special agents.
* Planned and presented briefings on terrorism, espionage, and subversion.
* Collected, analyzed, and reported information on foreign intelligence against the U.S.
* Earned a medal for my collection of Soviet intelligence information.

SPECIAL AGENT/COUNTERINTELLIGENCE MANAGER. U.S. Army, Korea (1987). Increased security awareness by preparing presentations for 1,500 personnel on subversion, espionage, and terrorist threats directed against the Army; trained and supervised two agents; conducted personnel security and counterintelligence investigations.
* Reviewed operational security procedures and advised executives on weaknesses in personnel, information, and physical security.
* Acted as liaison to Korean security organizations; coordinated Korean security presentations for U.S. personnel.
* Took over a disorganized operation and increased productivity 25%.

SPECIAL AGENT/SUPERVISOR. U.S. Army, Korea (1986-87). Was selected to collect, record, and analyze data on North Korean and Chinese forces; briefed executives.
* Used my management skills to increase information collection by 10%.

SIGNAL INTELLIGENCE SUPERVISOR. U.S. Army, Ft. Bragg, NC (1985-86). Increased efficiency while streamlining operations for a team operating signal interceptor equipment; coordinated scheduling and training.
* Received respected medals for streamlining operations/cutting costs 12%.

ELECTRONIC WARFARE EQUIPMENT OPERATOR. U.S. Army, Ft. Bragg, NC (1984-85). Intercepted/analyzed foreign noncommunication signals; presented reports.

EDUCATION & TRAINING	B.A. in **Criminal Justice**, University of South Florida, Tampa, FL, 1979. A.A. in **Criminal Justice**, Edison Community College, Ft. Myers, FL, 1976. Completed Army training in intelligence collection, counterespionage, security management, counterintelligence, and electronic warfare.
PERSONAL	Am able to work well with people and gain their confidence quickly.

Date

Exact Name of Person
Title or Position
Name of Company
Address (no., street)
Address (city, state, zip)

Dear Exact Name of Person: (or Dear Sir or Madam if answering a blind ad.)

I would welcome an opportunity to talk with you about how I could contribute to your company through my proven expertise in managing complex security programs as well as through my excellent personnel management and organizational skills.

While serving my country in the U.S. Marine Corps, I have achieved a "track record" of success in one of the world's toughest security roles: managing the security of U.S. embassies throughout Europe. In one recent job in Geneva, Switzerland, I received a distinguished commendation for "revitalizing" the embassy security program and providing security during the Strategic Arms Reduction Talks. In previous jobs in Belgium and the U.S.S.R., I developed security procedures for the NATO delegation area and implemented security plans for embassy buildings under construction.

I offer outstanding skills in developing security objectives, implementing programs, and training/managing security personnel. I possess expert knowledge of passive security equipment including motion detectors and CCTV systems and operate a wide range of firearms. Also, I have extensive hands-on experience in guard force management and scheduling. I hold a Top Secret security clearance based on a BI.

You would find me to be a highly motivated, people-oriented manager who thrives on meeting complex security challenges.

I hope you will welcome my call soon to arrange a brief meeting at your convenience to discuss your current and future needs and how I might serve them. Thank you in advance for your time.

Sincerely yours,

Atlas Hickman

Alternate last paragraph:
I hope you will call or write me soon to suggest a time convenient for us to meet and discuss your current and future needs and how I might serve them. Thank you in advance for your time.

ATLAS HICKMAN

1110½ Hay Street, Fayetteville, NC 28305   (910) 483-6611

OBJECTIVE   Security Program Manager

SECURITY   * Highly skilled in developing and managing comprehensive security programs; perform
EXPERTISE   security surveys and author program directives.
                         * Hands-on experience on guard force scheduling and management.
                         * Knowledgeable of passive security equipment including lighting, motion detectors, and
                           security containers.
                         * Offer experience with CCTV systems and classified material control.
                         * Experienced in providing VIP, site, and material security.
                         * Hold a TOP SECRET security clearance.

EXPERIENCE   **TRAINING MANAGER.** U.S. Marine Corps, Camp Lejeune, NC (1985-present).
                         Standardize weapon training objectives for an 800-person organization; training person-
                         nel in the operation, safety, and maintenance of sophisticated weapon/security systems.

                         SECURITY DIRECTOR. U.S.M.C., U.S. Embassy, Geneva, Switzerland (1983-85).
                         Awarded a medal by the Secretary of the Navy for "revitalizing" security procedures for an
                         embassy complex containing extremely sensitive classified materials and 600 personnel;
                         managed a 25-person security force.
                         * During the Strategic Arms Reduction Talks, improved site security systems.
                         * Coordinated personal protection of both American and Soviet delegates.
                         * Developed and implemented internal defense and counterterrorist procedures.
                         * Established and trained a reaction task force to meet the growing threat of terrorism
                           against Americans in Europe.
                         * Appraised and reorganized security procedures limiting duplication and reducing man-
                           power resources.

                         SECURITY SYSTEMS MANAGER. U.S.M.C., U.S. Embassy, Brussels, Belgium (1983).
                         Was selected to plan and manage security for the SHAPE NATO delegation area while train-
                         ing and supervising a staff of 22 at a busy U.S. Embassy complex.
                         * Advised top NATO and U.S. officials on security needs and procedures; acted as liaison
                           with foreign security agencies.
                         * Known for my problem-solving skills, resolved numerous security violations.

                         SECURITY MANAGER. U.S.M.C., U.S. Embassy, Moscow, USSR (1981-82).
                         Played a key role in the design and implementation of a personal access control system for
                         the U.S. Embassy; managed a security force of 34 people controlling internal security and
                         highly sensitive Embassy work areas.

                         * Managed security programs for a warehouse storing sensitive materials.
                         * Coordinated security for sites under construction; consulted with technicians on the
                           installation of passive security systems.
                         * During a Vice-Presidential visit, briefed Secret Service personnel on local security con-
                           cerns including communications, bomb disposal, and classified material control.
                         * Earned a respected commendation for my technical and management skills.

                         Highlights of other experience: Marine Officer. Serving in Vietnam, earned rapid promo-
                         tions while gaining surveillance/reconnaissance skills.

TRAINING   Excelled in college-level training related to security systems theory and personnel/security
                         systems management.

PERSONAL   Married with one child.

Date

Mr. Joseph G. Cincotti
Marketing Director
Dynateria, Inc.
P.O. Box 1106
Dunn, NC 28334

Dear Mr. Cincotti:

I would appreciate an opportunity to talk with you soon about how I could benefit your organization through my management skills as well as my expertise related to VIP/site security, counterterrorism, and security/ intelligence operations.

Currently I manage programs related to information collection and analysis, site/materials security, and personnel security investigations for the famed "Special Forces."

Previously I excelled in a demanding operations/security management position with the U.S. Embassy in El Salvador, where I established an airfield security system, coordinated activities for peacekeeping forces, acted as a U.S./Salvadoran liaison, and controlled a fleet of helicopters for transporting VIPs and others. I received a medal for my expert safeguarding of Vice President Quayle.

With a Top Secret security clearance with BI and experience in working in Central America, I offer the ability to speak, read, and write Spanish.

You would find me to be a dedicated professional known for giving "110%" to my job and my employees. I am single and willing to relocate worldwide to areas including Central and South America.

I hope you will call or write me soon to suggest a time convenient for us to meet and discuss your current and future needs and how I might serve them. Thank you in advance for your time.

Sincerely yours,

Edward Marsh

EDWARD MARSH

1110½ Hay Street, Fayetteville, NC 28305   (910) 483-6611

OBJECTIVE

To contribute to an organization that can use an outstanding motivator and communicator who offers expertise related to security management and intelligence as well as excellent skills in managing personnel and assets.

**LANGUAGE
CLEARANCE
&
SECURITY
EXPERTISE**

Speak, read, and write SPANISH.
Hold TOP SECRET security clearance with BI.
Am highly skilled in:

COUNTERTERRORISM	AIR-GROUND RECONNAISSANCE	SURVEILLANCE
VIP/SITE SECURITY	DEMOLITIONS	TRAINING

Certified as a senior advanced SCUBA diver; operate full range of weaponry.

EXPERIENCE

SECURITY PROGRAMS MANAGER. U.S. Army, Ft. Bragg, NC (1989-present). As senior intelligence manager of the 7th Special Forces Group, control a $100,000 budget and supervise 12 people while managing programs including:

information collection/analysis/security	crime prevention/inspections
personnel investigations	site/materials security

SECURITY OPERATIONS MANAGER. U.S. Army, El Salvador (1987-89). Working closely with the U.S. Embassy, excelled as a liaison between U.S. and Salvadoran executives while coordinating security and peacekeeping activities; played a key role in planning/administering a $14 million budget.
* Managed a fleet of helicopters used by military executives and the U.S. Ambassador.
* Combined patrolling and weapons to create an airport security system.
* Was described as being "the best anywhere" during a crisis.
* Received a distinguished medal for safeguarding Vice President Quayle.

SCUBA TEAM MANAGER. U.S. Army, Panama (1986-87). Received a respected medal while training and managing a team of 17 expert scuba divers in the famed "Special Forces."

SECURITY TRAINING CHIEF. U.S. Army, Panama (1984-86). Selected and prepared personnel for programs training the military's "best and brightest" security managers.

SECURITY TEAM MANAGER. U.S. Army, Honduras (1983-84). Led six security professionals involved in training/advising/supervising security teams providing site/VIP security for a military community.
* Was recognized by the Honduran government as a "soldier and diplomat."

RADIO SYSTEMS COMMUNICATIONS CHIEF. U.S. Army, Ft. Bragg, NC (1981-83). Managed the operation of state-of-the-art radio communications systems providing vital information; trained U.S. and foreign operators.

WEAPONS INSTRUCTOR. U.S. Army, Ft. Bragg, NC (1979-81). Instructed Special Forces professionals in the use of pistols, rifles, machine guns, and heavy weapons.

EDUCATION

Completed three years of college courses in Business.
Graduated from college-level Army courses in security, intelligence, and management.

PERSONAL

Known for my loyalty, courage, and integrity. Will relocate worldwide and offer extensive experience working in Central/South America.

Date

Exact Name of Person
Title or Position
Name of Company
Address (no., street)
Address (city, state, zip)

Dear Exact Name of Person: (or Dear Sir or Madam if answering a blind ad.)

I would appreciate an opportunity to talk with you soon about how I could contribute to your organization through my experience, knowledge, and skills related to law enforcement.

While serving my country in the U.S. Army, I have become known for my expertise with small arms and light crew-served weapons and am often singled out to give advice on weapons use. As you will see from my resume, I train and provide leadership to Special Forces personnel at Ft. Bragg, NC, the world's largest U.S. military base. During the war in the Middle East, I led a seven-person team in combat operations.

Currently I am studying Criminal Justice at Fayetteville Technical Community College in Fayetteville and have completed approximately 25 credit hours leading to an associate's degree. In addition to a six-month course for weapons specialists, my military training included such areas as a 400-hour Class II Sniper training course as well as first response, emergency life saving, and combat life saving programs.

Through training and experience, I have become familiar with a number of specialized areas including many foreign and domestic weapons, airborne manuevers, reconnaissance, patrolling, and surveillance.

While serving my country, I became accustomed to working in hazardous conditions in which there was "no room for error," and I have earned a reputation for my ability to make prudent decisions under pressure. My temperament and decision-making skills have been tested in combat conditions as well as in routine training activities.

I hope you will welcome my call soon to arrange a brief meeting at your convenience to discuss your current and future needs and how I might serve them. Thank you in advance for your time.

Sincerely yours,

John Van Hout, Jr.

Alternate last paragraph:
I hope you will call or write me soon to suggest a time convenient for us to meet and discuss your current and future needs and how I might serve them. Thank you in advance for your time.

JOHN VAN HOUT, JR.
1110½ Hay Street, Fayetteville, NC 28305 (910) 483-6611

OBJECTIVE

To contribute through my strong interest in the field of law enforcement by applying my military training/experience gained as a senior tactical adviser and weapons specialist known for excellent decision-making skills, sound judgment, and unlimited initiative.

EXPERIENCE

Advanced as a manager, senior tactical adviser, and weapons specialist in a Special Forces Group, U.S. Army, Ft. Bragg, NC:

SENIOR WEAPONS AND OPERATIONS SPECIALIST. (1993-present). Promoted based on my expertise with small arms and light crew-served weapons systems, act as an advisor on the use of these weapons in both conventional and unconventional warfare.
* Was handpicked to train and advise the Jamaican military's sniper team which was selected as the honor graduates in international competition.
* Conducted the training for company personnel which led to certification on all weapons.
* Developed guidelines and set up an internal equipment maintenance program.

WEAPONS AND OPERATIONS SPECIALIST. (1992-93). Continued to refine my leadership abilities and weapons proficiency working with a seven-person team.
* Qualified **Expert with the M-16 rifle** and achieved a maximum score in physical testing.
* Singled out for advanced training, completed the 400-hour Class II Sniper Program.

SUPERVISOR, ANTI-ARMOR SECTION. (1990-91). Trained and supervised seven people in an organization which had to remain in constant readiness to move anywhere in the world within 18 hours and be fully capable of going into combat on arrival.
* Applied my instructional skills and knowledge while training personnel, 95% of whom qualified as experts with the M-16 rifle.
* Controlled $500,000 worth of equipment and ensured maintenance was performed.

COMBAT WEAPONS SPECIALIST. U.S. Army, Saudi Arabia (1990-91). Earned several respected medals for my accomplishments during the war in the Middle East.
* Received the National Defense and Southwest Asia Service Medals.

SECURITY TEAM LEADER and **BORDER GUARD**. U.S. Army, Korea (1989-90). Supervised a team of six American and two Korean soldiers; saw that they were trained and ready to respond immediately to any threat or hostile action.
* Led the team throughout a 90-day security tour along the DMZ — the demilitarized zone between North and South Korea.
* Guided my section to consistently rate in the top 5% of the company.

RECONNAISSANCE TEAM LEADER. U.S. Army, Ft. Bragg, NC (1989). Became familiar with surveillance and reconnaissance techniques and was selected ahead of ten of my peers to lead a 4-person team; controlled a $1 million equipment inventory.

EDUCATION & TRAINING

Study **Criminal Justice**, Fayetteville Technical Community College, NC; 25 credit hours.
Completed the **six-month Special Forces Weapons Sergeant Qualification Course** as well as more than 1,500 additional hours of specialized training programs including:
Emergency/combat life saving — 44 hours each   Spanish — 510 hours
First Responder Course — 44 hours   leadership training — 200 hours
Anti-armor leaders course — 80 hours driver's training — 40 hours

SPECIAL KNOWLEDGE & HONORS

Through training and experience, offer special knowledge of areas such as:
working knowledge of many **foreign and domestic weapons**
familiarity with **airborne insertion techniques**: parachuting, rappelling, and fast rope
proficiency with **small arms, air defense systems, anti-armor weapons, and mortars**
small unit tactics, **reconnaissance, patrolling**, and unconventional warfare
Have won **numerous honors** including commendation and achievement medals, letters of commendation, and the **Parachutist and Expert Infantry Badges**.

PERSONAL

Hold a Secret security clearance. Am a proven combat leader with skills in training others.

Exact Name of Person
Title or Position
Name of Company
Address (no., street)
Address (city, state, zip)

Dear Exact Name of Person: (or Dear Sir or Madam if answering a blind ad.)

I would appreciate an opportunity to talk with you soon about how I could contribute to your organization through my management experience and technical expertise related to armed security operations, artillery and small arms, ammunition, as well as the management of service operations and daily organizational activities.

Expertise related to ammunition, artillery, and small arms

As you will see from my resume, I offer proven expertise related to ammunition, artillery, and small arms. In one job I trained more than 1,500 soldiers in marksmanship, small arms safety, guard duty, and military subjects. In another job as an Ammunition Specialist, I became an expert in handling small arms and artillery ammunition in all kinds of weather while simultaneously operating ammunition supply points. I have excelled as an instructor at the U.S. Army's Field Artillery School, and I have also acted as a consultant to the Virginia National Guard on artillery support and training.

Armed security knowledge

Most recently I have provided security protection at coal mines in Pennsylvania. During one assignment when the miners were on strike, I was night shift officer in charge of 12 to 20 security officers and I also trained new officers and managed crowd control. I am skilled at developing and implementing plans to protect people and property.

Management skills and leadership experience

You will also see from my resume that, while serving my country in the U.S. Army, I was promoted to the highest enlisted rank (Sergeant Major E-9) because of my proven leadership ability, capacity for hard work, and determination to excel. With excellent written and oral communication skills, I have excelled in management jobs which required me to prepare extensive written correspondence while also managing multimillion-dollar assets and dozens of people.

I hope you will call or write me soon to suggest a time convenient for us to meet and discuss your current and future needs and how I might serve them. Thank you in advance for your time.

Yours sincerely,

Donald Manning

Alternate last paragraph:
I hope you will welcome my call soon to arrange a brief meeting at your convenience to discuss your current and future needs and how I might serve them. Thank you in advance for your time.

DONALD MANNING
1110½ Hay Street, Fayetteville, NC 28305   (910) 483-6611

OBJECTIVE

To benefit an organization that can use a hard worker who offers versatile knowledge related to communications and security, inventory management and equipment maintenance, small arms operation and ammunition control, as well as personnel supervision and leadership.

EDUCATION & EXECUTIVE TRAINING

Earned **Associate's degree** in General Studies, Central Texas College, Killeen, TX, 1989.
Completed the graduate-level **Sergeants Major Academy** studying advanced concepts in leadership and management, Ft. Bliss, TX, 1990.
Received extensive training sponsored by the U.S. Army related to ammunition, artillery, and small arms; computer operations; supervision and management; and vehicle maintenance.

EXPERIENCE

SECURITY OFFICER. Falcon Global Corporation and Allied Security Corporation, Williamsport and Pittsburgh, PA (1993).
At two underground coal mines, provided physical security related to preventing property damage and guarding against unauthorized entry/exit on mine property while operating emergency personnel extraction equipment as needed; prepared hourly situation reports and monitored surveillance equipment.
* Found resourceful ways to reduce personnel expenses and equipment costs.
* At coal mines where miners were on strike, was night shift security officer in charge of 12 to 20 security officers; trained new officers and managed crowd control.

OPERATIONS CHIEF. U.S. Army, Ft. Stewart, GA (1989-93).
Was handpicked for this "hotseat" line management job after being promoted to the highest enlisted rank (E-9) in the U.S. Army; supervised 25 professionals and controlled $2.8 million in equipment while coordinating operations of an artillery operations center supporting seven organizations in combat-simulating training projects.
* Prepared maps and reports; maintained journals, files, and records.

SENIOR CONSULTANT. U.S. Army, Ft. Lee, VA (1984-88).
Oversaw a 15-person team providing artillery support and training for the Virginia National Guard during weekend drills and annual training.
* In a part-time job with Edwards & Edwards Associates in Chester, VA, from 1986-88, supervised security officers working under contract; recruited, screened, and trained new security officers, prepared payroll, maintained time sheets, and ordered supplies.

SERVICE OPERATIONS MANAGER. U.S. Army, Germany; Korea; and USA (1979-84).
As a "First Sergeant" in organizations all over the world, supervised up to 155 employees while supervising the provision of these and other support services:

employee training	supply and maintenance
food service	personnel administration

Other experience: U.S. Army, locations worldwide.
* **FIREARMS INSTRUCTOR.** During a two-year period, trained more than 1,500 soldiers in marksmanship, small arms safety, guard duty, and military subjects.
* **AMMUNITION SPECIALIST.** Became an expert in handling small arms and artillery ammunition in all types of weather; learned how to prepare and operate ammunition supply points.
* **FIRST-LINE SUPERVISOR.** In Vietnam, supervised six 155 mm howitzer sections, one ammunition section, and one centralized fire direction center while overseeing 85 employees in combat; was awarded the Bronze Star for heroism and was also awarded the Bronze Star for heroism as a Howitzer Section Leader.
* **INSTRUCTOR.** At a state-of-the-art Field Artillery School, earned a reputation as an outstanding instructor while training officers and enlisted soldiers in basic and advanced courses related to artillery.
* **RADIO AND TELEPHONE OPERATOR.** In an entry-level job in the U.S. Army in Germany, performed maintenance on vehicles, generators, and weapons.

PERSONAL

Have held a Top Secret security clearance. Offer proven leadership abilities. Have a capacity for hard work and long hours. Am always looking for ways to improve myself and to develop the skills of others. Have a reputation for resourcefulness.

Date

Exact Name of Person
Title or Position
Name of Company
Address (no., street)
Address (city, state, zip)

Dear Exact Name of Person: (or Dear Sir or Madam if answering a blind ad.)

I would appreciate an opportunity to talk with you soon about how I could contribute to your organization through my expertise in supervising people, controlling inventory, and managing the physical security of sites, assets, and data.

Experience in managing security of weapons and telecommunications
While proudly serving my country in the U.S. Army, I acquired extensive experience in managing the security of special weapons systems worldwide. Most recently, I was selected to oversee a team of five professionals using a sophisticated NATO intrusion system to safeguard a multimillion-dollar weapon system. In a previous job, I turned a communications security (COMSEC) facility known for low security standards into one with a perfect security record. With a Top Secret security clearance with BI, I am experienced in the preparation, distribution, and destruction of classified materials.

Inventory control and supply management "know-how"
As you will see from my resume, I was praised for dramatically improving operations at a nine-person supply facility. Regarded as one of the Army's "best and brightest" middle managers, I developed and implemented systems which made this facility the "best of its kind."

You would find me to be a dedicated and enthusiastic professional known for a "track record" of improving communication, morale, and efficiency in every organization I work in.

I hope you will welcome my call soon to arrange a brief meeting at your convenience to discuss your current and future needs and how I might serve them. Thank you in advance for your time.

Sincerely yours,

Robert Worley

Alternate last paragraph:
I hope you will call or write me soon to suggest a time convenient for us to meet and discuss your current and future needs and how I might serve them. Thank you in advance for your time.

ROBERT WORLEY

1110½ Hay Street, Fayetteville, NC 28305   (910) 483-6611

OBJECTIVE	To benefit an organization through my proven communication, management, and inventory control skills along with my specialized expertise related to the security of special weapons and telecommunications operations.

CLEARANCE & SPECIAL SKILLS

* Hold TOP SECRET security clearance with BI.
* Am highly skilled in **surveillance**, **reconnaissance**, and **counterterrorist** activities.
* Am familiar with security, ownership, and accounting procedures for special weapons systems worldwide.
* Operate, troubleshoot, and repair telecommunications assets including COMSEC equipment; prepare, distribute, and destroy classified materials.
* Offer knowledge of government supply systems.

EXPERIENCE

SPECIAL WEAPONS SECURITY MANAGER. U.S. Army, Germany (1989-present). Manage a security force of five people overseeing the safety and accountability of special weapons systems; use a sophisticated NATO intrusion detection system to constantly monitor security status.
* Developed and implemented a security program which reduced training time and labor costs 30%: this system is still in use today.
* Was praised for "flawlessly" managing the special security needs of weapons systems.

TELECOMMUNICATIONS SUPERVISOR. U.S. Army, Germany (1988-89). Took over a communications security (COMSEC) facility known for poor security and inefficiency and, within two months, transformed it into a productive operation with perfect security.
* Excelled in assessing and routing telecommunications messages and managing operations during the general manager's absence.

CLASSIFIED MATERIALS MANAGER. U.S. Army, Germany (1987-88). Supervised a team of 12 people involved in preparing, distributing, and destroying classified materials; operated COMSEC equipment; was selected to brief high-level U.S. and NATO officials on security matters.
* Turned around a "troubled" organization; by improving morale and communication, led this team which had been rated last to be rated **best in** its parent organization.

SUPPLY SUPERVISOR. U.S. Army, Ft. Sill, OK (1984-86). Was promoted ahead of my peers to train, motivate, and manage a nine-person supply team ordering and receiving supplies for a 600-person organization; controlled a $35,000 purchasing budget.
* Dramatically improved the accountability of supplies and budgetary funds; was praised for making this office the **best** in the entire organization.
* Developed and implemented a system which decreased the time needed to replace defective equipment.

SUPPLY/MAINTENANCE TECHNICIAN. U.S. Army, Ft. Sill, OK (1983-84). Was cited for creating and implementing new maintenance and supply systems while ordering supplies for and repairing 150 weapons; maintained records and transported materials.

TRAINING

Completed six months of college-level Army training related to special weapons security/operation, supply systems, and personnel management.

PERSONAL

Received numerous medals and commendations. As a hobby, repair handguns and rifles.

DANNY ANDERSON

1110½ Hay Street, Fayetteville, NC 28305   (910) 483-6611

OBJECTIVE

To contribute planning, coordination, motivational, and leadership skills to an organization that can use a dedicated young professional with experience related to security and law enforcement with an emphasis on weapons training, maintenance, and use.

SPECIAL SKILLS

Through training, have gained familiarity in specialized areas including the following:
Operational areas: combat and counter reconnaissance and counterterrorism with emphasis on planning and conducting tactical operations
Weapons: extensive training with foreign/domestic weapons including automatic, semiautomatic, mortars, and artillery, such as 9mm and .45 caliber pistols, as well as various shotguns and rifles
Communications: FM, HF, and satellite communications (DMDG); satellite communications radio with cryptographic equipment (LST 5C); equipment for transmitting/receiving secure digital data over radio and phone lines (KL 43C); HF radio used to transmit voice and data.
Clearance: was entrusted by the U.S. Army with a Secret security clearance.

EXPERIENCE

SENIOR WEAPONS SERGEANT. U.S. Army, Ft. Bragg, NC (1995-present).
Played an important role in finding ways to improve efficiency and capabilities as the specialist in charge of training personnel in technical proficiency, weapons knowledge, and weapons use in a Special Forces detachment at the nation's largest military base.
* Advised the general manager on weapons use and emplacement as well as overseeing security procedures when the unit was at its home site rather than in a training setting.
* Received an achievement medal for developing and implementing both force protection and security plans during U.N. assignments: these changes resulted in no incidents of security breaches while in a dangerous area.
* Learned to work in close cooperation with personnel from other countries and refined my public relations skills in overseas assignments and while training foreign personnel.
* Made important contributions toward revising standard operating procedures (SOPs).

STUDENT. U.S. Army, Ft. Bragg, NC (1994-95). Excelled after being selected to attend demanding professional development courses which had difficult requirements for entry and very high failure rates.
The Special Forces Assessment and Selection Course: this rigorous program was a physical and mental challenge: 160 people began the course and only 80 finished; of these 80 people only 59 were selected for the Special Forces Qualification Course.
The Special Forces Weapons Qualification Course: was one of only five people to complete this six-month course of the 25 selected to attend; subjects of main emphasis included small unit tactics, light and heavy weapons, hand-to-hand combat techniques, and dealing with foreign personnel.
Special Operations Basic Language School: completed a six-month French language program with an area study of the sub-Sahara region.

Was promoted ahead of my peers to Staff Sergeant with under five years in service, U.S. Army, Germany:
MAINTENANCE SUPERVISOR. (1993). Developed nine people into an outstanding maintenance team while also developing training schedules, supervising daily assignments, and counseling employees on a regular basis to instill self motivation and pride.
* Received commendable ratings during two consecutive annual logistics management evaluations and was awarded a commendation medal for meritorious service.

TEAM LEADER. (1992). Refined my supervisory and leadership skills while motivating and setting an example for four people in the areas of job performance and personal standards.

Other experience: As a SECURITY OFFICER and DISPATCHER at Emporia State University, gained exposure to police procedures while dispatching police officers and conducting nightly patrols.

EDUCATION & TRAINING

Have completed almost three years of college study in sociology and management.
Attended additional training in unit NBC (nuclear/biological/chemical) defense, leadership development, combat lifesaving, interpersonal relations, and physical fitness.

PERSONAL

Am mechanically inclined with a talent for being able to analyze how a piece of equipment works — especially weapons. Taught foreign students ideas, concepts, and technical facts.

JOHN J. DATES
1110½ Hay Street, Fayetteville, NC 28305   (910) 483-6611

OBJECTIVE

To offer my experience and strong interest in law enforcement to a police department that can use a dedicated, honest, and reliable young professional.

EXPERIENCE

INFANTRYMAN. U.S. Army, Ft. Bragg, NC (1993-96).
Completed extensive training and gained experience in a wide range of functional areas as a soldier in an infantry unit at the largest U.S. military base in the world:

TOW Missile qualified	airborne qualified
job-related education courses	bus driver school
emergency lifesaving school	pre-Ranger course
jungle operations training course	riot control training
desert training	survival training
SINGARS radio training	word processing

* Qualified with the following weapons:

TOW Missile	AT-4
hand grenades	M-16A2
50 caliber machine gun	claymore mine
9mm pistol	Mark 19 grenade launcher
M-60 machine gun	Squad Automatic weapon machine gun

MAINTENANCE SPECIALIST. Stanley Shane Construction, Park City, UT (1992-93).
Supervised grounds maintenance and applied skills in areas such as finish carpentry, framing, foundations, and driveways. Organized and supervised an inventory of tools.

SKI LIFT OPERATOR. Deer Valley Ski Resort, Park City, UT (1991-92).
Earned three "Deer Valley Difference Awards" in recognition of my hard work, ability, and strong personal relations with my peers and members of the public.

GOLF COURSE MAINTENANCE WORKER. Park Meadows Golf Course, Park City, UT (1990).
Operated a back hoe while completing maintenance on greens, fairways, and sand traps.

EDUCATION

Completed one year of general studies at Fayetteville Technical Community College, NC, and Salt Lake Community College, UT.

SKILLS

Through training and experience, am qualified to drive busses and the military HMMWV as well as offering experience with construction-related power tools, back hoe, and snow plow equipment.

CLEARANCE

Was entrusted by the U.S. Army with a Secret security clearance and have handled classified information.

PERSONAL

Am a hard-working young professional who gets along well with others.

GREY B. BURGESS

1110½ Hay Street, Fayetteville, NC 28305   (910) 483-6611

OBJECTIVE   To offer my background in law enforcement and security to an organization that can use an energetic fast learner who offers the proven ability to remain calm and in control and to make rapid decisions with objectivity under hazardous and stressful conditions.

EXPERIENCE   *Earned promotion ahead of my peers while ensuring that rules and regulations were enforced and that volatile situations were defused, U.S. Air Force:*

SUPERVISORY LAW ENFORCEMENT SPECIALIST. Italy (1992-present). Supervised four subordinates while investigating traffic accidents, patrolling the military community, responding to alarms and incidents, and taking the necessary actions to neutralize the situations.

* Provided physical security for personnel and multimillion-dollar aircraft and facilities.
* During a major training exercise, was instrumental in providing security for NATO personnel including handling two incidents where my coolness under pressure defused a fight and assisted local police in quickly rerouting traffic around a demonstration.
* Administered first aid to victims in an accident with a fatality and conducted a thorough investigation which determined who had been at fault.
* Helped evacuate innocent bystanders when a suspicious article was found and then located the owner of the package and brought the situation under control.
* Investigated the disappearance of two children, soon reunited with their families.
* Upon responding to the detonation of an explosive device near the security police living quarters, secured the area and helped keep the situation from escalating.
* Provided solid leadership for a unit recognized as "Best Security Police Large Unit."
* Investigated a hit-and-run accident and was able to locate and apprehend the suspect.

SECURITY POLICEMAN. Spain (1990-92). Enforced security for facilities, equipment, personnel, and large amounts of funds while providing a tactful and authoritative manner during random entry checks on a closed and guarded military base.

* Handled a variety of support activities including issuing temporary vehicle passes, patrolling the community, directing traffic, and investigating minor vehicle accidents.
* Responded to alarm activations and aircraft accidents both on and off the military base.
* Comforted a heart attack victim in his home, stabilized and prepared him for transport to a local hospital thereby minimizing discomfort and permanent injury.
* Participated in a fraud investigation: the property was recovered, the retail facility employee discharged, and her accomplice barred from using the facility.
* Assisted in raising funds and organizing a Christmas party which was very successful and helped build spirits and add to the enjoyment of the holiday season.

CORRECTIONS OFFICER. Philadelphia, PA (1989-90). Applied my ability to achieve and maintain control as the supervisor of a 40-person dormitory with the responsibility for guaranteeing safety for each inmate as well as seeing that living areas were clean.

* Ensured the safety and welfare of more than 460 prisoners at any given time.

BASE ENTRY CONTROLLER. Italy (1987-89). Ensured that any person who wished to enter the air force base grounds could display the proper identification and that visitors were given proper directions so they could easily locate the area they were visiting.

* Applied Air Force use-of-force criteria in determining the proper response to incidents.
* Handpicked to handle crowd control during the 1987 Aviano Air Show, was credited with making valuable contributions which ensured an incident-free day for 30,000 people.
* Responded to accidents, incidents, and alarms and made decisions on how to handle each situation depending on its severity and potential for harm.
* Identified a person suspected of being a threat during a large-scale training exercise: was credited with "decisive actions" which caused his apprehension and averted danger.
* Was officially evaluated as making "spectacular progress ... well ahead of his peers."
* While controlling entry to weapons storage areas, reacted quickly during an unscheduled intrusion test and resecured the area in minimum time.

AREAS of EXPERTISE

Through training and experience, have become skilled in VIP protection, escorting large sums of money, securing facilities, base clearance operations, entry control procedures, and nuclear and biological decontamination procedures.
Am knowledgeable and skilled in using weapons including pistols, rifles, and machine guns.
Use MAG 8 and Speedgun Magnum radar guns.

EDUCATION & TRAINING

Have completed 36 college-level credit hours, City Colleges of Chicago.
Certification in Industrial Drafting, Jefferson Vocational Technical Center, Watertown, NY.
Excelled in nearly 790 hours of specialized training including programs in air base ground defense/security; enforcing law and order; leadership and personnel management skills; and assembling, firing, and disassembling weapons including M-60 machine guns.

PERSONAL

Was entrusted with a Secret security clearance. Speak Italian. Am a fast learner who is meticulous about details. Will relocate according to employer need.

JANET LOWES
1110½ Hay Street, Fayetteville, NC 28305   (910) 483-6611

OBJECTIVE

To contribute to an organization that can use a poised communicator and well organized young professional who offers extensive experience in supervising administrative operations within an extremely busy legal jurisdiction.

EDUCATION

Have completed nearly **50 college credit hours** towards B.S. degree, Campbell University. Completed the U.S. Army two-month **Legal Specialist Course** which provided in-depth training in areas including application of rules of law, microcomputer applications, drafting documents, legal writing/correspondence, claims, and legal assistance.
As a **Legal Specialist**, gained hands-on training in legal research, civil litigation practices, military legal practices, and legal office management.
Completed a **Leadership Development Course** which emphasized public speaking as well as management/supervisory techniques.

COMPUTERS

Proficient at WordPerfect, Enable, LAAWS, Harvard Graphics, and Windows

EXPERIENCE

MAGISTRATE COURT ADMINISTRATOR and **LEGAL ASSISTANT**. U.S. Army, Office of the Judge Advocate, Ft. Bragg, NC (1993-present). Received a prestigious medal for the exceptional managerial skills and legal knowledge I demonstrated in this job; am the "internal expert" on legal processes, procedures, and practices in a staff section that sees many officer/attorney rotations.
* Obtain and review criminal citations, prepare and file all criminal information, court dockets, notice letters, discovery requests, warrants, and pretrial agreements.
* Supervise and train a paralegal and legal specialist while assisting three attorneys in preparation and trial of cases.
* On a daily basis, expertly apply my knowledge of the procedures required to assemble misdemeanor and petty offense cases; ensure the correct legal review of cases, the filing of charges in Federal District Court, and the informing of defendants of court dates.
* Oversee actions taken toward juvenile defendants who commit crimes on the base.
* Practice legal processes in alternate forms of justice, such as the voluntary Shoplifters Alternative Program and the Pre-Trial Diversion which requires investigation into a defendant's background to determine eligibility for the program.
* Write letters for attorneys informing defendants of court dates, missed appearances, and status of their offense; write letters to parents of juvenile offenders.
* Conduct interviews on behalf of attorneys to differentiate clients that require their assistance from those that need a quick answer.
* Answer hundreds of phone calls weekly from defendants and from agencies/offices including the Federal Marshals Office, Federal Probation Office, U.S. District Court, Criminal Investigation Division, Provost Marshals Office, Pre-Trial Diversion, Federal Public Defenders Office, Clerk of Courts Office, and defense attorneys; always maintain a professional and courteous attitude.
* Research Army regulations, state and federal statutes, legal documents, and publications.

ADMINISTRATIVE CLERK. U.S. Army, Office of the Staff Judge Advocate, Ft. Bragg, NC (1991-93). Supported the administrative needs of the Staff Judge Advocate's Office; controlled travel vouchers, ordered supplies, distributed information, ordered printed material including books and software, maintained the law library, and purchased furnishings.

LEGAL CLERK. U.S. Army, Office of the Staff Judge Advocate, Saudi Arabia (1991), During the war in the Middle East, assisted two attorneys in all facets of legal assistance including will preparation, powers of attorney, payment of foreign claims, and other matters.

CLAIMS LEGAL CLERK. U.S. Army, Office of the Staff Judge Advocate, Ft. Bragg, NC (1990-91). Processed claims forms for household goods claims while assisting in adjudication of household goods claims as well as minor tort claims; assisted in investigations of Federal Tort claims filed against government.

PERSONAL

Am known for my clear and courteous style of expressing myself, orally and in writing.

TIFFANY DOVE

1110½ Hay Street, Fayetteville, NC 28305   (910) 483-6611

OBJECTIVE   To offer my reputation as an articulate and intelligent young professional to an organization that can use a flexible and well-organized individual who can provide strong leadership and creative problem-solving skills along with the ability to rapidly master new ideas/methods.

EDUCATION & TRAINING

B.S., Mass Communications and Political Science, Miami University, Oxford, OH, 1991.
* Graduated *cum laude* with a 3.6 GPA; received a full scholarship, freshman year.
* Was the Distinguished Graduate of the School of Arts and Sciences.

Excelled in approximately nine additional months of training in leadership, language refreshers, electronic warfare/signals intelligence operations, and airborne operations.

EXPERIENCE

EXECUTIVE ASSISTANT. U.S. Army, Ft. Bragg, NC (1994-present).
Applied outstanding analytical, written, and verbal communication skills while introducing improvements to procedures which eliminated scheduling conflicts and improved the flow of communication among a senior executive, administrative staff members, and employees in a headquarters setting.
* Supervised two people and counseled them monthly on their job performance.
* Implemented a system for keeping the chief executive's schedule on a monthly basis and ensured that key personnel received weekly updates for their convenience.
* Determined the need for up-to-date information for new personnel and developed a "welcome packet" with maps and helpful information to make inprocessing smoother.
* Word processed, proofread, and produced sensitive documents including correspondence and annual performance evaluations of management personnel.
* Earned the praise of General Shelton, Commander of the 18th Airborne Corps, for translating a 32-page document used during a week-long visit by Russian dignitaries.

TECHNICAL OPERATIONS TEAM MEMBER/RUSSIAN LINGUIST. U.S. Army, Ft. Bragg, NC (1993-94).
Quickly assumed leadership roles in a department providing military intelligence operations with interception and jamming capabilities in order to disturb enemy radio communications.
* Assigned to receive additional training in a second foreign language, exceeded the Army's test standards and qualified as a Spanish linguist.
* Handpicked to lead a team during two major performance exercises, achieved an impressive success rate.

RUSSIAN LANGUAGE HONORS STUDENT. U.S. Army, Monterey, CA (1992).
Gained a high level of self discipline and displayed strong time management skills and perseverance while exceeding course standards in an intensive 47-week Russian instruction course at the Defense Language Institute.
* Honored as the Distinguished Graduate, also received the Literature Award from the Russian faculty members.
* Was singled out to supervise 15 students and see that living standards were enforced while assigning maintenance and cleaning duties and controlling supplies.
* Was selected as captain of the company's running team and achieved a perfect 300 in physical testing for nine consecutive months.

ASSISTANT MANAGER. Miami University, Oxford, OH (1988-91).
Worked full-time in this job throughout college to finance undergraduate education while also excelling academically; after seven months as a Utility Crew Member, was promoted ahead of four more experienced students to oversee a 15- to 20-person staff involved in preparing the university's Marcum Conference Center for a wide variety of events.
* Learned to be diplomatic and to tactfully handle customers.
* Was the recipient of the Parents Association Award for Excellence.
* Gained experience in operational areas such as building security and assisting the manager in designing floor layouts which would best accommodate each event.
* Constantly worked under tight deadlines while setting up for meetings and special events.

PERSONAL   Offer a working knowledge of WordPerfect 5.1 and Harvard Graphics. Believe that my success academically and in the military in becoming an expert marksman and parachutist has given me great physical and mental strength. Offer advanced research skills and creativity. Known for unquestioned integrity, was entrusted with a Top Secret clearance.

Date

Exact Name of Person
Title or Position
Name of Company
Address (no., street)
Address (city, state, zip)

Dear Exact Name of Person: (or Dear Sir or Madam if answering a blind ad.)

I would appreciate an opportunity to talk with you soon about how I could benefit your organization through my experience in managing personnel, resources, and projects as well as my skills as a communicator and motivator.

While serving my country in the U.S. Air Force, I have excelled in a wide range of management roles. Most recently I was handpicked to plan and implement the removal of a major weapon system from Europe. While working closely with high-level officials from the U.S., Germany, and the Soviet Union, I redistributed $15 million in property to the U.S. I have managed up to 115 people in activities ranging from maintenance production, to quality control, to hazardous materials distribution.

With a Top Secret security clearance with SBI, I offer knowledge of the Air Force quality control system and Department of Defense contracting procedures. I am regarded as an "expert" in all areas of logistics/ distribution management including strategic planning.

You would find me to be a dynamic professional with the ability to see the "big picture" while managing details.

I hope you will welcome my call soon to arrange a brief meeting at your convenience to discuss your current and future needs and how I might serve them. Thank you in advance for your time.

Sincerely yours,

Allan Barkley

Alternate last paragraph:
I hope you will call or write me soon to suggest a time convenient for us to meet and discuss your current and future needs and how I might serve them. Thank you in advance for your time.

ALLAN BARKLEY
1110½ Hay Street, Fayetteville, NC 28305 (910) 483-661

OBJECTIVE To benefit an organization that can use a dynamic and detail-oriented professional with expertise in managing personnel, resources, and projects along with proven abilities as an outstanding communicator and motivator.

CLEARANCE Hold TOP SECRET security clearance with SBI.

EXPERIENCE **PROGRAM CHIEF/LOGISTICS CONSULTANT.** U.S. Air Force, Germany (1988-89). Was handpicked to plan and implement the withdrawal of a major weapon system from Europe; worked with high-level American, German, Soviet, and other officials while supervising a team of professionals.
* Played a key role in drawing up detailed plans to close military bases and to withdraw the Ground Launched Cruise Missile System from Europe.
* Managed milestones related to withdrawal schedules, reporting, inspections, transportation, and manpower reductions.
* Redistributed $15 million in property to the United States.
* Have become known as an "expert" in all areas of logistics/distribution management including strategic planning, production control, and quality assurance.

MAINTENANCE PRODUCTION MANAGER. U.S.A.F., Netherlands (1987-88). Managed production and directed the utilization of all human and physical resources for a missile maintenance division.
* Supervised 115 people and $220 million in assets and munitions.
* Became known as a safety-conscious supervisor while motivating employees to achieve peak production.
* Set up a new advisory council that improved executive decision making.

QUALITY ASSURANCE DIVISION CHIEF. U.S.A.F., Italy (1986-87). Because of my ability to see the "big picture" while managing minute details, was specially selected to manage quality control programs related to multimillion-dollar missile assets.
* Selected, trained, certified, and supervised 18 inspectors; administered a reporting system that identified material deficiencies and automated quality assurance programs.
* Gained expertise in integrating many quality assurance programs into an overall system now regarded as an administrative "model."

Highlights of other experience: U.S.A.F., Wichita, KS (1981-86). **QUALITY CONTROL DIVISION CHIEF.** Supervised the removal and shipment of 700,000 lbs. of extremely hazardous propellants; was named "Manager of the Year" and received two respected medals for extraordinary achievements.
* Reorganized the quality control program; was promoted to this job after excelling in supervising 25 people in missile maintenance and hazardous material handling.

EDUCATION & TRAINING Bachelor of Arts degree in Business Management, University of La Verne, La Verne, CA, 1978. A.A. degree in Liberal Arts, Allan Hancock College, Santa Maria, CA, 1977. Completed college-level training related to quality assurance, personnel/resources management, and leadership.

PERSONAL Operate personal computers with word processing and spreadsheet software. Am knowledgeable of Air Force quality control programs and Department of Defense contracting procedures. Offer the ability to motivate personnel to excel.

Date

Exact Name of Person
Title or Position
Name of Company
Address (no., street)
Address (city, state, zip)

Dear Exact Name of Person: (or Dear Sir or Madam if answering a blind ad.)

Can you use a versatile and adaptable professional who offers strong hands-on managerial abilities, a keen intellect, and a strong background in research, technical writing, and public speaking?

While serving my country in the U.S. Army, I consistently excelled in demanding roles which varied from managing multimillion-dollar maintenance and logistics support operations, to instructing and counseling students at the U.S. Military Academy, to conducting studies and planning real-world activities for Special Operations Forces.

Throughout my career I have been handpicked for advanced training and educational opportunities as well as sensitive and critical jobs which required highly developed problem-solving, decision-making, and analytical skills.

I feel that I am a very versatile individual who has demonstrated the ability to think on my feet and adapt to change and pressure. Through my experience, excellent communication skills, and motivational abilities I could prove to be a valuable addition to an organization such as yours.

I hope you will welcome my call soon to arrange a brief meeting at your convenience to discuss your current and future needs and how I might serve them. Thank you in advance for your time.

Sincerely yours,

Haskell Dawkins

Alternate last paragraph:
I hope you will call or write me soon to suggest a time convenient for us to meet and discuss your current and future needs and how I might serve them. Thank you in advance for your time.

HASKELL DAWKINS

1110½ Hay Street, Fayetteville, NC 28305   (910) 483-6611

OBJECTIVE

To apply my reputation as an extremely adaptable, articulate, and innovative individual to an organization that can use a mature professional who has consistently excelled as a military officer through superior planning, communication, and leadership abilities.

EDUCATION & TRAINING

M.A., History, University of Georgia, Athens, GA, 1990.
B.S., Social Sciences, Campbell University, Buies Creek, NC, 1985.
* Maintained a 3.74 GPA and completed two years of courses in only ten months.
Completed in excess of 3,000 hours of advanced management and staff development programs as well as special coursework in effective teaching and counseling techniques.

EXPERIENCE

DIRECTOR OF LOGISTICS AND MAINTENANCE SUPPORT ACTIVITIES. U.S. Army, Ft. Bragg, NC (1994-present). Handled the intricate details of providing a 2,300-person organization with logistics and maintenance support while overseeing three dining halls, a $1.35 million annual budget, material reporting, and maintenance for 250 vehicles.
* Coordinated transport of 170 fully loaded vehicles to Wilmington, NC, and on to Haiti.
* Streamlined maintenance operations by instituting a system of twice-monthly meetings.

CURRENT OPERATIONS MANAGER. U.S. Army, Ft. Bragg, NC (1993-94). Conducted research, prepared reports, and presented briefings to a senior official while making decisions on when, where, and how to send Special Operations Forces personnel to real-world trouble spots.
* Communicated regularly with United Nations representatives and non-government organizations while arranging to send and bring back personnel from overseas activities.

ASSISTANT PROFESSOR. U.S. Army, The United States Military Academy at West Point, West Point, NY (1990-93). Handpicked from a pool of 200 highly qualified executives for one of only 20 instructor positions, was recognized with the Department of History's 1992 "Excellence in Teaching Award" for my effectiveness as a classroom instructor and mentor.
* Singled out as a course director, directed 19 instructors who dealt daily with 935 cadets during the 1991 fall semester.

GRADUATE STUDENT. U.S. Army, University of Georgia, Athens, GA (1988-90). Refined in-depth research and investigative skills while serving as an advisor for students in the university's ROTC program and earning a master's degree.
* Applied my outstanding written skills to develop a thesis which received a great deal of positive attention in scholarly history circles.

Excelled in highly visible and critical roles with the U.S. Army in West Berlin, Germany:
GENERAL MANAGER. (1987-88). Provided outstanding leadership and guidance for 155 personnel working in a highly stressful environment, which called for constant alertness.
* Applied my communication and diplomatic skills while dealing regularly with French and British allies and personnel from the West Berlin police.
* Was singled out as the "General Douglas MacArthur Leadership Award" winner.

OPERATIONS MANAGER. (1985-87). Was handpicked for the General Manager's position on the basis of the outstanding human and material resource management skills demonstrated while planning and scheduling training for this 750-person organization.
* Was cited as the area's best resource manager for my effectiveness in controlling the organization's $2.5 million annual ammunition budget.

Highlights of earlier U.S. Army experience: Consistently performed above standards as an officer, undergraduate student, and in previous leadership and supervisory roles.

SPECIAL SKILLS

Am familiar with WordPerfect, Word for Windows, Harvard Graphics, and Leading Edge.
Offer special knowledge of research libraries, archives, museums, and data collection facilities.

PERSONAL

Known for my loyalty and honesty, was entrusted with a Top Secret security clearance. Am very adaptable and able to handle stress and changing circumstances. Will relocate.

GABRIEL MARTIN

1110½ Hay Street, Fayetteville, NC 28305   (910) 483-6611

OBJECTIVE

To contribute to an organization that can use a dynamic communicator who offers exceptional public speaking and written communication skills, indepth technical knowledge of automated data processing and computer operations, along with extensive management experience in organizing new operations and streamlining the efficiency of existing ones.

EDUCATION

Masters in Education (M.Ed.), University of Oklahoma, Norman, OK, 1994.
Master of Science (M.S.) in International Relations, Troy State University, Troy, AL, 1980.
Bachelor of Science (B.S.) in Business Administration, Southern Utah University, 1973.
Completed extensive executive development training as a military officer including Command & General Staff College.

CLEARANCES

Hold one of the nation's highest security clearances: Top Secret based on a Special Background Investigation with Special Compartmented Information Access (TS\SBI\SCI).

COMPUTERS

Extremely computer proficient with knowledge of popular software including WordPerfect, MultiMate, Excel, Microsoft Word, PowerPoint, and PFS Professional Write.

EXPERIENCE

OPERATIONS DIVISION CHIEF. U.S. Army, Ft. Bragg, NC (1995-present).
Travel frequently in order to coordinate projects in Florida and Texas while managing day-to-day details of a 13-person operations division and am a deputy director of the Army's highly automated, state-of-the-art Battlefield Coordination Element, which simulates combat conditions and tests strategic planners in developing responses.
* Am excelling in a job which continually tests my ability to make prudent decisions, react wisely in emergencies, and organize human resources for rapid response to crises.
* On my own initiative, reorganized the operations division in such a way that it has been widely described as "the best of its kind ever seen."

STRATEGIC PLANNER & CHIEF, WAR PLANS BRANCH. U.S. Army, Germany (1992-94). In a job which required me to interact daily with international diplomats and NATO executives, traveled extensively throughout Europe in order to develop strategic plans for logistics activities throughout Europe, Africa, and the Middle East.
* Acted as Lead Logistics Planner for activities related to Bosnia-Herzegovina.
* On my own initiative, developed a plan to upgrade automated resources.
* Designed and implemented a new Logistics Operation Center (LOC) which elevated the capability for emergency logistics support and planning to its highest-ever level; this is considered the best mobile logistics center of its kind in the world.
* Was praised in writing as "the most proficient writer in the organization" and a "truly expert planner."

CHIEF, INTELLIGENCE & SECURITY DIVISION. U.S. Army, Germany (1990-92).
Was chief intelligence officer of a logistics organization responsible for a vast territory of 160,000 square miles in five European countries.
* Directed data collection and analysis as well as the preparation of written products containing information about various countries, terrorist threats, and other matters.
* Helped develop security procedures for more than 120 Local Area Networks (LANs) which involved over 3,000 personal computers.
* Was the driving force behind the acquisition and installation of state-of-the-art intelligence systems.

Page 2 of resume of Gabriel Martin

* In a formal evaluation, was praised as a "dynamic self-starter who took over a stagnant operation and began an unbelievable transition"; transformed an unmotivated group of professionals into a well-trained, highly proficient team who took pride in their work.
* *Special Project, 1991:* Played a key role in establishing the main logistics center which moved 600 tons of supplies daily to Kurds in Northern Iraq during the war in the Middle East; worked daily with French, Spanish, Italian, Turkish, British, and Iraqi personnel.

CHIEF OPERATIONS OFFICER. U.S. Army, Germany (1989-91).
In a NATO environment, oversaw the training of 750 military professionals while overseeing the maintenance of $350 million in sophisticated equipment; personally monitored frequent system upgrades.
* Was evaluated by NATO as the best organization of its kind during an annual inspection.
* Resolved thorny labor issues as we were all working up to 90 hours weekly.

CHIEF INTELLIGENCE OFFICER. U.S. Army, Germany (1988-89).
Managed numerous sensitive security programs including security for special weapons, programs granting Special Access to qualified personnel, security for covert operations, and background investigations for security clearances.
* Worked on a team that fielded a special weapons system, and was the expert on all security aspects of the system.
* Oversaw the security of $750 million in weapons systems and missiles.
* Created and maintained a thorough inspection system to ensure that every detail of daily operations conformed to exacting written policies and procedures.
* Was rated in writing as "the best intelligence officer" in our major command.

ASSISTANT PROFESSOR. University of Pennsylvania, Philadelphia, PA (1985-88).
Was selected for this teaching assignment at a major Ivy League university because of my outstanding communication skills; excelled in recruiting, enrolling, training, and evaluating qualified cadets for the Officer Training Program.
* Prepared and presented training on the defense establishment, principles of leadership, and the organization of the Army.
* Was credited in writing as orchestrating one of the best recruiting operations among the 21 competing programs in our area, and was praised for "earning the respect of students and faculty."
* Spearheaded marketing activities that resulted in a 167% increase in first-year enrollment.
* Also acted as Program Coordinator for Glassboro State College in New Jersey, with responsibility for growth and quality production of a four-year training program.
* Was honored by my selection as a member of the local school board in Deptford Township, and made several recommendations that strengthened the public school system.

Highlights of other experience:
GENERAL MANAGER. Managed 127 people as Battery Commander of a HAWK Firing Battery; was rated as "the best of the 11 commanders I've seen in this job."

PERSONNEL ADMINISTRATOR. After taking over a position managing personnel administration for 750 people, rapidly assessed the weaknesses in internal policies and procedures and charted a plan which brought all areas in line with goals .

PERSONAL

Offer a proven ability to handle multiple projects simultaneously. Have had extensive experience in planning and reacting to emergency situations, so I have cultivated the ability to rapidly analyze problems or opportunities and quickly develop appropriate responses.

Date

Exact Name of Person
Title or Position
Name of Company
Address (no., street)
Address (city, state, zip)

Dear Exact Name of Person: (or Dear Sir or Madam if answering a blind ad.)

I would appreciate an opportunity to talk with you soon about how I could contribute to your organization through my expert technical skills in the area of heating, air conditioning, and refrigeration.

As you will see from my resume, I have most recently excelled as a Utilities Equipment Repairer while serving my country in the U.S. Army at the world's largest U.S. military base. Although I now work with a team of people installing, repairing, and servicing a wide range of heating, air conditioning, and refrigeration equipment, I performed this work by myself for a period of 1 1/2 years during a period of severe understaffing. I have become known for my absolute reliability as well as for my unselfish support in training and developing junior technicians.

With a reputation as a highly motivated and intelligent technical professional, I am continuously seeking opportunities to refine my knowledge and skills through formal education and training on my own time. I completed with high honors all the units of study in the Master Course in Air Conditioning, Refrigeration, and Heating Course sponsored by NRI, and I excelled in the Army's Utilities Equipment Repairer Course. I have received several certificates from the EPA and other government agencies certifying my knowledge in specific areas. I have more than 7700 hours in the Apprenticeship Program working toward Journeyman status.

Although I am only 27 years old, I can guarantee that you would find me to be a highly experienced problem solver whom you could count on at all times for excellent customer service skills as well as in-depth technical knowledge. I can provide excellent personal and professional references.

I hope you will call or write me soon to suggest a time convenient for us to meet and discuss your current and future needs and how I might serve them. Thank you in advance for your time.

Sincerely yours,

James L. Tryon

JAMES L. TRYON
1110½ Hay Street, Fayetteville, NC 28305   (910) 483-6611

OBJECTIVE

I want to contribute to the growth and success of an organization that can use an air conditioning, refrigeration, and heating technician who offers excellent troubleshooting and problem-solving skills related to all phases of installation, repair, and service.

EDUCATION & CERTIFICATIONS

Completing Heating and Cooling Course, Fayetteville Technical Community College, 1996.

From the Department of Defense, Environmental Protection Agency Certification Program, received a Certificate for Processing CFC/HCFC Refrigerants, 1995.

Received a Certification from the Mobile Air Conditioning Society for completing training in CFC-12 refrigerant recycling and service procedures, 1994.

With High Honors, completed in 1½ years all units of study in the Master Course in Air Conditioning, Refrigeration and Heating Course sponsored by NRI, 1993-94.

Received a Diploma as a graduate of the Utilities Equipment Repairer Course, Ordnance Center and School, Ft. Belvoir, VA, 1992.

Completed extensive courses toward Associates Degree in Air Conditioning, Refrigeration, and Heating, Gwinnett Area Technical School, 1988-91; studied DC Circuit Analysis, Digital Electronics, Soldering/Assembly Technology, and other areas.

EXPERIENCE

UTILITIES EQUIPMENT REPAIRER. U.S. Army, Ft. Bragg, NC (1992-present). At the world's largest U.S. military base, work with a team of people installing, repairing, and servicing a wide range of air conditioning, heating, and refrigeration equipment in commercial and industrial properties; for 1 1/2 years during a period of severe understaffing, worked alone with the sole responsibility for installation, repair, and service.
* Have 7700 hours in the Apprenticeship Program working toward Journeyman status.
* Inspect equipment to determine extent of maintenance and repairs needed.
* Troubleshoot mechanical or electrical malfunctions in systems or components.
* Repair major components by complete disassembly, determination of serviceability, replacement of defective parts, and reassembly.
* Repair and fabricate new lines by cutting and bending tubing and installing fittings by flaring or soldering; repair electrical wiring and electromechanical controls.
* Inspect installation and condition of equipment systems.
* Control requisitioning, storage, and inventory of shop stock, materials, special tools, and necessary publications.
* Instruct lower-grade personnel in the use of applicable special tools, test equipment, and necessary publications.
* Administer quality control and quality assurance functions; inspect equipment.
* Received two Certificates of Achievement praising my "tireless efforts" and "unselfish support" during major projects.

MATERIAL CONTROL SPECIALIST. GEC Avionics, Norcross, GA (1991-92). Maintained various government forms including the 1149, 1348, and DD250 while selecting electronic components for repair, maintaining inventory at appropriate levels, and storing equipment needed for repair in bonded stores annex.

SELECTOR/MULTIFUNCTION PRODUCTION SPECIALIST. Northern Telecom, Inc., Stone Mountain, GA (1988-91). Became skilled in Just in Time Manufacturing and in statistical process control while putting orders together for customers in telecommunications.
* Packed ordered and performed data entry to assure customer satisfaction.
* Pulled various parts for a Manufacturing Flow Line to keep the line moving; input data.
* Performed wiring and soldering inspection and other assembly of Fiber Optics and other cables for Northern Telecom products.
* Received a prestigious safety award for my perfect safety record.

Other experience:
SHIPPING/RECEIVING CLERK. Tech Data Corporation, Norcross, GA. Received computer equipment, unloaded/loaded trucks, pulled and packaged inventory for shipping, and generated shipping documents.
COOK/CASHIER. McDonald's Corporation, Snellville, GA. Was trained in swing management techniques.
CLERK. Northern Telecom, Inc. and Rockwell International. Through temporary agencies, was involved in receiving and packing customer orders and in controlling inventory.

PERSONAL

Have become skilled in customer service, production management, and inventory control while working in electronics manufacturing, warehousing, and other areas. Am safety conscious, detail oriented, and career motivated with a strong work ethic.

Date

Exact Name of Person
Title or Position
Name of Company
Address (no., street)
Address (city, state, zip)

Dear Exact Name of Person: (or Dear Sir or Madam if answering a blind ad.)

I would appreciate an opportunity to talk with you soon about how I could contribute to your organization through my superior communication and management skills as well as my problem-solving and decision-making abilities refined as a military officer.

As a lieutenant in the U.S. Army, I have excelled in a "track record" of increasing productivity and efficiency in every organization I have worked in. Most recently I used my computer "know-how" to dramatically improve the accuracy of organizational reports. In previous jobs I became skilled in determining needs and trends while cutting costs and increasing administrative efficiency for three busy maintenance facilities, and I became known for devising customer service programs which raised customer satisfaction to an "all-time-high."

With a Master's degree in Business Administration, I have been described in writing as a "master of flexibility" and have received consistent praise for my writing and speaking abilities. Known for my outstanding computer skills, I use several popular software packages and program in several languages.

You would find me to be an innovative and adaptable executive with the ability to attend to minute details while keeping sight of the "big picture."

I hope you will welcome my call soon to arrange a brief meeting at your convenience to discuss your current and future needs and how I might serve them. Thank you in advance for your time.

Sincerely yours,

Robert Stokes

Alternate last paragraph:
I hope you will call or write me soon to suggest a time convenient for us to meet and discuss your current and future needs and how I might serve them. Thank you in advance for your time.

ROBERT STOKES
1110½ Hay Street, Fayetteville, NC 28305   (910) 483-6611

OBJECTIVE

To benefit an organization that can use an outstanding manager, logical analyst, creative problem solver, and dynamic communicator who offers excellent decision-making skills refined as a military officer.

EDUCATION & EXECUTIVE DEVELOPMENT TRAINING

M.S.B.A. in Business Administration, Boston University Overseas Program, 1989.
B.A. in Business Administration, Lakeland College, WI, 1985.
A.A. in Accounting, Madison Business College, WI, 1983.
* Earned a national scholarship and was on the Dean's List.
Excelled in Army training for junior executives related to leadership, project/personnel management, and supply/logistics.
* Graduated in the top 5% of my class from Officer Candidate School.

EXPERIENCE

MAINTENANCE SERVICES DIRECTOR. U.S. Army, Ft. Campbell, KY (1990-present). Because of my computer skills, was selected to manage automated services supporting a 800-person organization while overseeing maintenance operations for electronics systems worth $10 million.

* Developed and implemented an automated system which provided a direct interface between Army and personal computers.
* Led a 25-person team inspecting assets for a 800-person organization.
* Will be promoted to Captain in summer 1990.

Proven Expertise in Managing Supply and Logistics Activities while Increasing Productivity

DIRECTOR OF MAINTENANCE OPERATIONS. U.S. Army, Germany (1988-89). Became known for my keen analytical skills while determining supply needs and maintenance trends, cutting costs, increasing administrative efficiency, and providing logistical and maintenance guidance for three maintenance facilities supporting 6,000 people and $120 million in assets.

* Trained and led a team of six people which decreased by 86% the number of "old" maintenance projects awaiting completion.
* Improved efficiency and customer relations by encouraging communication among managers at all levels.
* Reduced by 30% the organization's maintenance backlog.

OPERATIONS MANAGER. U.S. Army, Germany (1987-88). Was described as a "master of flexibility" while managing a 175-person maintenance organization; reduced by 45% a maintenance backlog of transportation, electronics, and engineering assets.

* As a first lieutenant, was placed in a position normally held by a senior executive.
* Established an improved customer service program; by better serving equipment users, increased productivity throughout the organization.
* Used my computer skills to implement an automated maintenance supply system; was praised for the accuracy of automated reports.
  Maintained perfect accountability of $50 million of equipment.

FIRST-LINE SUPERVISOR. U.S. Army, Germany (1986-87). Became known as an energetic and innovative young executive while directing training and daily activities for a 22-person maintenance shop and a 16-person motor pool containing 70 vehicles.

COMPUTER SKILLS

Operate IBM computers with Lotus 1-2-3 and dBase III software.
* Program in FORTRAN, BASIC, and PASCAL.
* Knowledgeable of Lotus 1-2-3, WordPerfect, Harvard Graphics, and dBase.

CLEARANCE

Hold Top Secret security clearance

PERSONAL

A creative and adaptable professional, am known for learning new procedures quickly. Always give "110%." Will relocate worldwide and travel as extensively as my employer requires. Can provide outstanding personal and professional references upon request.

Date

Exact Name of Person
Title or Position
Name of Company
Address (no., street)
Address (city, state, zip)

Dear Exact Name of Person: (or Dear Sir or Madam if answering a blind ad.)

I would appreciate an opportunity to talk with you soon about how I could contribute to your organization through my superior motivational and communication skills as well as my proven management, problem-solving, and decision-making abilities.

As an Air Force lieutenant recently recommended for promotion to captain, I have excelled in "bringing together" complex production activities while setting goals and determining priorities for an organization with 550 aviation maintenance employees. In a previous job as the chief of transient maintenance at one of the military's busiest airlift centers, I oversaw maintenance, security, and parking services for over 7,000 aircraft en route to locations worldwide. Described as an "extraordinary young leader" with a "knack" for expertly coordinating services, I was awarded the Air Force's respected "General Lew Allen, Jr." award.

With a Bachelor's degree in Education and some graduate work in Guidance and Counseling, I am known for my ability to motivate others to set and achieve the highest goals. Praised in writing as a "natural" leader and "superb" communicator, I volunteer much of my spare time to public service in local "Find a Friend" and Jaycee activities.

You would find me to be an enthusiastic and energetic manager with the ability to "bring to life" your highest ideals.

I hope you will welcome my call soon to arrange a brief meeting at your convenience to discuss your current and future needs and how I might serve them. Thank you in advance for your time.

Sincerely yours,

Michael Jordan

Alternate last paragraph:
I hope you will call or write me soon to suggest a time convenient for us to meet and discuss your current and future needs and how I might serve them. Thank you in advance for your time.

MICHAEL JORDAN

1110½ Hay Street, Fayetteville, NC 28305   (910) 483-6611

OBJECTIVE   To benefit an organization that can use a dynamic motivator and enthusiastic communicator who offers proven management ability as well as problem-solving, planning, and decision-making skills refined as a mid-level executive.

EXPERIENCE   **CHIEF OF MAINTENANCE PRODUCTION.** U.S. Air Force, Pope AFB, NC (1989-90). Because of my managerial skills, was handpicked to set goals and determine priorities for 550 people maintaining 53 aircraft making over 900 flights monthly; analyze maintenance trends and supervise quality control.
* Played a key role in formulating and administering a $4.3 million budget.
* Increased efficiency by innovative inventory control techniques.
* Praised for my "aggressive leadership," was chosen to manage maintenance during three international projects.
* Received a respected medal for coordinating a multinational aviation competition; directed maintenance activities.
* Was regarded as one the Air Force's "best and brightest" young executives, and was recommended for promotion to captain.

A
"Track record"
of
Success
in
Coordinating
Complex
Activities,
Directing
Personnel,
and
Managing
Resources

TRANSIENT MAINTENANCE CHIEF. U.S.A.F., Pope AFB, NC (1988-89).
At the hub of one of the military's busiest airlift centers, oversaw maintenance, security, and parking facilities for over 7,000 aircraft stopping en route to worldwide locations; managed a team of 60 personnel.
* Was awarded the Air Force's prestigious General Lew Allen, Jr. Award.
* Was cited for maximizing the use of scarce maintenance resources during a training project; achieved a 100% reliability rate in rugged conditions.
* Was described as an "extraordinary young leader" with "outstanding knowledge of maintenance procedures and management principles."
* During an air show featuring over 40 aircraft, provided maintenance services for planes ranging from C-5s to the Thunderbird's F-16s.

MAINTENANCE MANAGER. U.S.A.F., Pope AFB, NC (1987-88). Was praised in writing as a "natural" leader with outstanding analytical skills while managing a 68-person shop maintaining 17 aircraft; developed a checklist for nuclear emergencies.
* Was cited with increasing the efficiency of maintenance operations by reorganizing activities and motivating personnel.
* Was evaluated as a "solid performer" and "superb communicator."

Other experience (1982-87).
SUBSTITUTE TEACHER. Earned a reputation as a powerful motivator while teaching children in grades seven to 12 in a variety of subjects.
TELECOMMUNICATIONS REPAIRMAN/MANAGER. In the U.S. Army, gained rapid promotion to middle management; trained, supervised, and motivated a team of six installing, maintaining, and repairing communications equipment.

**EDUCATION
&
EXECUTIVE
TRAINING**

B.S. in Education, Southwest Missouri State University, MO, 1981.
Completed a semester of graduate course work in Guidance and Counseling, Southwest Missouri State University, MO, 1986.
Excelled in U.S. Air Force training for executives related to management and aviation.

PERSONAL   Volunteer much of my spare time with the "Find a Friend" program and local Jaycees.

Date

Exact Name of Person
Title or Position
Name of Company
Address (no., street)
Address (city, state, zip)

Dear Exact Name of Person: (or Dear Sir or Madam if answering a blind ad.)

I would appreciate an opportunity to talk with you soon about how I could contribute to your organization through the experience I have gained in environmental engineering and monitoring.

During my eight years in the U.S. Navy, I have gained chemistry lab experience in a nuclear plant with three years in supervisory roles. I am familiar with proper procedures for operating nuclear plants under strict government guidelines due to two years of working under OSHA controls. As you will see from my resume, I was selected for specialized training emphasizing such areas as quality assurance inspection, fundamentals of chemical and radiological control, nuclear propulsion plant operation, and basic machinist's mate skills.

Throughout my years in the Navy I was handpicked for advancement ahead of my peers to handle sensitive, critical roles. Known for my own high standards and ability to quickly master new procedures and ideas, I excelled in passing my knowledge on to others and in building groups of employees into well-functioning teams.

I feel that my experience, skills, and knowledge combine effectively with my natural leadership and motivational abilities. As a professional who has a background of rapid advancement to increasingly responsible positions, I can offer strong self motivation and a drive to excel at anything I attempt.

I hope you will welcome my call soon to arrange a brief meeting at your convenience to discuss your current and future needs and how I might serve them. Thank you in advance for your time.

Sincerely yours,

Baxter Taylor

Alternate last paragraph:
I hope you will call or write me soon to suggest a time convenient for us to meet and discuss your current and future needs and how I might serve them. Thank you in advance for your time.

BAXTER TAYLOR
1110½ Hay Street, Fayetteville, NC 28305   (910) 483-6611

OBJECTIVE   To offer experience and training related to chemical and radiological engineering to an organization that can use my knowledge and interest in the environmental field, supervisory and leadership skills, and ability to easily master new procedures and pass knowledge on.

EXPERIENCE   *Promoted ahead of my peers to positions usually reserved for more experienced personnel, have consistently been cited for my motivational and leadership skills and excellent technical knowledge, U.S. Navy:*

SUPERVISORY ENGINEERING LAB TECHNICIAN and **MACHINIST'S MATE.** Charleston, SC (1994-95). Singled out to supervise five technical specialists, oversaw chemical and radiological control operations for a nuclear propulsion plant.

* Handpicked to receive specialized training, used my excellent communication skills to instruct other personnel in the operation of a prototype nuclear plant.
* Made significant contributions which allowed the ship to earn excellent ratings in examinations of operational reactor safeguards.
* Earned a Navy Achievement Medal for expertise demonstrated while upgrading training procedures and providing instruction for department personnel, thereby allowing them to increase their job knowledge while reducing the time it took to qualify as operators.
* Learned the value of being an effective supervisor while polishing my motivational and leadership skills.

SENIOR LAB TECHNICIAN and **MACHINIST'S MATE.** Alameda, CA (1988-94). Qualified ahead of my peers for critical leadership positions and was placed in charge of a 25-person department of chemical and radiological control technicians.

* Selected for the important position of Dosimetry Technician, handled the precise measuring necessary while checking radiation dosages and ensuring that records were totally accurate and always up to date.
* Earned qualification as the Engineering Watch Supervisor, the highest level available to a person in my career track.
* Was chosen ahead of 27 more experienced personnel based on my demonstrated technical abilities, job knowledge, and leadership potential.

SPECIAL KNOWLEDGE   Offer training and experience in procedures and activities such as:
     Maintaining proper power plant and secondary plant chemistry including water analysis and conducting some environmental sampling
     Performing radiation surveys in and around a nuclear power plant
     Completing quality assurance inspections
     Acting as a gas-free engineering technician

TRAINING   Was chosen to receive specialized U.S. Navy training in programs including the following:
— Quality Assurance Inspector: proper procedures for inspecting and assuring cleanliness during plant maintenance operations
— Engineering Laboratory Technician "C" School: fundamentals of chemistry and radiological controls for nuclear plants
— Nuclear Prototype: hands-on training in nuclear power plant operation
— Nuclear Power School: theory and principles of operating a nuclear propulsion plant
— Nuclear "A" School: basic machinist mate skills

CLEARANCE   Have been entrusted with a Secret security clearance.

EDUCATION   Am pursuing a degree in Environmental Studies.

PERSONAL   Am a fast learner with an aptitude for easily learning new technical advances. Consistently earned the respect and trust of superiors, peers, and subordinates for my high standards.

STEPHEN HENDERSON

1110½ Hay Street, Fayetteville, NC 28305   (910) 483-6611

OBJECTIVE   To benefit an organization that can use an adaptable professional who offers excellent electrical troubleshooting and technical skills as well as the ability to train and motivate others for maximum efficiency and quality.

CLEARANCE   Hold SECRET security clearance.

EXPERIENCE   **SUPERVISOR** and **NUCLEAR POWER PLANT ELECTRICIAN/INSTRUCTOR**. U.S. Navy, W. Milton, NY (1987-90). Because of my communication and technical skills, was handpicked to train 75 students every six months, in the classroom and on-the-job, on nuclear systems operations; supervised a team of 12 electricians operating and maintaining a nuclear power plant and supporting electrical equipment.

* Was selected to supervise the "refurbishment" of electrical control panels; by working 12-hour days, led the team to replace and test more than 75 relays in half the expected time.
* Led my team to achieve the "best" operational safety record in the plant for two years; was cited with increasing efficiency and raising morale to an "all-time" high.

NUCLEAR POWER PLANT ELECTRICIAN. U.S. Navy, Bangor, WA (1985-87). On a state-of-the-art submarine, earned unusually rapid promotion to "middle management" while overseeing the operation, maintenance, and repair of a nuclear power plant providing all power for this "floating hotel"; organized and assigned electrical systems training for personnel.

* Was selected "Technician of the Quarter" for maintaining excellent training programs and "flawless" training records.
* Received two respected commendations for providing at-sea turbine and motor generator repairs usually performed only at land-based facilities.
* As the ship's only electrical oxygen generator technician, ensured the operability of vital life-support equipment.

EQUIPMENT EXPERTISE   Can operate, troubleshoot and maintain electrical equipment including:

AC/DC motors	batteries	circuit breakers	generators
controllers	switchboards	oxygen generators	

* Operate electrical test equipment.
* Am familiar with "Woodward" governors for turbine and diesel generators.
* Knowledgeable with "SPD" breakers and switchboards.
* Am a qualified ISI Level II in-service nuclear plant inspector.

EDUCATION & TRAINING   Earning A.A. degree in Electrical Engineering, Delta College, Stockton, CA.
Graduated in top 10% from a number of college-level Navy training courses in electrical theory, maintenance, and schematic reading.
* Earned a 3.6 GPA in Nuclear Power School.

PERSONAL   Am a highly skilled troubleshooter who is known for learning new skills and systems quickly. Am an excellent supervisor, motivator, and teacher.

JOHN RADFORD

1110½ Hay Street, Fayetteville, NC 28305   (910) 483-6611

OBJECTIVE

To benefit an organization that can use a dedicated professional with excellent supervisory abilities along with top-notch mechanical skills in the maintenance and troubleshooting of diesel and gas-powered vehicles.

EXPERIENCE

MAINTENANCE MANAGER. U.S. Army, Ft. Bragg, NC (1988-present). At the nation's largest military base, manage ten mechanics in a shop providing vehicle maintenance.
* Diagnose and troubleshoot vehicle malfunctions to the component level.
* Perform quality assurance checks for vehicles/generator maintenance.
* Schedule services and maintain a variety of maintenance records.
* Interpret complex schematic diagrams and use technical manuals.
* Chosen "Manager of the Month" for my enthusiasm and technical knowledge.
* Earned a respected medal for leading my team to receive a "flawless" rating during a high-level inspection.
* Was praised in writing for "outstanding leadership" and "providing firm guidance and positive direction" to employees.

SHOP FOREMAN. U.S. Army, Korea (1986-87). Managed a maintenance team of 10 while overseeing the servicing/repair of vehicles from 1/4-ton pickups to five-ton trucks.
* Was commended for "exceptional" management.

MAINTENANCE SUPERVISOR and **SHOP FOREMAN.** U.S. Army, Ft. Bragg, NC (1981-86). Was promoted to supervise up to 10 mechanics troubleshooting and repairing malfunctions in these and other areas in a fleet of vehicles used worldwide:

engines	axles	transmissions
injector pumps	fuel pumps	steering systems
injector heads	transfer cases	brake systems

* Because of my leadership ability and mechanical skill, was selected to provide support to U.S. forces in Honduras; received a distinguished honor for keeping both vehicles and power generators operational.
* Refined my skills in managing and supervising others.
* Prepared vehicles for operation in extreme weather.
* Tested equipment and obtained replacement parts.
* Performed preventive maintenance on equipment and vehicles.

VEHICLE MECHANIC. U.S. Army, Korea and Panama (1978-81). Earned a reputation as an outstanding mechanic with the ability to troubleshoot complex problems.
* Was commended for excellent work maintaining vehicles for a military police operation; was praised for my positive and professional attitude.

EQUIPMENT EXPERTISE

Can fix any vehicle from 1/4-ton up to five-ton trucks; experienced in both diesel and gas-powered vehicles; maintain generators from 1.5 to 60kw.

EDUCATION & TRAINING

Maintained 3.5 GPA completing courses in Automotive Studies, Jamestown Community College, Jamestown, NY, 1971, and Central Texas College, 1984.
Completed college-level U.S. Army training related to:

leadership and management	maintenance management
operational safety	vehicle loading/maintenance

PERSONAL

Will relocate to any location including Africa, Australia, the Far East, and the Soviet Union.

Date

Exact Name of Person
Title or Position
Name of Company
Address (no., street)
Address (city, state, zip)

Dear Exact Name of Person: (or Dear Sir or Madam if answering a blind ad.)

I would appreciate an opportunity to talk with you soon about how I could contribute to your organization through my experience related to office operations along with my reputation as a fast learner who relates well to others as either a team member or supervisor.

While serving in the U.S. Army, I earned a reputation for sound judgment and strong organizational abilities while gaining a broad base of knowledge in all phases of supply operations and accounting for multimillion-dollar inventories. I am known for my ability to find ways to streamline procedures and reduce expenditures while rapidly adjusting to the differences in procedures from office to office.

I have earned four commendation medals and two achievement medals for my accomplishments, job knowledge, and professionalism. In addition to my background in office and supply support operations, I also was selected for an assignment as a Personnel Recruiter and was twice named as the top recruiter for the quarter for exceeding my sales quotas by 10%.

As you will see from my enclosed resume, I type 50 wpm and am familiar with most standard office equipment including microcomputers, adding machines, calculators, and multiline phones. I feel that through my experience and ability to adjust to change and pressure, I could make valuable contributions to an employer seeking a mature, reliable professional.

I hope you will welcome my call soon to arrange a brief meeting at your convenience to discuss your current and future needs and how I might serve them. Thank you in advance for your time.

Sincerely yours,

Samantha Jacobs

Alternate last paragraph:
I hope you will call or write me soon to suggest a time convenient for us to meet and discuss your current and future needs and how I might serve them. Thank you in advance for your time.

SAMANTHA JACOBS

1110½ Hay Street, Fayetteville, NC 28305   (910) 483-6611

OBJECTIVE

To offer my experience in office operations to an organization that can use a mature professional who is known as a quick learner, communicates effectively with others, and has a reputation for strong planning skills and dependability.

EXPERIENCE

Gained a strong base of knowledge in all phases of supply and inventory management while acquiring skills in training and supervising subordinates, U.S. Army:

ADMINISTRATIVE SPECIALIST. Ft. Lewis, WA (1993-95). Was known for my sound judgment and organizational abilities in this position which included preparing of official correspondence and posting transactions for 22 subaccounts worth over $90 million.
* Trained supply managers in supported units in the proper procedures for preparing documentation for the central master filing system.
* Cited for my "ability to make complex problems simple," also earned praise for my aggressiveness in meeting demanding challenges in an operation with a hectic pace.
* Excelled in passing my knowledge to others and played an important role in advising others so that the people I trained achieved a 100% pass rate on general skills testing.
* Identified $10 million in stock and funding shortages for upgraded and replacement equipment.
* Played an important role in arranging and overseeing the transfer of 100,000 pieces of equipment valued in excess of $5 million for a special project in Cuba.

PROPERTY ACCOUNTABILITY SPECIALIST. Korea (1992-93). Was placed in charge of accounting for 78 customer accounts; ensured that proper documentation was always current, accurate, and complete.
* Displayed a high level of knowledge of office operations and supply support activities, which resulted in my being selected to train new personnel.
* Coordinated arrangements for relocating 1,000 people and accomplished the training project with no damage or loss of equipment.

INSPECTOR and **SUPPLY SPECIALIST.** Ft. Bliss, TX (1989-92). Implemented time- and money-saving ideas while inspecting supply operations throughout this major military post; provided advice and guidance on proper procedures for maintenance, safety, and property book accountability as well as supply operations.
* Rewrote the procedural guidelines for inspectors: units who applied the new methods saved anywhere from $2,000 to $10,000.

LOGISTICS OPERATIONS SUPERVISOR. Germany (1986-88). Maintained accountability for a $7 million operating budget while supervising 24 specialists.
* Maintained a $200,000 local purchasing account and a 750,000-gallon fuel account.
* Counseled subordinates and prepared them for professional competitions: one won an "Employee of the Quarter" award.

PERSONNEL RECRUITER. Landover, MD (1983-86). Used my communication and interpersonal skills while becoming visible in the community and locating qualified young adults, prescreening them, and selling them on the advantages of a military career.
* Exceeded my sales goals 10% and was twice named "Recruiter of the Quarter."
* Singled out over eight other qualified professionals, served as Acting Operations Manager for six months.

TRAINING

Completed more than six months of training in professional leadership development, instructional and counseling techniques, and supply operations.

SPECIAL SKILLS

Type 50 wpm; operate standard office machines including microcomputers, adding machines, copiers, microfiche, and multiline phones.

PERSONAL

Was awarded four commendation and two achievement medals for outstanding accomplishments. Held a Secret security clearance. Can handle pressure and time constraints.

Date

Exact Name of Person
Title or Position
Name of Company
Address (no., street)
Address (city, state, zip)

Dear Exact Name of Person: (or Dear Sir or Madam if answering a blind ad.)

I would appreciate an opportunity to talk with you soon about how I could benefit your organization through my outstanding management and leadership skills refined as a military officer.

As a Captain in the U.S. Army, I have excelled in some of the Army's toughest jobs: as "commander" of a nuclear security organization, a headquarters operation, and a recruiting company. In each case I have transformed mediocre organizations into "top performers" showing dramatic increases in efficiency and productivity. In the top 1% of officers, I have been selected for promotion to major.

Previously I was chosen to manage 75 people and $1.2 million in assets in northern Italy where I often functioned in "diplomatic" roles. I am fluent in Italian. Because of my integrity and honesty, I was entrusted with a Cosmic Top Secret Atomal security clearance with Background Investigation.

You would find me to be a dynamic and versatile leader who offers the ability to make any operation the "best of its kind."

I hope you will welcome my call soon to arrange a brief meeting at your convenience to discuss your current and future needs and how I might serve them. Thank you in advance for your time.

Sincerely yours,

Tony Canupp

Alternate last paragraph:
I hope you will call or write me soon to suggest a time convenient for us to meet and discuss your current and future needs and how I might serve them. Thank you in advance for your time.

TONY CANUPP

1110½ Hay Street, Fayetteville, NC 28305   (910) 483-6611

OBJECTIVE

To benefit an organization that can use a dynamic and versatile leader who offers an outstanding "track record" of achievements as well as management and communication skills refined as a junior military officer.

CLEARANCE

Hold Cosmic Top Secret Atomal security clearance with BI.

SUMMARY

WAS SELECTED THREE TIMES FOR THE TOUGHEST JOB IN THE MILITARY: "COMMANDER" (CHIEF EXECUTIVE OFFICER) OF A NUCLEAR SECURITY ORGANIZATION, A HEADQUARTERS OPERATION, AND A RECRUITING COMPANY.
* In every case, transformed mediocre organizations into top performers.
* In the top 1% of officers, am scheduled for promotion to major.

EXPERIENCE

MARKETING MANAGER. U.S. Army, Olean, NY (1988-present). As a captain in the U.S. Army, was chosen as the "company commander" of a fast-paced recruiting organization operating in eight locations.
* Took control of this troubled organization and within 90 days turned it into one of the five best of 56 in the parent organization.
* Transformed this company into the top "quality enlistment" organization in the northeastern U.S; led the organization to be in the top 1% of 260 U.S. recruiting companies.

GENERAL MANAGER. U.S. Army, Italy (1986-87). In this "chief executive officer" role, managed a 75-person organization and $1.2 million in assets; often functioned as an "international diplomat" with Italian and American executives.

MANAGEMENT CONSULTANT. U.S. Army, Italy (1985-86). Learned the Army's planning system used to modernize assets while advising 11 organizations supporting nuclear-capable NATO units.
* Played a key role in guiding nuclear weapons facilities to outstanding inspection scores.

GENERAL MANAGER. U.S. Army, Italy (1983-85). In this "company command" role, led a 50-person organization which was picked for the European commanding general's "Unit of Excellence" award in 1985.
* Functioned as the equivalent of a "mayor" for the local American community.

Highlights of other Army experience (1978-82):
FIRST-LINE SUPERVISOR. Learned to build effective teams while managing up to 34 people and $14 million in assets.
ADMINISTRATOR. Managed administrative services for up to 1,500-person operations, one of which was rated "best" in its parent organization.
GENERAL MANAGER. Implemented a training program for 25 directorates.

EDUCATION & TRAINING

B.S. degree in Biology/Education, Upper Iowa University, Fayette, IA, 1978.
Completed graduate-level U.S. Army professional training.
* Graduated with the highest GPA from management and language schools.
* Refined my analytical and problem-solving skills while excelling at the Combined Arms and Services Staff School for military executives, 1987.

PERSONAL

Am fluent in Italian. Known for my integrity and loyalty, offer the ability to motivate personnel and build productive teams. Have won numerous distinguished awards.

Date

Exact Name of Person
Title or Position
Name of Company
Address (no., street)
Address (city, state, zip)

Dear Exact Name of Person: (or Dear Sir or Madam if answering a blind ad.)

I would appreciate an opportunity to talk with you soon about how I could contribute to your organization through my management and supervisory skills as well as through my technical abilities in the areas of logistic systems management, training development, assets accountability, and inventory control.

As you will see from my resume, I have rapidly risen to the rank of Captain while serving my country in the U.S. Army. Evaluated in the top 10% of all officers, I have been selected for two "company command" assignments, which essentially put me in the position of being the "chief executive officer" of companies with hundreds of employees. In one company I developed a family support program which greatly decreased employee stress and boosted morale. In the other company, I took over the management of dysfunctional property accounting systems and quickly developed new procedures that reduced excess inventory and eliminated "lost" equipment. In that same company, I was placed in charge of a two-month project where I was responsible for setting up, from scratch, a vast logistics "service station" in the hostile desert environment of Kuwait which supported the needs of 1,039 people for food, water, fuel, repair parts, ammunition, vehicles, and other equipment.

During my management experience as an officer, I have come to believe strongly that continuous training of human resources is often the key to an organization's superiority in the marketplace. Skilled in diagnosing training needs and conceptualizing methods needed for improvement, I have earned a reputation among employees as a manager who is skilled at balancing company goals and employee needs.

You would find me in person to be a highly motivated young executive who takes pride in my ability to communicate visions and motivate personnel to achieve them. I can provide outstanding personal and professional references. I am cheerfully willing to relocate.

I hope you will welcome my call soon to arrange a brief meeting at your convenience to discuss your current and future needs and how I might serve them. Thank you in advance for your time.

Sincerely yours,

James Edwards

Alternate last paragraph:
I hope you will call or write me soon to suggest a time convenient for us to meet and discuss your current and future needs and how I might best serve them. Thank you in advance for your time.

JAMES EDWARDS
1110½ Hay Street, Fayetteville, NC 28305   (910) 483-6611

OBJECTIVE

To benefit an organization that can use a junior executive evaluated as one of the U.S. Army's most outstanding captains based on achievements in managing people, developing logistical systems, creatively solving problems, and motivating employees to excel.

EDUCATION

Bachelor of Business Administration (B.B.A.) degree, Campbell University, NC, 1986.
As an officer, successfully completed Combined Armed Services Staff School.

EXPERIENCE

COLLEGE INSTRUCTOR. Campbell University, Buies Creek, NC (1994-present).
Teach Army ROTC subjects in the university's Department of Military Science.

GENERAL MANAGER. U.S. Army, Ft. Stewart, GA (1992-94). In this job as a Company Commander, was ranked in the top 10% of U.S. Army officers and described as being a "multitalented officer on the fast track who has demonstrated keen intelligence and common sense in all situations"; was recommended for rapid promotion to major and described in writing as "the best company commander in this brigade" based on my results in managing a 323-person headquarters company providing medical, maintenance, transportation, and other support services to an 800-person organization.
* **Systems management**: Took over the management of dysfunctional property accounting systems which had resulted in extensive "lost" equipment and expensive "excess" inventory; on my own initiative, computerized many tasks while transforming internal systems into "the best" in the division.
* **Logistics/project management**: Was put in charge of a two-month special project in Kuwait which involved my establishing a new logistics base supporting 1,039 people in a hostile environment; set up highly efficient systems for food/water/fuel/ammunition resupply, for personnel/equipment transport, and for repair parts.
* **Assets accountability**: Maintained 100% accountability of $36 million in vehicles and equipment, sustained a 97% vehicle availability rate, and reduced the carrying costs of the repair part inventory without sacrificing results.

COMPANY COMMANDER. U.S. Army, Ft. Stewart, GA (1991-92). Was selected for this highly sought-after job over more senior officers, and was promoted to the job above based on my success in managing $28 million in property while molding human resources into a highly motivated, well trained team.
* **Program development**: Developed and implemented a family support program which decreased employee stress and improved employee morale.
* **Leadership**: Was described in writing as possessing "keen intelligence complemented by unwavering integrity, candor, and common sense" based on my management of a 79-person company.
* **Training management**: Developed a strong belief in the fact that continuous training of employees and strong motivation are the keys to organizational effectiveness.

TRAINING ADMINISTRATOR. U.S. Army, Ft. Stewart, GA (1990-91). Was credited with "working tirelessly" to develop and initiate programs that significantly improved operations.
* **Communication skills**: Developed the organization's standard operating procedures.

FIRST-LINE SUPERVISOR. U.S. Army, Ft. Irwin, CA (1989-90). Conceived of, developed, and implemented a comprehensive training program that improved the individual skills of every employee while pushing marginal performers to new levels.
* **Training expertise**: Became skilled in diagnosing training needs and conceptualizing methods needed for improvement.

HONORS AND AWARDS

Earned #1 ranking (honor graduate) in School of Cadet Command, 1994.
Inducted into Loyal Order of St. George for outstanding performance as a tanker, 1994.
Selected as battalion representative for Army-wide MacArthur Leadership Competition, 1992.
Named to Commandant's list (top 20%) during Infantry Officer Advanced Course, 1990.
Ranked #3 in leadership out of 66 in Armor Officer Basic Course, 1987.

Date

Exact Name of Person
Title or Position
Name of Company
Address (no., street)
Address (city, state, zip)

Dear Exact Name of Person: (or Dear Sir or Madam if answering a blind ad.)

I would appreciate an opportunity to talk with you soon about how I could benefit your organization through my experience in word/data processing as well as my proven ability to solve tough administrative problems and streamline office operations.

While serving my country in the U.S. Air Force, I have earned respected commendations while providing administrative support to NATO and Air Force executives working in a fast-paced diplomatic environment. Known for my ability to identify potentially serious problems and motivate personnel to correct them, I was recently selected to manage a "troubled" operation. Through creative solutions I developed, the operation is now a model of efficiency and boasts very high employee morale.

With extensive experience using a number of word processing and computer systems, I have been entrusted with some of the nation's highest security clearances, Top Secret with BI and Cosmic Top Secret Atomal. I have earned a reputation as an excellent communicator with the ability to explain complex concepts clearly and concisely.

You would find me to be a dedicated worker with the ability to get along with people from all backgrounds.

I hope you will welcome my call soon to arrange a brief meeting at your convenience to discuss your current and future needs and how I might serve them. Thank you in advance for your time.

Sincerely yours,

Francis Kelley

Alternate last paragraph:
I hope you will call or write me soon to suggest a time convenient for us to meet and discuss your current and future needs and how I might serve them. Thank you in advance for your time.

FRANCIS KELLEY

1110½ Hay Street, Fayetteville, NC 28305   (910) 483-6611

OBJECTIVE   To benefit an organization through my skill in streamlining office operations, my proven ability to create and implement solutions for tough problems, and my experience in word and data processing.

CLEARANCE   Because of my integrity and loyalty, have been entrusted with some of our nation's highest security clearances: TOP SECRET with BI and COSMIC TOP SECRET ATOMAL.

EXPERIENCE   **OFFICE ADMINISTRATOR.** U.S. Air Force, Oslo, Norway (1989-90). Was selected for this job managing a "troubled" operation because of my problem-solving ability and administrative knowledge: took over an office with serious control problems and restored control of classified documents, increased office efficiency, and strengthened employee morale.
* Maintained an extensive filing system including over 3,000 classified materials, correspondence, and executive reports.
* Identified and corrected a document flow problem which had created a bottleneck of unnecessary documents.

DEPUTY CHIEF OF ADMINISTRATION. U.S.A.F., Oslo, Norway (1986-89). Received two prestigious medals and unusually rapid promotion to "sergeant" because of my outstanding administrative support of two generals and 32 international officers working in a fast-paced diplomatic environment; managed six employees.
* Routinely coordinated with high-ranking NATO and Air Force executives.
* Developed and implemented an automated system which cleared the files of outdated materials twice yearly; operated three sophisticated word processing systems.
* Was praised in writing for my initiative in learning all office jobs in three months.

PERSONNEL ADMINISTRATION SPECIALIST. U.S.A.F., Offutt AFB, NE (1984-86). Received several honors and a promotion recognizing my contributions in designing, writing, communicating, and implementing new procedures used in personnel administration by nearly 250 organizations.

SERVICE OPERATIONS MANAGER. U.S.A.F., Offutt AFB, NE (1984-86). Learned to control a fast-paced service operation while managing the distribution of 74,000 pounds of mail weekly; named "Airman of the Quarter."

Other experience:
DOOR-TO-DOOR SALESMAN (1982-84). Refined my communication skills.
MANAGER (1981-82). Managed a busy Dunkin' Donuts store; hired employees.

COMPUTER SKILLS   Operate CPT 8100T, CPT 9000T, and NOTIS word processors and Zenith 100 computers with CPT Lazer Printer-8, CPT Rotary VIII, and Genicom printers.

EDUCATION & TRAINING   Completed college courses in Administration Management, Community College of the Air Force, a branch of the University of Maryland.
Completed college-level U.S.A.F. training courses in areas including office management, computer operation, personnel administration, and word processing.

PERSONAL   Work well with people from all backgrounds. Am an excellent motivator.

Date

Dear

I would appreciate an opportunity to talk with you soon about how I could contribute to your organization through my outstanding administrative, secretarial, and office management skills as well as through my creative and hard-working approach to work.

As you will see from my resume, most recently I have excelled as an Executive Secretary/ Office Manager at a fast-paced office at Ft. Bragg, the world's largest U.S. military base. On my own initiative, I computerized four separate departments which were totally lacking in computer support capability, and I trained several secretaries to use WordPerfect 6.0. I became the trusted confidante of key executives and received the highest evaluations of my proficiency and attitude.

Prior to that job, I was handpicked as the youngest Human Resources Manager ever to hold that job in a 200-person military organization. I earned widespread praise for my quality approach to employee training, and I played a major role in improving communication between supervisory staff and human resources executives.

Prior to serving my country in the Army, I earned promotion to the job of Production Controller at an international company which had offices throughout Europe. I was involved in analyzing profit/loss conditions using spreadsheets and presented my analyses of labor and production costs to upper management orally and in visual formats. I routinely dealt with sale reps from numerous European countries while working as part of a team to optimize factory production results.

You would, I am sure, find me to be a congenial individual who prides myself on strong customer relations and public relations skills. I can provide top-notch personal and professional references.

I hope you will call or write me soon to suggest a time convenient for us to meet and discuss your current and future needs and how I might serve them. Thank you in advance for your time.

Sincerely yours.

Amy Tagliat

AMY TAGLIAT

1110½ Hay Street, Fayetteville, NC 28305   (910) 483-6611

OBJECTIVE   I want to contribute to the efficiency and productivity of an organization that can use a resourceful and versatile young professional who offers excellent secretarial and administrative assistant skills along with proven administrative ability and office management experience.

COMPUTERS   Proficient with WordPerfect 6.0, Lotus 1-2-3, Harvard Graphics, dBase, and Windows.

EXPERIENCE   **EXECUTIVE SECRETARY/OFFICE MANAGER.** U.S. Army, Ft. Bragg, NC (1994-96). At the world's largest U.S. military base, received two prestigious awards recognizing my excellent on-the-job performance as well as my 100% formal proficiency rating.
* Became the trusted confidante and advisor of a high-ranking executive and was selected to act as chairman and manager of all administrative matters.
* Composed and processed all outgoing mail for a 100-person organization.
* On my own initiative, implemented standardized filing and distribution systems in three departments which were totally lacking in existing procedures.
* Modernized two office computer systems with WordPerfect 6.0; taught myself to use new software and then trained several secretaries to use the software which dramatically increased efficiency and staff morale by reducing duplicated efforts and creating professional-looking documents.
* Designed and created visual presentations for upper management on a weekly basis which showed the results of my review/analysis of personnel data and proficiency trends.
* Compiled and reported daily personnel status reports to higher management.
* Created several interoffice forms/documents related to personnel attendance, status, and absences which were used to streamline procedures, enhance communication, speed up decision making, and reduce excess paperwork.

HUMAN RESOURCES MANAGER. U.S. Army, Ft. Bragg, NC (1993-94). Became the youngest person ever to hold this job in a 200-person organization; acted as chief liaison between supervisory staff and human resources executives while also personally analyzing personnel proficiency ratings, scheduling training to correct deficiencies, and implementing all office systems to support a Total Quality Management approach to training.
* Through my style of "leadership by example" as well as through my aggressive and creative approach to reorganizing internal office systems, created an administrative staff admired as a model by other companies.

PRODUCTION CONTROLLER. Foster Refrigeration, United Kingdom (1989-92). Began in an entry-level position and was rapidly promoted to Production Controller for this commercial refrigeration factory which had sister companies throughout Europe.
* Dealt daily face-to-face and by telephone with sales reps from Europe.
* Reviewed and analyzed profits/costs using a spreadsheet format, and was frequently commended for my excellent analytical skills.

EDUCATION   Excelled in extensive college-level training sponsored by the U.S. Army in office management, computer operations, and personnel administration.
Received extensive training in production control and quality control through corporate training sponsored by Foster Refrigeration.

PERSONAL   Am a cheerful hard worker known for integrity and creativity. Can provide excellent references upon request. Hold a Secret security clearance. Will relocate as needed.

Date

Exact Name of Person
Title or Position
Name of Company
Address (no., street)
Address (city, state, zip)

Dear Exact Name of Person: (or Dear Sir or Madam if answering a blind ad.)

I would appreciate an opportunity to talk with you soon about how I could contribute to your organization through my background of outstanding performance in positions emphasizing office administration, computer operations, and information security.

With a reputation as a highly motivated professional, I excel at finding ways to increase productivity and achieve outstanding results in all rated areas of performance. I offer a high degree of administrative know how and a history of maximizing human resources under severe time constraints and during periods of high personnel turnover.

As you will see from my resume, I gained extensive skills in computer operations, general office operations, records management, and handling sensitive materials while serving in the U.S. Air Force. Consistently able to find ways to streamline procedures, I also have become known for my effectiveness in interpersonal communications, leadership roles, and training as well as for my abilities in technical writing and briefing.

An enthusiastic professional, I have always excelled in positions which require high levels of integrity and good character. I feel that I have a lot to offer a company such as yours through my history of achievements in clerical and office administrative roles.

I hope you will welcome my call soon to arrange a brief meeting at your convenience to discuss your current and future needs and how I might serve them. Thank you in advance for your time.

Sincerely yours,

Louise Jarvis

Alternate last paragraph:
I hope you will call or write me soon to suggest a time convenient for us to meet and discuss your current and future needs and how I might serve them. Thank you in advance for your time.

LOUISE JARVIS

1110 ½ Hay Street, Fayetteville, NC 28305 (910) 483-6611

OBJECTIVE

To offer extensive experience in office administration to an organization in need of a mature self starter with a talent for finding methods of increasing productivity and efficiency while maximizing individual employee's strengths for the benefit of the company as a whole.

SPECIAL SKILLS & TRAINING

Am familiar with computer hardware and software including the following:
Hardware: Zenith 200, 150, and 486; UNISYS
Software: Microsoft Windows, WordPerfect up through Version 6.0, and the RIMS program used by the U.S. military to maintain files.
Other skills include answering multiline phones and using manual and electric typewriters.
Experienced in information security, have held a Top Secret security clearance.
Was selected for training in leadership, postal operations, and supply management.

EXPERIENCE

Consistently excelled in positions of trust and responsibility while broadening my base of knowledge and experience of office automation and administration, U.S. Air Force:
ADMINISTRATIVE MANAGER. Pope AFB, NC (1993-95). Improved several aspects of daily operations overseeing training, cooperation during interagency actions, and records management in a 900-person organization; supervised three administrative specialists.
* Applied my knowledge and expertise to successfully train 10 administrative technicians who received career advancement and upgrades.
* Discovered and corrected 200 discrepancies in an inventory of security badges.
* Implemented procedural changes which greatly reduced security incidents and also a successful suggestions program.
* Prepared and presented weekly information security reports for the senior executive.

ADMINISTRATIVE ASSISTANT. The Netherlands (1991-93). Praised for my attention to detail, knowledge, and abilities, received excellent ratings during NATO inspections in a job which included document security, records management, typing, and filing.
* Ensured classified documents were filed, distributed, logged, and destroyed in accordance with all applicable regulations while closely coordinating document management with my counterparts from other NATO member-countries.
* Received a certificate of achievement for contributions while rewriting a critical emergency action plan under severe time constraints: the plan vastly improved operations.

PUBLICATIONS, FORMS, AND ADMINISTRATION MANAGER. Turkey (1990-91). Operated an information transfer center which processed official mail; provided advice and guidance to smaller departments and sections throughout the community.
* Implemented the Record Information Management System (RIMS) ahead of schedule.
* Displayed strong managerial skills providing 24-hour-a-day support services during the war in the Middle East and its aftermath.
* Developed a strong team of employees despite an early 50% personnel turnover.
* Totally reorganized the filing system which eliminated the possibility of lost records.

ADMINISTRATIVE BRANCH MANAGER. Robins AFB, GA (1989-90). Promoted to this position on the basis of my ability to work under pressure and offer outstanding managerial abilities as a Control Center Manager, proceeded to find ways to eliminate wasted time and efforts in this operations center.
* Streamlined record-keeping and reporting procedures and completed a major reorganization project ahead of schedule.
* Managed a $250,000 account for sensitive and secure communications equipment.

ADMINISTRATIVE ASSISTANT, OPERATIONS AND PLANS BRANCH. Belgium (1986-87). Contributed to the smooth operation of a regional headquarters by providing control, records maintenance, and distribution for both classified and unclassified materials and by administering personnel actions including performance reports and awards.

PERSONAL

Earned four commendation medals for outstanding performance, loyalty, and dedication. Offer proven abilities as a planner and organizer. Challenge employees to high standards.

Date

Exact Name of Person
Title or Position
Name of Company
Address (no., street)
Address (city, state, zip)

Dear Exact Name of Person: (or Dear Sir or Madam if answering a blind ad.)

I would appreciate an opportunity to talk with you soon about how I could contribute to your company through my outstanding communication, motivational, problem-solving, and decision-making skills.

As a captain who has recently earned my M.B.A. degree at night while excelling in my full-time jobs, I offer experience in managing multimillion-dollar budgets and supervising hundreds of people.

Handpicked for the Army's most competitive line management job —"company commander" — I managed a 180-person company and $20 million in sophisticated electronics assets. By applying my problem-solving and motivational skills, I led the organization to improve inventory control, employee training, and data processing.

In previous jobs, I managed a $5 million budget, supervised a fleet of vehicles, and directed all administrative services supporting a 140-person organization operating around-the-clock.

You would find me to be an energetic, dynamic, and versatile professional who thrives on meeting a challenge. Known for my "common sense" approach to making decisions, I offer proven analytical ability.

I hope you will welcome my call soon to arrange a brief meeting at your convenience to discuss your current and future needs and how I might serve them. Thank you in advance for your time.

Sincerely yours,

James Garrison

Alternate last paragraph:
I hope you will call or write me soon to suggest a time convenient for us to meet and discuss your current and future needs and how I might serve them. Thank you in advance for your time.

JAMES GARRISON

1110½ Hay Street, Fayetteville, NC 28305   (910) 483-6611

OBJECTIVE   To benefit an organization that can use an energetic and innovative manager who offers a dynamic communication style, superior motivational skills, as well as problem-solving and decision-making abilities refined as a military officer and corporate manager.

EDUCATION   Completed Graduate Management Program, American Express, 1991.
Earned M.B.A. degree, Fayetteville State University (a campus of the University of North Carolina), NC, 1990.
* Led a team to earn honors in a statewide competition in which M.B.A. students solved profitability problems of real companies.
Received B.S. in Business Administration, South Carolina State College, SC, 1983.
* Received a full athletic scholarship; was captain of the track team.
Completed graduate-level management training for selected Army officers.

EXPERIENCE   **EXECUTIVE CONSULTANT.** U.S. Army, Ft. Bragg, NC (1990). Used my expert writing and speaking skills to articulate concepts and resource requirements to top-level military executives.
* Improved project management by streamlining information processing.

GENERAL MANAGER. U.S. Army, Ft. Bragg, NC (1989-90). As chief executive officer of 180 employees, managed these areas while controlling sophisticated electronics equipment valued at $20 million:

employee training	assets repair/maintenance	personnel administration
strategic planning	budgeting and finance	inventory control

* In this job reserved for the top 1% of officers, gained valuable expertise in "managing managers."
* Implemented automated systems which improved management decision-making and increased efficiency.
* Boosted productivity by implementing a comprehensive training program.
* Developed decentralized inventory control procedures which enabled the organization to achieve an equipment accountability of 100%.
* Devised a preventive maintenance program which increased from 86% to 96% the availability of a fleet of 65 vehicles.

OPERATIONS OFFICER. U.S. Army, Ft. Bragg, NC (1987-89). Became known for my ability to rapidly analyze information and make sound decisions while advising top strategic planners; supervised 25 specialized electronics technicians operating 15 communications systems.

Highlights of other experience: U.S. Army, Germany (1983-86). Managed a $5 million operating budget while directing administrative services for a 140-person organization staffed 24 hours a day.
* Strengthened productivity and morale by reorganizing work schedules.
* Earned five distinguished medals while creating a training plan rated as "exceptional"; managed 65 employees.

COMPUTERS   Operate computers with Lotus 1-2-3 and Harvard Graphics software.

PERSONAL   Held SECRET security clearance. Known for my "common sense" planning skills.

Date

Exact Name of Person
Title or Position
Name of Company
Address (no., street)
Address (city, state, zip)

Dear Exact Name of Person: (or Dear Sir or Madam if answering a blind ad.)

I would appreciate an opportunity to talk with you soon about how I could benefit your organization through my communication, management, and decision-making skills refined as a junior military officer.

A West Point graduate with a B.S. degree in Operations Research, I have acquired a reputation as a dynamic leader and motivator while serving my country as a Captain in the U.S. Army. Recently I was chosen to manage financial and supply operations for a troubled 682-person operation. I rapidly established budgetary guidelines and dramatically improved the accountability of millions of dollars in assets.

I offer the proven ability to "revitalize" troubled operations and coordinate major projects. Noted for my "clear, concise, and to the point" communication style, I have been chosen to write detailed operations plans adopted for worldwide use.

You would find me to be a dedicated professional with the ability to set and achieve goals.

I hope you will welcome my call soon to arrange a brief meeting at your convenience to discuss your current and future needs and how I might serve them. Thank you in advance for your time.

Sincerely yours,

Charles Dwight Heckler

Alternate last paragraph:
I hope you will call or write me soon to suggest a time convenient for us to meet and discuss your current and future needs and how I might serve them. Thank you in advance for your time.

CHARLES DWIGHT HECKLER

1110½ Hay Street, Fayetteville, NC 28305   (910) 483-6611

OBJECTIVE   I offer outstanding leadership, communication, management, and decision-making skills to an organization that can use a dynamic and innovative professional who has excelled as a junior military officer.

EDUCATION   B.S. degree in **Operations Research**, U.S. Military Academy at **West Point**, 1984. Completed U.S. Army training in leadership and management.
* Excelled in **Ranger School**, the Army's "stress test" designed to test the limits of the "best and brightest" young officers.
* In high school, excelled as both a scholar and athlete.

EXPERIENCE   **OPERATIONS MANAGER.** U.S. Army, Ft. Bragg, NC (1989). As a captain, was specially chosen for this "company command" position "reinvigorating" a 165-person organization previously noted for low morale and achievements.
* Used my counseling and training skills to dramatically increase employee performance in training projects and knowledge tests.
* Was praised in writing for my ability to handle stress as well as my "clear, concise, and to the point" communication style.

BUDGET/SUPPLY MANAGER. U.S. Army, Ft. Bragg, NC (1989). Refined my financial skills while managing all logistics and supply operations for a 682-person organization; controlled a $250,000 annual budget.
* Established budgetary guidelines and held weekly conferences to monitor spending; prepared monthly budget reports for top executives.
* Conducted bi-weekly meetings to monitor supply trends.
* Took control of a troubled operation and enforced budgetary standards.
* Set up logistical operating procedures which improved equipment accountability.

ASSISTANT PLANNING MANAGER. U.S. Army, Ft. Bragg, NC (1988-89). Was chosen to develop and present strategic plans for "the most all-important" project ever undertaken by this 682-person team; created highly-detailed plans which have been adopted by the organization as "standards."
* Coordinated an evaluation plan which conducted three-day checks of nine operations teams in one week.

ADMINISTRATOR/PROJECT MANAGER. U.S. Army, Germany (1987-88). Was evaluated in writing as "one of the best" lieutenants in the parent organization while handling administrative duties for an operation frequently training throughout Europe.
* Maintained perfect equipment accountability while managing supplies for training.
* Was commended for creating dynamic training projects.

FIRST-LINE SUPERVISOR. U.S. Army, Germany (1985-87). Led two teams to be rated as "best" in their parent organizations; managed a $1 million inventory of equipment.
* Was selected from 22 lieutenants to represent the U.S. at the Spandau Prison changeover ceremony for the guarding of Rudolf Hess.
* Because of my technical knowledge, was chosen to represent the organization at a conference at the White Sands Missile Range.

PERSONAL   Hold Secret clearance. Excelled in academics and wrestling in high school.

201

Date

Exact Name of Person
Title or Position
Name of Company
Address (no., street)
Address (city, state, zip)

Dear Exact Name of Person: (or Dear Sir or Madam if answering a blind ad.)

Can you use an enthusiastic and energetic young professional who offers a strong customer service orientation along with a work history which includes experience related to office operations, planning and scheduling, dispatching, and contract management?

While serving in the U.S. Air Force, I earned a reputation as a talented performer who could be counted on to go the extra mile and not quit until I found a way to get the job done. As a Production Control Specialist for civil engineering operations, I prioritized work requests, inspected work sites, and provided support by coordinating human and material requirements as well as performing data entry functions. I have consistently been described as being capable of handling details so that each job is coordinated properly and completed on time.

As you will see from my resume I am familiar with business software including MS Word. Powerpoint, Excel, and Harvard Graphics. I have a great deal of experience in preparing and presenting briefings and am accustomed to dealing with people ranging from city government officials, to civil engineers, to supervisory personnel, to a variety of mechanics.

I am a highly motivated individual with a reputation for honesty and integrity in all my relationships. I excel in finding ways to streamline daily operations and bring about improvements in productivity, customer service, and efficiency.

I hope you will welcome my call soon to arrange a brief meeting at your convenience to discuss your current and future needs and how I might serve them. Thank you in advance for your time.

Sincerely yours,

Kitty Gail King

Alternate last paragraph:
I hope you will call or write me soon to suggest a time convenient for us to meet and discuss your current and future needs and how I might serve them. Thank you in advance for your time.

KITTY GAIL KING
1110½ Hay Street, Fayetteville, NC 28305   (910) 483-6611

OBJECTIVE

To contribute through a versatile background which includes outstanding performance in customer service, job scheduling and planning, and office operations as well as through my reputation as a dedicated, enthusiastic, and creative young professional.

EXPERIENCE

PRODUCTION CONTROL MANAGER & QUALITY CONTROL SPECIALIST. *Consistently earned praise for my ability to remain in control while overseeing the details of scheduling and coordinating multiple simultaneous civil engineering work requests and projects, U.S. Air Force: Pope AFB, NC (1993-1995).* Prioritized work requests and entered essential data into computer records while ensuring that routine and emergency service calls were responded to promptly and that activities were tracked and recorded accurately.
* Initiated a series of computer reports which streamlined operations by allowing foremen to analyze potential problem areas and see that personnel were assigned in a way which maximized their particular skills.
* Assured that $775,000 worth of work was carried out by reorganizing the work order priority program and then maintaining the proper computer records.
* Prepared and organized slides and other materials used in weekly operations briefings.
* Set up and managed regular weekly work request review meetings.
* Was cited for my professionalism in controlling and allocating emergency human and material resources in response to a major aircraft accident.

Bergstrom AFB, TX (1991-93). Received a commendation medal for my efforts in overseeing activities related to preparing the military complex for closure: worked closely with officials from the City of Austin as the Air Force's representative for monitoring more than $1 million worth of contracts which studied the potential for civilian reuse of the facilities.
* Managed more than $500,000 in preliminary engineering studies.
* Contributed after-hours time providing typing and computer support for the Air Force Base Disposal Agency (AFBDA) team in order to allow them to complete the turnover of facilities to the City of Austin on schedule.
* Streamlined the self-help program so that recordkeeping and customer service became more efficient and of a noticeably higher quality.

Germany (1989-91). Was evaluated as being someone who always took the "extra steps beyond expected performance standards" which resulted in reducing problems and improving customer service in a civil engineering organization; maintained strict attention to detail in order to ensure work requests were completed in a timely and efficient manner.
* Contributed to the "excellent" rating received during a NATO evaluation by finding ways to eliminate conflicting information and control communication lines more effectively.
* Provided a levelheaded approach and ability to handle stress as a controller in an operations center providing communications links during the war in the Middle East.

Bergstrom AFB, TX (1987-89). Became skilled in taking care of the details of answering service calls, entering appropriate information into computer records, prioritizing requests, dispatching work crews, and keeping the necessary personnel informed of changing priorities and schedules.
* Controlled communications which allowed flood damage repairs at a recreational area to be coordinated and completed in the minimum amount of time.
* Learned to use grid maps to plot damage control requirements and to coordinate with fire, security, hazardous material, medical, explosive ordnance, and bioenvironmental units.

EDUCATION & TRAINING

Completed one year of general studies, St. Andrews Presbyterian College, Laurinburg, NC. Excelled in training programs including one leading to a certificate in Production Control, a Total Quality Management (TQM) course, and a leadership/management school.
* Earned a prestigious award as the top student in the leadership/management school and graduated in the top 2% from the Production Control class.

PERSONAL

Secret security clearance. Understand heating, air conditioning, plumbing, carpentry, electrical, and sheet metal work from eight years of daily exposure to civil engineering activities.

Date

Mr. Jack W. McGuinness
Advisor, United Arab Emirates
PO Box 41184
Abu Dhabi, UAE

Dear Mr. McGuinness:

I would appreciate an opportunity to talk with you soon about how I could contribute to your organization through my expertise in planning and conducting Special Operations training, my extensive experience in Mideast affairs and culture, and my versatile technical knowledge and competence. Please be assured that I am available for relocation worldwide immediately, and I will provide outstanding personal and professional references upon your request. I am particularly interested in a job as Operations Officer/Office of Defense Advisor within the United Arab Emirates.

As you will see from my resume, while serving my country I have worked at the highest enlisted rank — Sergeant Major. I speak Arabic, Egyptian, German, Spanish, and French, and I hold a Top Secret security clearance with SBI. I offer expert knowledge of military contracting procedures, diving and scuba operations, navigation and demolitions, as well as marine and optical and airborne/parachute equipment.

Most recently I have been involved in product testing of equipment related to airborne and parachute operations as well as underwater and waterborne operations. I have fully tested and authored reports containing recommendations related to demolitions, underwater, and parachute products.

With a reputation as an outstanding communicator, I have excelled as a Special Forces instructor and I have written Special Operations policies and procedures related to a wide variety of areas. I am skilled at all aspects of planning training and authoring training doctrine.

You would find me to be a resourceful manager and problem-solver who is known as a thoroughly honest, adaptable, and versatile professional.

I hope you will contact me soon to suggest a time when we might meet in person to discuss your needs and goals and how I might serve them. Thank you in advance for your time.

Yours sincerely,

Scott L. Toomy

SCOTT L. TOOMY

1110½ Hay Street, Fayetteville, NC 28305   (910) 483-6611

OBJECTIVE

To benefit an organization that can use a resourceful manager and problem-solver who offers expertise in testing and fielding new equipment, designing and implementing new systems, and managing the change of physical assets and operating procedures.

EXPERIENCE

DIRECTOR OF SPECIAL SKILLS AND TECHNICAL PROFICIENCY. U.S. Army Special Operations Command, Ft. Bragg, NC (1993-present). At the world's largest U.S. military base, am considered the technical expert on matters related to airborne and parachute operations for all units within the Army's famed Special Operations; also assist in assuring the technical proficiency of underwater and waterborne operations.
* Wrote a regulation for Army personnel on airborne operations that defines standard operating procedures used worldwide.
* Authored policies for Special Operations for all branches of the service.
* Developed a Jumpmaster Guide for the Army's Special Operations.
* Have earned a reputation as an exceptional technical writer: produced a major change to USASOC Regulation 350-2 (Airborne Operations) and produced the final draft of USSOCOM Directive 350-3 (Parachute Operations).

PRODUCT TEST OFFICER. U.S. Army Airborne/Special Operations Test Directorate, Ft. Bragg, NC (1992-93). Conducted tests involving demolitions and new Army equipment, including underwater gear; also directed testing of parachute equipment and airborne items.
* Fully tested, evaluated, and prepared formal reports with recommendations related to three demolitions items, two underwater projects, and two parachute products.

STUDENT, EXECUTIVE DEVELOPMENT PROGRAM. U.S. Army Sergeants Major Academy, Ft. Bliss, TX (1992). Graduated in the top 10% of the class from the highest-level military school for enlisted officers; this graduate-level school is designed to refine the management abilities of the Army's "best and brightest" mid-level managers.

GENERAL MANAGER. U.S. Army Special Forces, Ft. Campbell, KY (1990-91). In this Sergeant Major position, supervised a 110-person Special Forces company, and directed the involvement of this company in the war in the Middle East.

OPERATIONS MANAGER. U.S. Army Special Forces, Ft. Campbell, KY (1988-91). Directed the often-classified activities of a Special Forces "A" team during special projects in Jordan, Egypt, and Saudi Arabia.
* Became intimately familiar with Mideast affairs and cultures.

INSTRUCTOR SUPERVISOR. U.S. Army Special Warfare Center, Ft. Bragg, NC (1985-88). Designed major changes in the program of instruction related to construction, civil actions, and demolitions while excelling as an instructor of Special Forces engineering.
* Taught more than 1,000 people during three years.

Other U.S. Army experience: Was singled out for rapid promotion while distinguishing myself academically and professionally: was named "Soldier of the Year" for the 3rd Armored Division, 1977, and was "Distinguished Graduate" of the NCO Course, 1974.

SPECIAL SKILLS & KNOWLEDGE

Languages: Speak Arabic, Egyptian, German, Spanish, and French
Clearance: Top Secret security clearance with SBI
Computers: Use software including WordPerfect, OfficeWriter, Harvard Graphics
Military contracting: Expert knowledge of how Department of Defense buys equipment
Piloting: FAA certified Private Pilot, single-engine land
Special equipment: Offer special knowledge of marine and optical equipment
Navigation and demolitions: Am a demolitions instructor; proficient with navigation aids
Diving and scuba operations: Directed worldwide projects as a Dive Officer/Scuba Officer

EDUCATION

Completed four years of college-level training in management, electrical engineering, technical military subjects, business, and other areas; Liberty University, Clemson University, and U.S. Army.

PERSONAL

Am known as a thoroughly honest, resourceful, adaptable, and versatile professional.

Date

Exact Name of Person
Title or Position
Name of Company
Address (no., street)
Address (city, state, zip)

Dear Exact Name of Person: (or Dear Sir or Madam if answering a blind ad.)

I am seeking an opportunity to discuss with you how I can contribute to your organization through my diversified experience in personnel and resource management, as well as my proven problem-solving and decision-making abilities.

Community services management ability
As an Army Colonel, I managed educational, public works, retail, and recreational service programs for 14,000 people living in 20 dispersed communities in three culturally differing countries. With limited financial resources, I have met an increasing demand for services, and saved hundreds of thousands of dollars through disciplined budget execution and a creative approach to programming. I am widely respected for my ability to maximize the effectiveness of every budgeted dollar.

Personnel administration/management expertise
Considered an "expert" in the field of personnel administration, I directed the placement, training, and administration of executives, mid-managers, and technical specialists worldwide. I also developed highly effective programs to reward employee excellence, increase operational efficiency, improve employee working conditions and morale, strengthen environmental/industrial safety, and increase substance abuse awareness.

I am a dedicated executive who leads by example, delegates, and is a team participant. I am also recognized for my tireless energy and spirited efforts in producing outstanding results.

Please advise me of a convenient time for us to discuss options you may have available and how I might serve you. Thank you for your time.

Sincerely yours,

Frank Reynolds

FRANK REYNOLDS

1110½ Hay Street, Fayetteville, NC 28305　　　　　　　　(910) 483-6611

OBJECTIVE　　To benefit an organization needing a skilled executive with diverse personnel and resource management experience as well as problem-solving and decision-making abilities.

SUMMARY　　WHILE ACHIEVING THE RANK OF COLONEL IN THE U.S. ARMY, ESTABLISHED A "TRACK RECORD" OF ACHIEVEMENT IN PERSONNEL ADMINISTRATION, COMMUNITY SERVICES MANAGEMENT, AND PUBLIC ADMINISTRATION.

EXPERIENCE　　**DIRECTOR OF COMMUNITY SERVICES.** Italy, Greece, and Turkey (1987-90). Managed personnel, educational, public works, retail, family support, and recreational services for 14,000 people living in 20 communities in three countries; supervised 128 professionals; managed $14 million in budgets.
* Automated budget operations and increased services, through streamlining, with limited financial resources.
* Formed a team of experts to extend services to remote communities.
* Programmed needed services — for example, child care and youth services — and maximized the use of financial resources.
* Dealt with the National Italian unions on issues of mutual concern to the U.S. forces and the Italian unions.

CHIEF OF PERSONNEL ADMINISTRATION. Ft. Bragg, NC (1984-87). Was handpicked to develop and implement plans for the placement, training, and administrative support of management-level personnel for organizations with 9,000 employees working in five different countries at 11 locations.
* Controlled an $864,000 operating budget; supervised 141 people.
* Developed a popular and diverse leisure recreational program that included golf, tennis, racquetball, basketball, flag football, soccer, and softball.
* Designed/implemented a program which drastically reduced substance abuse.
* Created a comprehensive safety plan that included inspection checklists, incident/accident reporting procedures, and strategic objectives.

DIRECTOR, SPECIAL PERSONNEL ASSIGNMENTS. Alexandria, VA (1982-84). Refined worldwide personnel assignment operations by developing/implementing a "total person" qualifying process. Concurrently selected/placed 10,000 executives and area technical experts in highly visible leadership positions to include the Office of the Joint Chiefs of Staff and DOD level assignments; cited for special achievement.

DIRECTOR OF EXECUTIVE PLACEMENT. Alexandria, VA (1980-82). Viewed as the "expert" on executive placement while coordinating training and professional assignments for top executives including colonels and promotable lieutenant colonels.
* Worked with high-level Department of Defense military and civilian officials.

INSPECTOR GENERAL. Korea (1979-80). As confidential advisor to three general officers, created a program to "teach" organizational standards and evaluate achievement; authored and published a popular monthly newsletter for managers.

EDUCATION & TRAINING　　M.A. in Personnel Management and Administration, Webster College, 1978.
B.S. in Physical Education and History, University of California at LA, 1963.
Completed specialized Army training for officers in personnel management.
Completed two years of graduate-level education for military executives.

Date

Exact Name of Person
Title or Position
Name of Company
Address (no., street)
Address (city, state, zip)

Dear Exact Name of Person: (or Dear Sir or Madam if answering a blind ad.)

I would appreciate an opportunity to talk with you soon about how I could contribute to your organization through my leadership skills combined with my background in program development, strategic planning, personnel supervision, and financial management.

While achieving the rank of Colonel in the U.S. Air Force, I have excelled in a wide variety of jobs. In one job as a "city manager" I managed a 29,000-acre industrial/housing community. In another job I supervised financial administration and numerous services for 4,000 people. I have also played a key role in planning and implementing support programs for newly fielded defense systems. Many facilities and programs I have managed have been judged "the best" in the Air Force, including a 1,300-room hotel, a natural resources program, and a fuels management program.

Recently chosen to administer an $84 million budget, I have earned a reputation as a expert financial planner who "makes the most" of every dollar. While managing teams of up to 1,500 diversified professionals, I have become skilled in motivating people to work for a common goal. With an M.B.A. degree, I have managed "from scratch" some of the Air Force's largest logistics programs.

You would find me to be a talented communicator and adaptable executive with a proven ability to turn ideas into operating realities.

I hope you will welcome my call soon to arrange a brief meeting at your convenience to discuss your current and future needs and how I might serve them. Thank you in advance for your time.

Sincerely yours,

Patrick Marks

Alternate last paragraph:
I hope you will call or write me soon to suggest a time convenient for us to meet and discuss your current and future needs and how I might serve them. Thank you in advance for your time.

PATRICK MARKS

1110½ Hay Street, Fayetteville, NC 28305 (910) 483-6611

OBJECTIVE

To benefit an organization that can use a versatile leader and talented communicator who offers proven expertise in managing human and physical resources, multimillion-dollar budgets, and top-level planning operations.

EDUCATION & TRAINING

M.B.A. degree in Business, Auburn University, Auburn, AL.
B.S.B.A. degree in Accounting, Tennessee Technical University, TN.
Completed extensive graduate-level courses for U.S.A.F. executives.

EXPERIENCE

WHILE ACHIEVING THE RANK OF COLONEL IN THE U.S. AIR FORCE, EARNED A REPUTATION AS AN UNPARALLELED DECISION-MAKER, MANAGER, AND MOTIVATOR.

CHIEF OF FACILITIES PLANNING. Tyndall AFB, FL (1990). Managed a budget of $84 million and 500 people while creating programs for worldwide services ranging from airfield repair, to computer support, to hospitality management.

Hospitality & Recreation Services

GENERAL MANAGER (CITY MANAGER). Tyndall AFB, FL (1989-90). As "city manager" of a 29,000-acre industrial/housing community, administered a $25 million budget and supervised 1,300 people providing services such as:

police/fire	personnel administration	civil engineering
recreation	hotels/hospitality	dining/housing

* Directed the U.S.A.F.'s **best** hotel and food services team, 1989, and managed its **top** natural resources management program, 1990.

RESOURCES DIRECTOR. Tyndall AFB, FL (1988-89). Negotiated over $200 million in contracted services while overseeing supply/transportation activities and financial/pay services for 12,000 people; managed an $80 million budget.

Human & Physical Resources

RESOURCES MANAGER. Turkey (1986-88). Led this 4,000-person organization to operate at an all-time high level of efficiency; controlled a 1,000-vehicle fleet operating throughout Turkey while managing a $125 million payroll and a $50 million operating budget.

* Worked with foreign and U.S. contractors to provide a range of goods and services rated **best** in Europe in 1987.
* Created the U.S.A.F.'s **most efficient** fuels management program, 1988.

Top-Level Planning

PROJECT DIRECTOR. Wright-Patterson AFB, OH (1984-86). Created, from planning through budgeting and integration phases, a total logistics and maintenance support program for a $5 billion defense system; coordinated the efforts of 1,500 technical experts and senior executives.

* Put in place a cost-effective system which included maintenance programs, training programs and materials, and automated logistics systems.

PROGRAM MANAGER. Wright-Patterson AFB, OH (1983-84). "Sold" to executives and implemented a $1.6 billion spare part procurement program for the B-1 bomber — the Air Force's largest such program at the time — while managing 70 personnel developing a $3 billion maintenance/logistics program.

EXECUTIVE AIDE. Wright-Patterson AFB, OH (1982-83). Served as the "right arm" for three generals directing Air Force logistics operations; managed 43 personnel and formulated policies for 95,000 U.S.A.F. logistics managers.

* Implemented the office's first administrative computer system.

RESOURCES MANAGER. Eaker AFB, AR (1980-83). Managed a $25 million procurement program, a $125 million supply account, and a $70 million budget.

PERSONAL

Hold TOP SECRET security clearance with SBI. Use personal computers.

Date

Exact Name of Person
Title or Position
Name of Company
Address (no., street)
Address (city, state, zip)

Dear Exact Name of Person:`(or Dear Sir or Madam if answering a blind ad.)

I would appreciate an opportunity to talk with you soon about how I could contribute to your organization through my management experience, problem-solving skills, and "track record" of results in cutting costs and increasing productivity.

As you will see from my resume, I have excelled as an Air Force officer in finding optimum solutions at least cost for large-scale problems.

While earning my M.S. in Systems Management, I authored a Master's thesis hailed as a "breakthrough" in the development of a multiple-source procurement strategy which is saving an estimated $4.5 billion in jet engine costs in only five years.

In one job as a computer project manager, I managed multimillion-dollar projects through all stages, from identifying requirements, to justifying requirements for DOD funding, to final project acceptance.`One plan I conceived of integrated 165 devices into a state-of-the-art network.

In every job I have held, I have excelled in reducing costs, increasing productivity, and solving tough problems while working with the "experts" to bring out their best.

I hope you will welcome my call soon to arrange a brief meeting at your convenience to discuss your current and future needs and how I might serve them.`Thank you in advance for your time.

Sincerely yours,

Raymond McCran

Alternate last paragraph:
I hope you will call or write me soon to suggest a time convenient for us to meet and discuss your current and future needs and how I might serve them.`Thank you in advance for your time.`

RAYMOND MCCRAN

1110½ Hay Street, Fayetteville, NC 28305   (910) 483-6611

OBJECTIVE   To contribute to an organization that can use a talented manager with a "track record" of accomplishments in reducing costs, improving morale, increasing productivity, solving problems, and implementing solutions.

EDUCATION   M.S. in Systems Management, Air Force Institute of Technology, 1979.
B.S. in Engineering Management, U.S. Air Force Academy, 1970.

PUBLICATION   Authored a Master's thesis hailed as "a real breakthrough" in the development of a multiple-source procurement strategy which is saving the U.S. an estimated $4.5 billion in jet engine costs in just five years.
*   Persisted in authoring this thesis and developing this idea despite major obstacles.

CLEARANCE   Top Secret security clearance with SBI.

EXPERIENCE   **OPERATIONS CENTER DIRECTOR.** `U.S. Air Force, Japan` (1987-present). Have been promoted to manage 15 people coordinating/supporting 525 monthly reconnaissance flights flown by the Air Force, Navy, Army, and Marine Corps.
*   Greatly improved morale in a 75% minority organization.
*   Reduced labor costs 20% while providing quality services.
*   Decreased by 50% the time involved in obtaining vital information.

OPERATIONS CHIEF. `U.S.A.F., Greece` (1983-87). Managed dozens of people, supervised the movement of reconnaissance crews and aircraft, and led politically sensitive international projects requiring my coordination of these areas:

housing   communications   labor
maintenance   security   diplomatic clearances

*   Led the smallest reconnaissance unit with the heaviest flying schedule to maintain an extraordinary, four-year, 99% "mission effectiveness" rate, despite frequent terrorist problems and labor turmoil.
*   Originated simple graphics tools to explain complex problems visually.
*   Reduced annual fuel costs $325,000 by astute forecasting.
*   Cut scheduling and reporting errors 99%; saved 600 manhours yearly.

COMPUTER PROJECT MANAGER and **PILOT.** `U.S.A.F., Offutt AFB, NE` (1978-83). Saved millions of dollars while managing computer projects worth $6 million through all stages, from identifying requirements, to justifying requirements for DOD approval/funding, to final project acceptance.
*   Conceived of and developed a five-year, seven-million-dollar plan to integrate 165 devices into a state-of-the-art network.
*   Saved $80,000 by disproving the need for one project.
*   Reduced the cost of one five-year project from $200,000 to $2,000.
*   Taught this organization to apply queuing theory with marginal cost analysis in determining computer needs: this technique was copied by the Army, Navy, and Marine Corps.
*   As a pilot, 1981-83, with a commercial multi-engine, single-engine, jet instrument license, supervised a 33-person crew in worldwide missions.

PERSONAL   Logged total flight time of 3,200 hours in fixed-wing aircraft. `Will relocate worldwide.

Date

Exact Name of Person
Title or Position
Name of Company
Address (no., street)
Address (city, state, zip)

Dear Exact Name of Person: (or Dear Sir or Madam if answering a blind ad.)

I would appreciate an opportunity to talk with you soon about how I could contribute to your organization through my versatile accomplishments and my success in ever-increasing levels of management and supervision.

Personnel management and communication skills

Throughout my career in the U.S. Navy, I have advanced because of my natural skills in communicating with others. I have supervised departments with as many as 89 employees, administered budgets of varying sizes, and controlled inventories valued in excess of $820 million. While serving my country in the military, I have advanced to the highest possible enlisted rank while completing some course work leading to a graduate degree in management and earning both a B.S. in Business Administration and A.A. in Criminology.

Production management and quality control know-how

In several line management positions, I have proven my ability to manage fast-paced production operations. In a recent job as a production supervisor, I significantly reduced production costs while actually improving quality control for an $820-million electronics inventory. In another job in the production and logistics area, I am proud to have managed, without a single safety incident, the extremely hazardous activities associated with handling and testing weapons.

Security and law enforcement expertise

As you will see from my resume, I offer specialist knowledge and experience in the areas of security, law enforcement, and firefighting. Selected to receive advanced Department of Defense training in special weapons handling, the dynamics of international terrorism, as well as techniques for small arms instruction and safety, I am qualified on several small arms.

Extensive international travel and proficiency with foreign languages

Living, working, and traveling in international settings have allowed me many opportunities to become knowledgeable of other cultures. I speak some Italian and German.

I hope you will welcome my call soon to arrange a brief meeting at your convenience to discuss your current and future needs and how I might serve them. Thank you in advance for your time.

Sincerely yours,

Harold S. Myatt

Alternate last paragraph:

I hope you will call or write me soon to suggest a time convenient for us to meet and discuss your current and future needs and how I might best serve them. Thank you in advance for your time.

HAROLD STANLEY MYATT
1110½ Hay Street, Fayetteville, NC 28305   (910) 483-6611

OBJECTIVE   To offer my versatile background of success in production and personnel management, logistics, quality control, and security to an organization that can benefit from my talents in training and building personnel into effective and productive teams.

EDUCATION   B.S., Business Administration, Hawaii Pacific University, Honolulu, HI; minor in Accounting.
A.A., Criminology, University of Maryland, College Park, MD.
Have begun graduate course work in Management; earlier studied Computer Science.

EXPERIENCE   *Achieved the military's highest enlisted rank during a distinguished career, U.S. Navy*:
PERSONNEL MANAGER/DEPARTMENT ADMINISTRATOR. Sardinia, Italy (1993-present). Recognized as a detail-oriented professional with excellent planning and organizational skills, am involved in scheduling and overseeing the performance of an 89-person work force maintaining and operating state-of-the-art weapons systems.
* Made determinations on how to best use personnel for maximum productivity.
* Prepared and reviewed a variety of official correspondence including regular performance reports, recommendations for awards and honors, and information.
* Refined my hands-on computer skills using WordPerfect as a tool in coordinating security personnel for a 1,200-person organization while at sea and in port.
* Specialized in training managers and technicians though my ability to sell my knowledge and insights as well as my outstanding motivational and communication skills.

PRODUCTION SUPERVISOR and **LOGISTICS MANAGER.** Pearl Harbor, HI (1990-93). Earned a respected commendation medal for my outstanding performance in dual roles of supervising 70 production workers and controlling an $820 million weapons inventory.
* Reduced monthly production costs as much as $10,000 while ensuring electronic test equipment was available with minimum downtime in a 24-hour-a-day-operation.
* Coordinated logistics aspects of weapons movements between Guam, Hawaii, Japan, and the continental U.S. by air or surface transportation.

PHYSICAL SECURITY OPERATIONS MANAGER. Charleston, SC (1987-89). Promoted and selected for advanced training, was recognized for my expertise in providing industrial security at a sensitive strategic missile facility.
* Trained and supervised personnel protecting twelve production buildings, 100 ammunition storage sites, perimeters, intrusion detection systems, and lighting systems.
* Applied my tactful and effective communication skills as liaison with Marine personnel.
* Completed the advanced training in special weapons security and counterterrorism.
* Instructed personnel in safe handling of small arms at a weapons range.

WEAPONS DEPARTMENT ADMINISTRATOR. Charleston, SC (1984-86). Handled a variety of activities ranging from supervising weapons-handling personnel, to overseeing safety in ship/pier crane operations, to coordinating weight testing and calibration.
* Trained and then supervised 40 employees in safety procedures for handling ordnance.
* Coordinated more than 360 procedures with no accidents or incidents during the transfers of more than 7,000 missiles and torpedoes.

Highlights of earlier U.S. Navy experience: Advised personnel of educational opportunities available in military career development courses and civilian programs; supervised as many as 20 people as a security specialist and law enforcement professional.

SPECIAL KNOWLEDGE   <u>Security and law enforcement procedures</u>: industrial security, counterterrorism, surveillance, physical security, incident reporting, night stick/handcuffs, frisking/take downs, special weapons security, intrusion detection systems (IDS), and range management
<u>Weapons skills</u>: M-14, M-16 rifles; .45-cal. and .38-cal. pistols; shotgun and M-79 grenade launcher.
<u>Other special skills</u>: maintaining and handling MK48/ADCAP torpedoes, Tomahawk, TASM, TLAM, and Harpoon missiles; electronics troubleshooting; welding and brazing.

PERSONAL   Entrusted with a Secret NAC/DIS security clearance. Speak Italian and conversational German. Enjoy traveling, living, and working in international locations.

Date

Exact Name of Person
Title or Position
Name of Company
Address (no., street)
Address (city, state, zip)

Dear Exact Name of Person: (or Dear Sir or Madam if answering a blind ad.)

I would appreciate an opportunity to talk with you soon about how I could contribute to your organization through my versatile skills related to personnel administration, counseling, and operations management.

As will see from my resume, I hold a master's degree in divinity and have most recently served my country as a chaplain. Prior to entering the service at the onset of the Gulf War, I served as senior minister of a Baptist church.

A creative person by nature, I have acquired extensive experience in fundraising and public relations through working off Broadway for four years in church plays to raise money for missions trips. I also offer exceptionally strong writing skills, and I have supervised the writing of newspaper articles for the last four years while also serving as chaplain.

When working in churches, either in youth ministries or as a senior minister, I have earned a reputation as a creative programmer and exciting preacher. I have also utilized my communication skills as an effective counselor, both with individuals and in groups. I am trained to administer tests including the Myers-Briggs Personality Inventory Profile.

Although I am highly regarded by the U.S. Army and am being scheduled for further promotion in rank ahead of my peers, I am writing you because I am interested in utilizing my creativity, education, counseling expertise, and varied experience in some role within your organization which involves human resources administration. My background is well suited to human resources administration, and I would like to discuss with you in person how my skills and experience could be used.

I hope you will call or write me soon to suggest a time convenient for us to meet and discuss your current and future needs and how I might serve them. Thank you in advance for you time.

Sincerely yours,

Jon Gustin

Alternate last paragraph:
I hope you will welcome my call soon to arrange a brief meeting at your convenience to discuss your current and future needs and how I might serve them. Thank you in advance for your time.

JON GUSTIN
1110½ Hay Street, Fayetteville, NC 28305   (910) 483-6611

OBJECTIVE	To benefit an organization that can use an experienced manager and communicator with particular strengths related to creative programming, the resourceful management of human and material resources, as well as the process of professional counseling and skilled problem-solving in both group and one-on-one situations.
EDUCATION	**Master of Divinity with Religious Education**, Southeastern Baptist Theological Seminary, Wake Forest, NC, 1982. **Bachelor of Science in Human Services**, Wingate College, Wingate, NC, 1979. * Was active in the Pep Club, Drama Club, Track, Circle K, and Christian Student Union. * During my spring breaks in 1977 and 1978, worked with missionaries in Mexico City. * Was elected Student Government Representative, Puppet Chairman, and Christian Student Union Activities Chairman. Completed these three units in Clinical Pastoral Education: * 1989, Third Unit: North Carolina Baptist Hospital, Winston-Salem, NC. * 1987, Second Unit: North Carolina Baptist Hospital, Winston-Salem, NC. * 1985, Basic Unit: Roanoke Mental Health Center, Roanoke, VA.
EXPERIENCE	**CHAPLAIN & WRITER/EDITOR. *U.S. Army***, Ft. Bragg, NC (1991-present). Entered the military at the onset of the Gulf War and have supervised the preparation of newspaper articles while also serving as a chaplain in four organizations. * Completed Airborne School, Officer Training for Chaplains, the Walter Reed Army Hospital Ministry Course; was trained to administer the Myers-Briggs Personality Inventory Profile. * Received several awards including medals for my work in Haiti and the Middle East. * For military newspapers write articles such as *"What Makes an American Commander Great?"*, *"Life in a Combat Medic Station"*, and *"Remembering the Vietnam War"*. **SENIOR MINISTER. *First Baptist Church***, Ridgeway, VA (1988-90). Served as pastor of a 175-person church and became known for strong skills related to education, worship, pastoral ministry, development of lay leadership, and growth in spiritual life and service. **ASSOCIATE MINISTER/YOUTH & OUTREACH COORDINATOR. *First Baptist Church***, Martinsville, VA (1984-87). Took over a wobbly youth ministry and transformed it into a vibrant ministry through my creativity and professional management skills; was involved in programs including Sunday School, Youth Fellowship, Acteens and Royal Ambassadors, Youth Choir, and youth activities including retreats, lock-ins, recreational events, and community services. **CAMPUS MINISTER INTERN. *Gardner-Webb College***, Boiling Springs, NC (1982-83). Planned worship services as a part of the worship team, planned and coordinated retreats, and handled pastoral care and church administration. **Other experience:** **CHAPLAIN, NORTH CAROLINA BAPTIST ASSEMBLY**. (Summer 1982). Coordinated a leadership team and all staff activities such as luaus, cookouts, and pool parties; on my own initiative, established a worship team which aided in creative worship activities. **DEAN OF MEN, NORTH CAROLINA BAPTIST ASSEMBLY**, (Summer 1981) as Caswell-Staff House Supervisor and Assistant to the Chaplain.
THEATER EXPERIENCE	Offer considerable theater experience, which included working off Broadway for four years in church plays to raise money for mission trips to New York City, New Orleans, and Chicago; dinner theaters and plays I have performed in have included *"Cheaper by the Dozen"*, *"You Can't Take It with You"*, *"Time Out for Ginger"*, and *"Papa Was a Preacher"*.
PERSONAL	Offer exceptionally strong skills related to personnel administration and counseling and have been blessed with a creative mind capable of figuring out new solutions to old problems. Can offer excellent personal and professional references upon request.

Date

Exact Name of Person
Title or Position
Name of Company
Address (no., street)
Address (city, state, zip)

Dear Exact Name of Person: (or Dear Sir or Madam if answering a blind ad.)

I would appreciate an opportunity to talk with you soon about how I could benefit your organization through my experience in management, my knowledge of government contracting, as well as my skills as a communicator and problem solver.

While serving my country as a Captain in the Marine Corps, I have acquired experience in many management roles. Currently I screen applicants to find the "best and brightest" prospects for future military executives. In my previous job I dramatically improved operations at a supply facility, turning a "troubled" operation into "one of the best in Japan." I have led several teams to be evaluated as "the best" among their counterparts. I am respected for my ability to train, motivate, and manage others.

Having held a Top Secret security clearance with SBI, I have a strong knowledge of government supply and contracting procedures. I have managed inventories of up to $47 million and budgets of $2.5 million.

You would find me to be a dedicated professional known for a positive, "can-do" attitude. I have a reputation for providing both excellent "quick fixes" and long-term solutions to problems.

I hope you will welcome my call soon to arrange a brief meeting at your convenience to discuss your current and future needs and how I might serve them. Thank you in advance for your time.

Sincerely yours,

Richard Young

Alternate last paragraph:
I hope you will call or write me soon to suggest a time convenient for us to meet and discuss your current and future needs and how I might serve them. Thank you in advance for your time.

RICHARD YOUNG

1110½ Hay Street, Fayetteville, NC 28305   (910) 483-6611

OBJECTIVE

To offer my management experience along with my superior communication and problem-solving skills to an organization that can use an outstanding motivator and leader who has excelled as a junior military officer.

EXPERIENCE

MARKETING DIRECTOR. U.S. Marine Corps, Cincinnati, OH (1988-present). As a Captain in the Marines, select the "best and brightest" of prospective young executives to train as military officers; handle all recruiting of officers in southern Ohio and northern Kentucky.
* Present lectures on military careers; interview recruits; present ROTC scholarships.
* Learned to sell an intangible product.
* Refined my public speaking skills dealing with people from all backgrounds.

SUPPLY OPERATIONS MANAGER. U.S. Marine Corps, Okinawa, Japan (1987-88). Was handpicked to take over a "troubled" operation, and turned it into a highly efficient and professional supply service; controlled an $8 million inventory account and a $200,000 annual operating budget while managing nine employees.

"Track Record" of Success in Versatile Management Roles

* Learned Department of Defense purchasing and contracting procedures.
* Reorganized this operation "from the ground up": trained personnel and restructured disorganized inventory control procedures.
* Earned a reputation as a talented problem solver and troubleshooter.

GENERAL MANAGER. U.S. Marine Corps, Camp Pendleton, CA (1986-87). Oversaw the management of a $47 million inventory and controlled a $2.5 million yearly supply budget while managing 75 people.
* Increased productivity by consolidating many accounts.
* Developed and implemented a new and effective equipment turn-in system.

LOGISTICS MANAGER. U.S. Marine Corps, Camp Pendleton, CA (1985-86). Implemented a logistics system which could be set up and operating anywhere in the world within 72 hours; managed a 75-person team providing all logistics support for a 770-person organization.
* Led a team regarded as the best among its 40 counterparts.

FIRST-LINE SUPERVISOR. U.S. Marine Corps, Camp Pendleton, CA (1984-85). Led a team of 80 specially trained personnel evaluated as "the best" in the parent organization; controlled $2 million in assets.

COMPUTER SYSTEMS MANAGER. U.S. Marine Corps, Camp Pendleton, CA (1984). Earned a reputation as an excellent manager while overseeing training and daily activities for ten professionals working in a state-of-the-art computer center.
* Established "model" inventory control procedures.

EDUCATION & TRAINING

Bachelor of Arts in Economics, Ursinus College, Collegeville, PA, 1982.
Excelled in U.S. Marine Corps college-level training for officers in supply, personnel, and human resources management.
* After completing the Marine Corps' challenging Officer Candidate School, was awarded a regular commission, an honor received by only a few at that time.

PERSONAL

Have held Top Secret clearance with SBI. Known for my leadership ability.

Date

Exact Name of Person
Title or Position
Name of Company
Address (no., street)
Address (city, state, zip)

Dear Exact Name of Person:`(or Dear Sir or Madam if answering a blind ad.)

I would appreciate an opportunity to talk with you soon about how I could contribute to your organization through my proven management skills as well as my extraordinary ability to motivate and train others to achieve peak productivity.

While serving my country in the U.S. Army, I have acquired extensive experience in management.`Currently I manage 40 personnel in three states, and I have used my management and motivational skills to increase the operation's performance to its highest level in 10 years.`Previously I developed plans enabling offices from Maine to Virginia to analyze and determine their best operations strategies.

With a reputation for increasing "bottom-line" sales figures in any organization, I offer the ability to motivate employees and provide excellent training for personnel.

You would find me to be a "seasoned" manager who is dedicated to producing the best possible results in any job.

I hope you will welcome my call soon to arrange a brief meeting at your convenience to discuss your current and future needs and how I might serve them.`Thank you in advance for your time.

Sincerely yours,

Gary Povill

Alternate last paragraph:
I hope you will call or write me soon to suggest a time convenient for us to meet and discuss your current and future needs and how I might serve them.`Thank you in advance for your time.`

GARY POVILL

1110½ Hay Street, Fayetteville, NC 28305   (910) 483-6611

OBJECTIVE

To offer my background in management and human resources to an organization that can use a "seasoned" management professional with a proven ability to motivate employees to reach for and achieve the highest possible goals.

EXPERIENCE

MARKETING MANAGER/OFFICE MANAGER. U.S. Army, Greenville, SC (1989-90). Managed and trained 40 middle managers involved in the marketing of U.S. Army employment in upstate South Carolina, a territory covering 5,400 square miles; administered a budget of $100,000.
* Through my management and motivational skills, increased the operation's performance to its highest level in 10 years.
* Developed an employee training/development program which was adopted and implemented by the parent organization.

SALES OPERATIONS MANAGER. U.S. Army, Pittsburgh, PA (1986-89). Supervised and trained 50 personnel recruiters covering a three-state area.
* Within 18 months "turned around" an operation rated "last" within its parent organization into one rated "best."

OFFICE MANAGER/PRODUCTION SUPERVISOR. U.S. Army, Pittsburgh, PA (1986). Supervised a team of eight professionals at one of the nation's largest personnel processing centers.
* Cut computer operation errors by over one third through instituting a quality control program.

STRATEGIC PLANNER/OPERATIONS CONSULTANT. U.S. Army, Ft. Meade, MD (1985-86). Designed plans for personnel recruiting offices to analyze their marketing needs; advised offices with serious negative trends.
* Excelled in leading an operation serving needs from Maine to Virginia.
* Led a company ranked 39th out of 46 to first place.

OFFICE MANAGER. U.S. Army, Ft. Meade, MD (1972-85). Managed dozens of recruiters involved in interviewing clients; made presentations on military career fields to civic and service organizations.
* Wrote and presented advertising materials to local media.
* Achieved the highest recruiting award in the shortest period of time.

Other experience: Learned leadership skills as a soldier in Vietnam.
* Earned the Purple Heart, Bronze Star for valor, and Vietnamese Cross for gallantry.

EDUCATION & TRAINING

Associate's degree in **Psychology**, Columbia College, Columbia, MO, 1976.
Completed college-level U.S. Army and civilian training in areas including:
     management and leadership   employment counseling
     professional salesmanship   career planning

COMPUTER SKILLS

Operate IBM personal computers with various software packages including spreadsheets and bar graphs; familiar with the Techtronics System, laser disk players, and joint optical information networks.

PERSONAL

Hold Top Secret security clearance. Am willing to give "110%" in any job.

Date

Exact Name of Person
Title or Position
Name of Company
Address (no., street)
Address (city, state, zip)

Dear Exact Name of Person: (or Dear Sir or Madam if answering a blind ad.)

Can you use an aggressive, articulate, and innovative professional with a reputation as a persuasive individual with well-developed sales and communication skills?

As a U.S. Army officer I have become adept at developing plans, molding teams, and ensuring the success of organizational goals. I have managed companies with as many as 125 employees, controlled multimillion-dollar inventories, and directed a variety of activities ranging from training programs and formal classroom instruction, to technical support center operations, to long-range planning and program development.

I have consistently placed at the top in all phases of job performance while in the military, during extensive executive training programs, and in college. Currently completing requirements for a Master of Public Administration degree, I have received several medals and awards for exceptional service including the Bronze Star Medal for contributions during the war in the Middle East.

Well-traveled and accustomed to dealing with people of other cultures, I spent two years in Australia as a missionary and teacher during my days as a college student. In that job as well as in later jobs while in military service, I have been commended for my natural skills in dealing with people and for my ability to "sell" ideas. From a young age I learned how to set and achieve difficult goals; for example, I earned my Eagle Scout rank in Boy Scouts at age 12!

I hope you will welcome my call soon to arrange a brief meeting at your convenience to discuss your current and future needs and how I might serve them. Thank you in advance for your time.

Sincerely yours,

Richard Wade

Alternate last paragraph:
I hope you will call or write me soon to suggest a time convenient for us to meet and discuss your current and future needs and how I might serve them. Thank you in advance for your time.

RICHARD WADE
1110½ Hay Street, Fayetteville, NC 28305   (910) 483-6611

OBJECTIVE

To add value to a company that can use a persuasive communicator, creative organizer, and talented manager who has excelled as a military officer while earning respect for the ability to develop and implement ambitious plans, perform under pressure, and "sell" ideas.

EXPERIENCE

DIRECTOR OF PUBLIC AFFAIRS. U.S. Army, Ft. Polk, LA (1994-present). Apply my outstanding human relations and communication skills while managing an organization which provides public affairs support to companies whose employees are on temporary overseas assignments.
* Oversaw a two-month project to establish a Haitian migrant worker camp in the Republic of Surinam; edited a bi-weekly newspaper for 550 Americans involved in the set up.
* Represented U.S. interests while coordinating visits by more than 20 ambassadors and issuing press releases in cooperation with State Department and embassy personnel.

ASSISTANT PROFESSOR and **TRAINING PROGRAM MANAGER.** U.S. Army, Provo, UT (1991-94). Credited with doubling the enrollment in the Brigham Young University Military Science Department, developed a very demanding Reserve Officer Training Corps (ROTC) whose students led the nation in the levels of their scores for physical fitness.
* Selected as Training Manager for a 120-person organization, also coached an award-winning athletic team and taught Military Science courses.
* Polished my skill at long-range planning while working with representatives of other agencies to develop a successful and highly effective 18-month training program.
* Played a critical role in selling talented and highly motivated young adults on the advantages of a military career and grooming them to be the leaders of the future.

Advanced in roles calling for outstanding management skills, U.S. Army, Ft. Riley, KS:
GENERAL MANAGER. (1989-91). Promoted based on my success in running a highly technical support center, transformed a group of poorly motivated, low-performing employees into a team recognized for its high morale and outstanding performance.
* Controlled maintenance and operations for more than $10 million worth of vehicles and equipment as manager of a 125-person organization.

COMBAT OPERATIONS MANAGER. Saudi Arabia (1990-91). Awarded the respected Bronze Star Medal for "exceptional service in combat" during the war in the Middle East, led 125 employees to consistently top performance levels in defense of the people of Kuwait.

TECHNICAL OPERATIONS CENTER MANAGER. (1988-89). Honed my ability to work under the pressure of ensuring the smooth operation of a 24-hour-a-day technical support center while overseeing activities including inputting and relaying constantly changing data.
* Reached unit achievement levels never seen before at a national training center.

Refined my management skills, U.S. Army, Germany:
FIRST-LINE SUPERVISOR. (1986-87). Directed activities ranging from supervising the training and performance of 50 employees, to overseeing maintenance/record keeping for 25 vehicles, to guaranteeing safety and maintenance of an inventory of nuclear weapons.
* Developed innovative maintenance methods recognized as best in the organization.

TECHNICAL OPERATIONS MANAGER. (1984-85). Led a team of technical specialists.

EDUCATION, TRAINING

Completing Master of Public Administration degree, Brigham Young University, Provo, UT.
B.S., Corporate Physical Education, University of Utah, Salt Lake City, 1983.
* Honored as the Distinguished Military Graduate with a 4.0 GPA in Military Science, also received a prestigious award as the university's top military science graduate.
Excelled in more than 3,020 hours of training for military executives in areas including staff and technical operations management, public speaking, editing, and media relations.

PERSONAL

Became an Eagle Scout at age 13. Am known for remaining calm and unflappable in difficult situations. Have a highly developed ability to express myself verbally and in writing.

Date

Exact Name of Person
Title or Position
Name of Company
Address (no., street)
Address (city, state, zip)

Dear Exact Name of Person: (or Dear Sir or Madam if answering a blind ad.)

Can you use an enthusiastic and energetic young professional who offers exceptional motivational and communication skills? With a reputation as someone "who has never met a stranger," I have become known for my insistence on exceeding high performance standards in every position I have held.

As you will see from my resume, I was selected to become a personnel recruiter involved in "selling" the idea of a military career to qualified young people. I had a reputation as an articulate, enthusiastic, and dedicated professional and had been promoted ahead of my peers while advancing in the intelligence field. I "stood out" as one of the best in every position I held while advancing in supervisory roles and in my technical knowledge of security and intelligence analysis both in international and domestic locations.

Since entering the sales and recruiting field, I have consistently exceeded goals and set records and soon was promoted to train new personnel and oversee the operational aspects of the field. I placed in the top 5% of **all recruiters in the United States** after many occasions when I was the region's top producer. As a trainer and administrator, I managed security and operations while molding new personnel into "top-notch" performers.

While exceeding the expectations of my superiors in the Army, I completed an associate's degree in Business Management and am presently pursuing a bachelor's degree in Business Management. I am proud of my reputation as a "perfectionist" and feel that I can be counted on to give 100% of my efforts to anything I attempt.

I hope you will welcome my call soon to arrange a brief meeting at your convenience to discuss your current and future needs and how I might serve them. Thank you in advance for your time.

Sincerely yours,

Floyd Lee Smith

Alternate last paragraph:
I hope you will call or write me soon to suggest a time convenient for us to meet and discuss your current and future needs and how I might serve them. Thank you in advance for your time.

FLOYD LEE SMITH
1110½ Hay Street, Fayetteville, NC 28305   (910) 483-6611

OBJECTIVE

To contribute my energy and enthusiasm to an organization in need of an exceptional motivator and communicator who has excelled in sales, personnel recruiting, and training and who also offers experience in the specialized fields of intelligence analysis and security.

EXPERIENCE

Consistently exceeded corporate goals and set "sales" records in the areas of personnel recruiting and training with the U.S. Army at various locations in West Virginia:

ASSISTANT TO REGIONAL ADMINISTRATOR. Charleston (1993). On the basis of my previous successes, was selected to assist a regional administrator and won several awards for no deficiencies in any areas during important operational inspections.

RECRUITING STATION MANAGER. Hurricane (1990-92). Evaluated as "the best" trainer at a facility rated as the state's top producer for two straight years, managed security and administrative support while developing inexperienced personnel into a "top-notch" team.
* Was named #1 "Large Station Recruiting Manager" out of 56 managers in a six-state area, 1991 and 1992.
* Received a commendation medal for providing lifesaving aid to eight victims of a three-car accident: treated them for shock, bleeding, and a head wound.

TRAINING MANAGER. St. Albans (1989-90). Placed in the top 5% of all military recruiters nationwide while overseeing training scheduling and planning, advising managers on training needs and requirements, and conducting one-on-one training sessions.
* Developed training improvements which resulted in a 30% increase in production.

FIELD RECRUITER. U.S. Army, Cullman and Troy, AL (1987-89). Earned the highest possible ratings in all evaluated areas including professional competence, performance, and standards while continuing to exceed goals after evaluating applicants, pre-qualifying, and counseling them.
* Refined my public speaking and communication skills while visiting area high schools and talking with interested young people, their parents, and others involved.
* Achieved quotas as high as 300% over station goals and was, on several occasions, honored as "top producer" for an eight-state region.

OPERATIONS SUPERVISOR. U.S. Army, Ft. Bliss, TX (1986-87). Honored with a commendation medal for "professionalism and leadership skills which far exceeded expectations," oversaw the receipt, analysis, and storage of intelligence information and also helped organize and conduct intelligence training programs.

SUPERVISORY INTELLIGENCE ANALYST. U.S. Army, Ft. Hood, TX (1984-86). Promoted ahead of my peers and then placed in a job usually held by more experienced personnel, ensured the security and safety of communications secure (COMSEC) and operations secure equipment and information vital to national security.
* Gained a strong sense of the value of teamwork in working with others to guarantee the security of valuable intelligence assets.

INTELLIGENCE ANALYST. U.S. Army, Germany (1982-84). Assigned to the intelligence section of a headquarters operation, maintained secret documents and was involved in breaking codes and alerting military units of terrorist threats or potential enemy actions.
* Quickly earned the respect of senior officials and was entrusted with responsibilities not normally given to someone of my rank and experience level.

EDUCATION

Attend the University of Charleston, WV, working toward a B.A. in Business Management/Associate's degree in Business Management, Vincennes University, IN; degree expected 1990.

TRAINING

Completed extensive military training programs in air defense missile, computer, and intelligence operations.

PERSONAL

Top Secret security clearance with BI. Completed two years of high school ROTC training and was the Honor Graduate of an intelligence specialists' school I was sent to by the Alabama National Guard while still in high school. Qualified "expert" with the M-16 rifle.

Date

Exact Name of Person
Title or Position
Name of Company
Address (no., street)
Address (city, state, zip)

Dear Exact Name of Person: (or Dear Sir or Madam if answering a blind ad.)

I would appreciate an opportunity to talk with you soon about how I could contribute to your organization through my versatile skills in sales and marketing, management and administration, personnel training and development, as well as in conducting investigations and solving a wide range of problems.

As you will see from my resume, I began my career in the Air Force in the inventory control and material management field and was quickly identified as a dynamic manager and motivator. I then was promoted rapidly into jobs which involved training people and managing sales/recruiting activities. In one job in Brooklyn, I took over a recruiting operation cited for "low production and deep-rooted problems" and transformed employees with a reputation as "losers" into the #1 sales team in the parent organization. I have won the Air Force's highest honors given for excellence in training, communication, and sales; I was named Top Salesman in the northeast, Top Sales Manager, and received the Silver Badge twice.

With a belief that communication skills are the key to success in nearly any job, I believe I could become a valuable asset to your organization in a number of areas. I am a hard-working and congenial individual who truly enjoys helping my organization prosper and who takes pride in my ability to develop the skills of less experienced colleagues.

I hope you will call or write me soon to suggest a time convenient for us to meet and discuss your current and future needs and how I might serve them. Thank you in advance for you time.

Sincerely yours,

Michael Ray Gilmour

Alternate last paragraph:
I hope you will welcome my call soon to arrange a brief meeting at your convenience to discuss your current and future needs and how I might serve them. Thank you in advance for your time.

MICHAEL RAY GILMOUR

1110½ Hay Street, Fayetteville, NC 28305   (910) 483-6611

OBJECTIVE   To contribute to an organization that can use a dynamic manager who has excelled in a "track record" of challenging assignments through applying my skills in training and motivating people, directing sales operations at multiple locations, and solving a wide range of problems using proven analytical, investigative, and decision-making abilities.

EXPERIENCE   **OPERATIONS SUPERVISOR.** United States Air Force, New Windsor, NY (1993-present). Because of my reputation as an exceptional manager with an unusual ability to "see the big picture" while managing hundreds of operational details, was specially selected for this job which involves extensive responsibilities related to strategic planning and operations management.

* Supervise six sales/recruiting offices with 42 employees in five states (PA, NJ, NY, CT, and MA) who recruit health professionals, officers, and enlisted personnel while also supervising five separate stations processing new employees for military service; in addition, manage an operations center which is the central hub of administrative control and strategic planning for Air Force recruiting activities in the northeast.

* Act as the "right arm" of the chief executive officer and keep him continuously informed of trends and problems affecting the recruitment and retention of quality employees; write briefings and position papers which he delivers to higher levels of management.

* While managing the five stations processing new employees for military service, oversee the skillful utilization of a computer bank matching employees with jobs.

* While managing the operations "nerve center" of Air Force recruiting in the northeast, am extensively involved in analyzing data and in preparing charts, graphs, and other visual aids that display production and competition statistics on the sales force and on sales results; write monthly production reports.

* Conduct formal Background Investigations in order to verify applicant data and moral character; routinely work with local police departments.

* Conduct random analyses and investigations of all sales and processing operations.

* Have reduced costs by restructuring the computerized applicant tracking system, thereby permitting quicker access to critical data.

* Drastically revised procedures of the operations section; after an extensive analysis, redesigned internal operating procedures to eliminate cumbersome administrative procedures and improve communication.

SALES MANAGER. U.S. Air Force, Brooklyn, NY (1991-93).
Took over a recruiting operation cited for "low production and deep-rooted problems"

225

and transformed employees with a reputation as "losers" into the #1 sales team in the parent organization; retrained, motivated, and supervised six sales professionals recruiting individuals for careers in maintenance, electronics, medical, administrative, and management fields.

* Planned and orchestrated highly effective activities related to advertising and promotion while working with print, radio, and television media.

* Led this organization to achieve or exceed all goals despite being understaffed.

* Was named **Top Sales Manager**, **Top Salesman in the northeast**, and **Senior NCO of the Year**.

TERRITORY MANAGER. U.S. Air Force, Roslyn, NY (1986-92).
Trained and managed 12 people involved in recruiting health professionals including RNs, nurse practitioners, and anesthesiologists for Air Force careers; visited hospitals and schools, created exhibits, performed phone prospecting, bought mailing lists of prospective candidates, and attended conferences and job fairs in order to meet prospects.

Other experience: Excelled in jobs as a **Training Instructor** teaching military subjects and skills and as an **Officer Recruiter** recruiting pilots, engineers, and navigators.
* In earlier jobs, excelled in managing warehouses and controlling inventories.

SALES HONORS   Received the Air Force's highest awards given for excellence in communication and sales, received the respected Silver Badge twice, and won many management awards.

EDUCATION   Completed more than three years of college-level education and training in areas including personnel administration, sales and marketing, and financial and resource management.

COMPUTERS   Proficient with Microsoft Excel, Harvard Graphics, and Microsoft Word.

PERSONAL   Am a congenial fellow who truly enjoys helping my organization grow and lending a hand to less experienced colleagues. Secret security clearance. Will travel and relocate as needed.

THOMAS NUNNERY
1110½ Hay Street, Fayetteville, NC 28305   (910) 483-6611

OBJECTIVE

I want to contribute to an organization that can use a dynamic and results-oriented sales professional who offers a proven ability to meet or exceed quotas while also training and developing other sales professionals.

SALES PHILOSOPHY

* Am a highly motivated individual with a winning attitude!
* Have learned how to make the best out of bad situations.
* Believe in leading by example rather than by talking.
* Understand the value of time management and the critical nature of planning in order to maximize the efficiency of each minute on the job.
* Instilled inside me is the concept of accountability, and believe in taking total responsibility for my results with a "no-excuses" attitude.
* Am thoroughly diligent in maintaining paperwork and understand the importance of not falling behind in that area.
* Believe genuine concern for the customer is a critical ingredient to success in sales; always approach a sales situation as though I am trying to solve the customer's problem or help the customer find a new opportunity to succeed.

EXPERIENCE

TERRITORY MANAGER/RECRUITER. U.S. Army, Hickory, NC (1986-present). Have earned the distinction as the Top Salesman in North Carolina because of my exceptional results in recruiting individuals for careers in the U.S. Army.

* Became known for my ability to sell the U.S. Army with enthusiasm and honesty; while managing other individuals, personally set the standard for performance excellence: with a personal goal of 24 enlistment contracts, achieved 43 contracts and thereby personally made 75% of the entire recruiting station's quota.
* Took over a territory ranked #53 (at the bottom) among U.S. Army recruiting stations, and transformed it into #7 in total sales.
* Was generous with my time in mentoring new sales professionals, and am proud of my results in transforming many rookies into award winners and top producers.
* Oversaw an office of five people, and molded personnel into a high-spirited team of employees dedicated to achieving the highest results.
* Managed our sales and recruiting activities within prescribed budgets; solved numerous problems through skillful cost-cutting without sacrificing results or quality — for example, introduced new planning techniques which improved effectiveness even though I reduced the travel expenditures portion of the budget.
* Became skilled in prospecting for customers and in customer relations.

COMPUTERS

Have utilized computers on a daily basis for word processing, statistical analysis, data collection, and information processing.

SALES HONORS

In addition to a dozen Army Commendation Medals for exceptional performance, received the Army's top awards for sales achievements.

* Received the Gold Recruiter Badge with 3 Sapphire Achievement Stars and won the Gold Recruiter Badge with 3 Gold Achievement Stars.
* In addition to the above-mentioned rarely given honors, received the Recruiter of Excellence Award presented by the Chief of Staff, U.S. Army.

EDUCATION & TRAINING

Completed North Central Area Vocational-Technical School, Farmerville, LA; developed proficiency in plate and pipe welding.
While in military service, completed more than two years of college-level training related to sales, marketing, management, and supervision and also completed rugged physical training which qualified me as an expert marksman, combat infantryman, and parachutist.

* Graduated with honors from Primary Leadership Development Course, a management program designed to refine the skills of the Army's best middle managers.
* Excelled in completing the Noncommissioned Officer Academy, an executive development program for enlisted managers.

PERSONAL

Am an outgoing and friendly individual who enjoys meeting strangers and helping others.

Date

Exact Name of Person
Title or Position
Name of Company
Address (no., street)
Address (city, state, zip)

Dear Exact Name of Person: (or Dear Sir or Madam if answering a blind ad.)

I would appreciate an opportunity to talk with you soon about how I could contribute to your organization through my versatile experience, team building and supervisory skills, and reputation for high personal standards and a strong work ethic.

While serving in the U.S. Army, I gained knowledge of supply and inventory control procedures while involved in activities ranging from operating material handling equipment, to maintaining records, to training new employees to my own high performance standards.

I have directly supervised as many as nine people while overseeing the receipt, issue, and storage of an inventory of more than $7 million worth of supplies for a 140-person organization. I have been awarded two achievement medals and several certificates and letters of achievement for my professionalism and accomplishments.

I am enthusiastic and not afraid of hard work. I feel that I have a lot to offer an organization that needs a team player with strong motivational skills and a drive to excel.

I hope you will welcome my call soon to arrange a brief meeting at your convenience to discuss your current and future needs and how I might serve them. Thank you in advance for your time.

Sincerely yours,

Forrest Gumper

Alternate last paragraph:
I hope you will call or write me soon to suggest a time convenient for us to meet and discuss your current and future needs and how I might serve them. Thank you in advance for your time.

FORREST GUMPER
1110½ Hay Street, Fayetteville, NC 28305   (910) 483-6611

OBJECTIVE

To offer my experience in the acquisition, storage, and distribution of equipment and supplies to an organization that can use a detail-oriented professional with skills related to employee supervision, material handling equipment operations, and postal procedures.

EXPERIENCE

SUPERVISORY SUPPLY SPECIALIST. U.S. Army, Ft. Bragg, NC (1991-95).
Advanced in the supply management field to this role overseeing all details of controlling more than $7 million worth of equipment used to provide for the needs of the 140-person headquarters department of an engineering company.

* Supervised six specialists involved in keeping automated records of all supply transactions and ensuring adequate quantities of all vital supplies and equipment.
* Was awarded an achievement medal in recognition of my contributions toward reestablishing control of supply operations upon the company's return from the Middle East.
* Played a valuable role in identifying excess equipment, establishing up-to-date records of shortages, and accounting for all equipment.
* Earned the respect of superiors for successfully training a supply specialist and a weapons specialist to my own high standards.

SUPPLY OPERATIONS SPECIALIST/VEHICLE OPERATOR. U.S. Army, Saudi Arabia (1990-91).
Received an achievement medal and other certificates of appreciation for my accomplishments while supervising three subordinates and handling arrangements for moving large amounts of equipment and supplies to various sites during preparations for combat and throughout the war in the Middle East.

* Cited for my "unparalleled enthusiasm" and ability to work long hard hours, earned a reputation as a self starter who could be counted on to see that the work was done.
* Handled the stress of frequently moving entire support operations — including vehicles and large items of engineering equipment — from site to site.
* Gained further experience in operating the 300-foot sky crane while unloading equipment at the port and during moves.

SUPPLY SPECIALIST. U.S. Army, Ft. Bragg, NC (1988-90).
Performed a variety of activities related to the receipt, issue, replenishment, and interim storage of authorized supply items for an engineering organization.

* Became skilled in operating heavy equipment including forklifts and sky cranes to load and unload trucks and move materials to and from their proper storage areas.
* Was recognized by my superiors as being dedicated to training and self improvement while always being willing to share my knowledge with others.
* Provided supported units with guidance and found ways to save funds by emphasizing the importance of complete accountability.

POSTAL CLERK. U.S. Army, Ft. Bragg, NC (1986-88).
Completed special training resulting in qualification as a Postal Clerk: provided services related to the sorting, handling, and dispensing of mail to individuals and companies.

SPECIAL KNOWLEDGE

Through training and experience, am qualified to operate vehicles and equipment including:
     up to 5-ton dump trucks   up to 10k forklifts
     up to 2 1/2-ton cargo trucks   tractor trailers
Use office machines and equipment including typewriters, adding machines, calculators, copiers, and microfiche.

TRAINING

Completed military training programs in the areas of supply operations, leadership development, and postal operations as well as airborne training and emergency lifesaving.

PERSONAL

Have been entrusted with a Secret security clearance. Have some knowledge of German.

Date

Exact Name of Person
Title or Position
Name of Company
Address (no., street)
Address (city, state, zip)

Dear Exact Name of Person: (or Dear Sir or Madam if answering a blind ad.)

I would appreciate an opportunity to talk with you soon about how I could benefit your organization through my background in supply management as well as my proven expertise in training and motivating employees.

As you will see from my resume, my most recent position as an Inventory Control Manager gives me the opportunity to directly supervise as many as 30 personnel while managing a $10 million supply house. On my own initiative I completely restructured warehouse operations, resulting in a significant increase in efficiency and accountability.

Throughout my career I have gained a reputation as a "go-getter" who can be counted on to set high performance standards and guide employees to achieve their own high goals. I feel that my ability to respond to rapidly changing circumstances calmly and with control is one of my greatest strengths.

I hope you will call or write soon to suggest a time convenient for us to meet and discuss your current and future needs and how I might serve them. Thank you in advance for your time.

Sincerely,

Raleigh Bunce

Alternate last paragraph
I hope you will welcome my call soon to arrange a brief meeting at your convenience to discuss your current and future needs and how I might serve them. Thank you in advance for your time.

RALEIGH BUNCE
1110½ Hay Street, Fayetteville, NC 28305   (910) 483-6611

OBJECTIVE

To benefit an organization that can use an enthusiastic and highly motivated young professional who offers a background in supply management and inventory control along with a proven ability to "turn around" troubled operations, train employees and motivate them to achieve outstanding results, and figure out resourceful solutions for stubborn problems.

COMPUTERS

Am proficient in a wide range of hardware and software, including IBM-compatible, Macintosh, Apple II, PRC-27, WordPerfect, Multimate, and spreadsheets.

EXPERIENCE

SUPPLY MANAGER. U.S. Army, Fort Bragg, NC (1992-present).
At the world's largest U.S. military base, have transformed a disorganized supply operation into a model of efficiency, and have received several awards in recognition of my exceptional management skills and supply knowledge.
*   In 1992, walked into a supply operation where no records were being kept, stockout problems were common, and employees were untrained; decided to start "from scratch" and then trained employees, set up internal procedures, and ensured compliance with generally accepted supply practices.
*   In my first job in the supply field, managed an arms room stocked with weapons and sensitive items; applied textbook theories related to supply along with "common sense" in order to produce an arms room respected for outstanding customer service.
*   Was promoted in 1993 to become the organization's senior Supply Manager; currently manage a diversified inventory valued at $10 million of property and supplies that include clothing, office materials, and vehicles while also managing three people.
*   Have become skilled at projecting long-range needs and planning for future purchases.
*   Earned praise for my ability to maintain perfect accountability of all equipment and assets and was commended for my meticulous and timely completion of all paperwork.
*   Acquired a "bottom-line" focus while continuously adjusting priorities and finding more cost-effective ways to satisfy organizational needs while working within a $30,000 budget.
*   Managed the activities of up to 30 people during special projects for which I coordinated supply administration.

STUDENT, SUPPLY MANAGEMENT COURSE. U.S. Army, Ft. Jackson, SC (1991-92).
Excelled academically in a rigorous, three-month supply management course designed to train the Army's executives in the supply management/inventory control field.

CREW LEADER. Texas Department of Highways, San Augustine, TX (1986-91).
Supervised three highway maintenance workers repairing highways and erecting road signs while simultaneously attending college full-time.
*   Commended for consistently completing projects before deadline.

DELIVERY DRIVER. The Flower Shop, Nacogdoches, TX (1988-91).
Acted as part-time delivery man and jack-of-all-trades for a busy floral business.
*   Performed maintenance and repair work.
*   Handled receiving and inventory of stock.
*   Closed store, including balancing the till and making deposits.
*   Created and implemented a new route system that significantly decreased delivery time.

VETERINARIAN ASSISTANT. San Augustine Animal Clinic, San Augustine, TX (1982-87).
Refined my time management skills while assisting in the operation of a fast-paced clinic.
*   Cleaned kennels, answered phones, scheduled appointments, and performed various accounting procedures.

EDUCATION

Received a **Bachelor of Science degree in Public Administration** from Stephen F. Austin State University, Nacogdoches, TX, 1991.
Graduated at top of Advanced Individual Training class, Ft. Jackson, SC, 1992.

PERSONAL

Am a flexible, versatile professional who is known for my "attention to detail." Received numerous commendation and medals. Was entrusted with a Secret security clearance.

Exact Name of Person
Title or Position
Name of Company
Address (no., street)
Address (city, state, zip)

Dear Exact Name of Person: (or Dear Sir or Madam if answering a blind ad.)

I would appreciate an opportunity to talk with you soon about how I could contribute to your organization through my expertise related to logistics, inventory control, and warehousing.

As you will see from my resume, I have acquired expert skills in warehouse management while being promoted to increasingly more responsible jobs in the U.S. Air Force. Most recently I took over the management of a warehouse which was inefficient and disorganized. I conducted an inventory of this multimillion-dollar operation and saved $250,000 right away by correcting errors in over 600 line items. Through combining my creativity with my techical expertise, I expanded warehouse space by 20% and saved 15% in requisition costs.

In my previous job I was handpicked from among 20 candidates for a job which involved designing a new, state-of-the-art warehouse for more 55,000 line items. After designing the new warehouse, which was cited as the "best ever seen" by fire inspectors, I directed the efficient relocation of one million items from the old to the new warehouse. New storage procedures I implemented resulted in 100% account-ability of all stored stock and, through devising a new filing system and checklists, we reduced excess manhours by 10%.

I am even proud of my accomplishments in the "building-block" jobs of my career, including de-livery driver, bench stock clerk, and warehouseman. In those jobs, I earned a reputation as a safety-con-scious professional with an unblemished safety record in operating all the equipment and vehicles in-volved in the warehouse/supply field.

I hope you will welcome my call soon to arrange a brief meeting at your convenience to discuss your current and future needs and how I might serve them. Thank you in advance for your time.

Sincerely yours,

Arthur P. Vick

Alternate last paragraph:
I hope you will call or write me soon to suggest a time convenient for us to meet and discuss your current and future needs and how I might serve them. Thank you in advance for your time.

ARTHUR P. VICK
1110½ Hay Street, Fayetteville, NC 28305   (910) 483-6611

OBJECTIVE
To benefit an organization that can use an innovative problem solver and logistics expert knowledgeable about all aspects of inventory management including shipping, receiving, and warehousing as well as automated systems, personnel supervision, and budgeting.

EXPERIENCE
LOGISTICS MANAGER. U.S.A.F., Robins AFB, GA (1994-95).
Took over a warehouse with a multimillion-dollar inventory and immediately made changes that improved efficiency while decreasing costs; managed three people.
* Identified errors on 600 line items that reduced excess inventory by $250,000.
* Developed new receiving procedures that ensured 100% accountability of store assets.
* Expanded warehouse space by 20% by rewarehousing techniques; reduced requisition costs 15%.

WAREHOUSE SUPERVISOR. U.S.A.F. Base Supply Warehouse, Japan (1992-94).
Was handpicked over 19 other logistics experts to provide leadership in designing a new, state-of-the-art 112,000 sq. ft. warehouse which allowed the location, at a moment's notice, of more than 55,000 items worth $3.5 million; managed nine people.
* Relocated more than one million products in 3,000 line items from the old to the new warehouse with no disruption of customer service and perfect accountability; coordinated the movement of sensitive and classified materials.
* Reduced excess man-hours by 10% by implementing a new filing system and checklists.
* Designed a warehouse which fire inspectors said was "the best ever seen."
* Developed a user-friendly warehouse refusal checklist that allowed new recruits to resolve potential warehouse refusals.
* Perfected the procedures for producing and processing error-free shipment documents.

PROPERTY DISPATCH SUPERVISOR. U.S.A.F. Base Supply Warehouse, Japan (1991-92).
Supervised 10 people while managing the utilization of over 5,000 pieces of property, including 30 vehicles, with a perfect safety record.
* Creatively overcame a labor shortage by implementing a new personnel utilization plan.

TRAINING MANAGER. U.S.A.F., Sheppard AFB, TX (1987-91).
Was noted as being a "stronghold of character" while excelling in conducting briefings, planning and conducting training, and providing guidance to more than 100 people daily.
* Became known for my contagious enthusiasm and for my capacity for hard work.

WAREHOUSEMAN. U.S.A.F. Base Supply, Holloman AFB, NM (1986-87).
Handled the prompt and accurate receipt, storage, and distribution of 12,000 highly specialized "war readiness" items valued at over $115 million.
* Ensured correct shelf life of all items; prepared items for worldwide distribution.
* Became proficient in warehousing and transporting hazardous materials.

BENCH STOCK CLERK. U.S.A.F. Base Supply, Holloman AFB, NM (1986).
Inventoried and replenished bench stocks while also utilizing LOGMARS for input into the main computer system.

DELIVERY DRIVER. U.S.A.F. Base Supply, Holloman AFB, NM (1984-85).
Maintained a perfect driving and safety record operating assigned vehicles and material handling equipment while delivering supplies and equipment to government agencies.

STOCK SPECIALIST. Sears Roebuck & Co., Troy, MI (1980-84).
Reduced catalog department assets by 25% by returning property to store or shipping it back to distribution center while also coordinating a new tagging and location system.

EDUCATION
Completed extensive college course work in logistics management, Community College of the Air Force, Maxwell AFB, AL, 1986-95.
Completed extensive training sponsored by the Air Force in advanced warehousing techniques, automated inventory control systems, personnel supervision, and management.

PERSONAL
Am known for my supervisory skills, leadership qualities, strong initiative, communication skills, as well as my ability to learn quickly and rapidly master new systems.

WILLIAM COURTNEY

1110½ Hay Street, Fayetteville, NC 28305   (910) 483-6611

OBJECTIVE

To benefit an organization that can use a talented manager and motivator who offers proven communication, problem-solving, and financial skills as well as a "track record" of achievements related to supply management and inventory control.

KEY STRENGTHS & SKILLS

Personnel management: During my career, have often been faced with "turning around" organizations plagued by low morale and non-productivity: in every case have created cohesive, finely tuned teams willing to "go the extra mile."
* Have led numerous teams to be rated the best on the continent.

Resource management: While controlling multimillion-dollar budgets and assets, have learned to optimize the use of resources and reduce operating costs.

Training development: In every organization I've worked in, have established or re vamped training programs; believe thorough training and cross-training are essential to success in any field.

Supply management: Have consistently increased efficiency while managing supply services providing everything from household goods to computer and aircraft parts.

CLEARANCE

Hold SECRET security clearance; have gained valuable knowledge of international relations while living and working in countries throughout Europe.

LANGUAGES

Speak some Italian and Spanish.

COMPUTERS

Use Burroughs Word Processor, Sperry 1100/60, and Commodore 40-40 computers.

EXPERIENCE

BRANCH SUPERVISOR. U.S. Air Force, England (1986-present).
Earned formal recognition from top executives for taking charge of a 15-person organization which had been rated last in its parent organization and turning it into the **best of its kind** in Europe.
* Supervise procurement, storage, distribution, and repair of $7 million of furnishings and appliances for 4,000 people living in 10 locations in Europe.
* Perform quality assurance evaluations on two government contracts valued at over $1 million each.
* Saved $1 million in rental fees and 2,400 man hours yearly by creatively reorganizing six storage facilities.
* Implemented a repair system which saved over $250,000 annually.
* Developed a cross-training program which enabled all personnel to do every job in the office.

COMPUTER OPERATIONS MANAGER. U.S.A.F., Iceland (1985-86).
Managed a computer center which was the "focal point" of supply processing for a 3,000-person organization; managed 20 supply specialists involved in processing and researching orders 24 hours a day, 365 days a year.
* Transformed a poorly trained and unmotivated organization into one rated first in its parent organization.

EMERGENCY SUPPLY COORDINATOR. U.S.A.F., George AFB, CA (1984-85).
Used my knowledge of the U.S.A.F. supply system to "save" numerous aviation projects; ensured that vital aircraft parts were obtained from sources all over the world within 72 hours.

* Created a "card catalog" system and a worldwide Air Force directory which reduced the time needed to research supply sources.
* Despite reductions in personnel, ran the operation at 24-hour-a-day capacity with in creased efficiency.

DATA PROCESSING SUPERVISOR. U.S.A.F., England (1981-83).
Led a previously unproductive team of eight people to become the highest rated data processing organization in Europe; oversaw a center processing supply orders 24 hours a day, seven days a week.
* Increased efficiency 20% by revamping distribution systems.

Highlights of other U.S.A.F. experience:
ASSISTANT SUPPLY SUPERVISOR. Supervised nine people providing inventory data for 25 organizations using over 6,000 different line items; controlled hazardous material handling.
* Developed "self pickup" and computer card distribution systems which saved hundreds of man hours yearly.
* Presented an information seminar cited as the "best ever."

MATERIAL CONTROL SPECIALIST. While managing procurement, budgeting, and inventory control for a 120-person organization, eliminated superfluous supply requests by implementing a written justification/approval system; reduced expenses from $2 million to $750,000.
* Became known as an expert on munitions supply.
* Learned these valuable keys to effective leadership: remain flexible, think clearly, and get to know your people.

RESEARCH CLERK. Developed procedures for ordering supplies, purging records of unwanted data, and maintaining files of over 25,000 stock and part numbers.

EDUCATION & EXECUTIVE TRAINING

B.S. degree in Sociology, University of Maryland, MD, degree to be awarded 1991.
A.A. degree in Sociology, University of Maryland, MD, 1986.
A.A. degree in Inventory Management, Community College of the Air Force, AL, 1984.
Completed U.S.A.F. training for supply executives related to personnel management, hazardous materials handling, and inventory control.

PERSONAL

Am a creative professional who always tries to increase efficiency without compromising quality. Known as a "take charge" leader who sets clear goals and always achieves them. Motivate others to become "productive and proud" workers. Will relocate worldwide.

Exact Name of Person
Title or Position
Name of Company
Address (no., street)
Address (city, state, zip)

Dear Exact Name of Person: (or Dear Sir or Madam if answering a blind ad.)

I would appreciate an opportunity to talk with you soon about how I could contribute to your organization through my public speaking and written communication skills, my scholastic achievements and academic potential, and my leadership experience as a military officer.

Scholastic Achievements
As you will see from my resume, I offer a background of academic accomplishments. In 1987 I received a Master's degree in Military Art and Science from the U.S. Army Command and General Staff College. After earning all As, I was selected through a rigorous screening process to complete a second year of study in which I earned a second Master's degree in Advanced Military Studies. I combined my military aviation experience with extensive research to author a master's thesis entitled "The MI-24 Hind: Soviet Attack Helicopter Close Air Support vs. U.S. Army Air Assault Division" and two monographs. I have also authored articles published in professional journals.

Leadership Accomplishments
In my current job I have been evaluated as the most outstanding officer in this position in more than 30 years. I have excelled in developing classified strategic operations plans for a 10,000-person division. In my previous job I was handpicked to establish a new school providing intensive technical training for 120 professionals every two weeks.

You would find me to be a devoted worker with a dedication to high academic ideals along with the intelligence, creativity, and communication skills to bring those ideals to life.

I hope you will welcome my call soon to arrange a brief meeting at your convenience to discuss your current and future needs and how I might serve them. Thank you in advance for your time.

Sincerely yours,

Archibald Reid

Alternate last paragraph:
I hope you will call or write me soon to suggest a time convenient for us to meet and discuss your current and future needs and how I might serve them. Thank you in advance for your time.

ARCHIBALD REID III

1110½ Hay Street, Fayetteville, NC 28305   (910) 483-6611

OBJECTIVE

To benefit an educational institution through my outstanding skills as a public speaker and published author, my extraordinary achievements as a scholar, and my leadership experience as a military officer.

EDUCATION

Master of Military Art & Science (M.M.A.S) degree in Advanced Military Studies, U.S. Army Command and General Staff College, Ft. Leavenworth, KS, 1988.
* Was selected for this program after a rigorous screening process.
* Successfully completed two monographs.

Master of Military Art & Science (M.M.A.S.) in Military Studies, U.S. Army Command and General Staff College, Ft. Leavenworth, KS, 1987.
* Earned all As; graduated **with honors**.
* Combined my background as an Army aviator with my excellent research skills to author a master's **thesis** entitled "The MI-24 Hind: Soviet Attack Helicopter Close Air Support vs. U.S. Army Air Assault Division."

Bachelor of Science in Education, Old Dominion University, Norfolk, VA, 1975.

Completed graduate-level Army training in aviation and management/leadership.
* Excelled in **Ranger School**, the Army's management "stress test" designed to test the mental and physical limits of the Army's best and brightest.

PUBLICATIONS

Authored articles in professional journals including "Campaign Planning: Paradigm or Paradox," accepted for publication by the Military Review.

EXPERIENCE

STRATEGIC AND TACTICAL PLANNING MANAGER. U.S. Army, Ft. Drum, NY (1988-90). Was handpicked for this job developing and publishing classified strategic and tactical operations plans for a 10,000-person division; am cited as responsible for the division's ability to plan operations on short notice.
* Excel in developing complex plans in a "crisis action" environment.
* Transformed a section described as "disorganized and ineffective" into an operation praised as the "best of its kind" in the Army.
* Created a crisis planning system which enabled vital plans to be developed, approved, and implemented in a very compressed time period.
* Represented the division at planning conferences worldwide.
* Was evaluated as the best officer in this job in more than 30 years.
* Was praised as a "superb coach" who "takes the time to train others."

EDUCATOR/ADMINISTRATOR. U.S. Army, Ft. Rucker, AL (1985-86). Was chosen to set up and manage the Aviation Center Air Assault School training 120 students every two weeks; was selected as "1985 Army Aviation Trainer of the Year" for my contributions to "the development and prestige" of Army aviation.

LANGUAGE, COMPUTERS

Conversant with Spanish and French.
Use IBM and MacIntosh computers with Microsoft Word, Lotus 1-2-3, and Harvard Graphics software.

PERSONAL

Have been described as a "natural leader" and "top leader" with outstanding analytical ability and communication skills. Hold Top Secret security clearance with SBI.

Date

Henry County Public Schools
Attn: Mrs. Johnson
Personnel Office
P.O. Box 8958
Collinsville, VA 24078-8958

Dear Mrs. Johnson:

With the enclosed resume describing my exceptional track record as a leader and communicator, I would like to formally express my interest in joining Henry County Public Schools as a Junior ROTC Instructor.

As you will see from my resume, I have advanced to the rank of lieutenant colonel while serving my country in the U.S. Army. Although I have excelled in "line management" jobs such as two separate positions as a company commander, for the past 10 years I have worked primarily in jobs which involved teaching as well as developing/managing training programs. In one job at the U.S. Army National Training Center, I was handpicked as a resource to teachers, line managers, and staff personnel. In a previous job, I planned and directed training programs for Reserve Components and Readiness Groups in Hawaii, and many innovative techniques of mine were adopted by other organizations.

Now that I have served my country with distinction, it is my desire to help inspire and educate future military leaders, and I believe I can best do that as a Junior ROTC Instructor. I can provide outstanding personal and professional references, and I would be delighted to make myself available at your convenience to discuss the qualifications and talents I could put to work for you.

You would find me to be a congenial person who offers an innate ability to work well with people and inspire them to peak performance. I believe strongly in leadership by example.

I hope you will welcome my call soon to arrange a brief meeting at your convenience to discuss your current and future needs and how I might serve them. Thank you in advance for your time.

Sincerely yours,

Ivan Demetrius

IVAN DEMETRIUS
1110½ Hay Street, Fayetteville, NC 28305   (910) 483-6611

OBJECTIVE

To contribute to an organization that can use an exceptionally strong communicator who has excelled as a military officer while being promoted to the rank of lieutenant colonel.

EXPERIENCE

MANAGEMENT CONSULTANT. U.S. Army, Korea (1993-94).
Was in charge of a team of management and logistics professionals providing expert advice to military organizations in Asia in the areas of budgeting, personnel planning and administration, operations management, logistics and supply services, and special projects.

TRAINING CONSULTANT. U.S. Army National Training Center, Ft. Irwin, CA (1991-93).
Was handpicked for this job as a resource to teaching professionals, staff personnel, and line managers; demonstrated my skill at organizing complex training missions while training, coaching, and advising others in how to plan, prepare, and implement a wide variety of service operations supporting organizational needs.
* Conducted formal reviews of operational effectiveness and prepared written reports designed to boost efficiency of dining operations, supply services, logistics procedures, personnel administration procedures, and computer support services.

SERVICE OPERATIONS MANAGER. U.S. Army, Ft. Bragg, NC (1988-91).
Developed supply, maintenance, and medical support requirements for three battalion-size organizations with a combined labor force of 2,500 people; oversaw all areas affecting the quality of life of these soldiers.
* During the war in the Middle East, set up "from scratch" logistical support operations which were commended for their efficient movement of heavy equipment and other assets as well as perishable, nonperishable, and hazardous supplies.
* Received my second Bronze Star for exceptional performance in building logistical systems that performed flawlessly during wartime.

COMMANDER. U.S. Army, Korea (1987-88).
Functioned as the "chief executive officer" of two separate organizations while overseeing support services provided to 750 civilians and military professionals; acted as the public relations spokesperson for the military base to the adjacent Korean city.

TRAINING DIRECTOR. U.S. Army, Ft, Shafter, HI (1984-87).
Planned and directed training programs for Reserve Components and Readiness Groups; developed a master training calendar and developed training evaluation reports which were highly effective in improving the skills of individuals and overall organizational effectiveness.
* Became skilled in managing multiple projects and in synchronizing training events.

COMPANY COMMANDER/GENERAL MANAGER. U.S. Army, Ft. Bragg, NC (1981-84).
As company commander of a 142-person headquarters and headquarters company, was personally responsible for multimillion-dollar equipment and property, and managed all support services including payroll preparation, food service, personnel administration, and transportation operations.

COMPANY COMMANDER/GENERAL MANAGER. U.S. Army, Korea (1980-81).
Was company commander of a rifle company with 155 people; developed a training program which was adopted by other organizations and which was praised for its exceptional results in teaching technical skills.

EDUCATION

B.S., Agricultural Sciences, N.C. Agricultural & Technical State University, Greensboro, NC. Extensive executive development coursework as a military officer.

COMPUTERS

Proficient with software including Microsoft Word and PowerPoint.

PERSONAL

Am known for my sound judgement, integrity, and ability to motivate others to excel. Enjoy the challenge of teaching young people and take pride in instilling in them a disciplined approach to work and study. Can provide outstanding personal/professional references.

Date

Exact Name of Person
Title or Position
Name of Company
Address (no., street)
Address (city, state, zip)

Dear Exact Name of Person: (or Dear Sir or Madam if answering a blind ad.)

I would appreciate an opportunity to talk with you soon about how I could contribute to your organization through my versatile technical and management skills as well as my proven ability to teach and train others.

I am proud of the fact that I began serving my country as an enlisted soldier and then, after earning my college degree in Business Administration with honors, I was commissioned as an officer and handpicked for jobs which required excellent human relations skills as well as technical expertise.

In one job in Korea, I managed 54 people while also acting as a Basketball Coach. I led my basketball team to win the championship in Korea and Japan! In a job teaching communications classes to more than 350 people, I was chosen as **Top Instructor**. In another job I was involved in training and certifying instructors for a variety of military schools.

With technical expertise in the computer and communications field, I can operate, install, and maintain any computer system and I am proficient with Windows, Harvard Graphics, and other popular software packages. In one job as a Computer/Communications Consultant, I developed a computer architecture that saved the parent organization over a quarter million dollars. I offer the ability to design computer or telephone architecture using secure or non-secure means.

You would find me in person to be a congenial individual who prides myself on my ability to motivate others and help them develop their skills to much higher levels. I sincerely believe I have a gift for teaching and training people and for "translating" abstract concepts into understandable language. I can provide outstanding personal and professional references.

I hope you will welcome my call soon to arrange a brief meeting at your convenience to discuss your current and future needs and how I might serve them. Thank you in advance for your time.

Sincerely yours,

Warren Holcomb

Alternate last paragraph:
I hope you will call or write me soon to suggest a time convenient for us to meet and discuss your current and future needs and how I might serve them. Thank you in advance for your time.

WARREN HOLCOMB
1110½ Hay Street, Fayetteville, NC 28305   (910) 483-6611

OBJECTIVE

To contribute to an organization that can use a polished teacher, motivator, and manager who excels in coaching, training, developing, and mentoring others in both academic and professional situations.

EDUCATION

B.S. degree in Business Administration, Xavier University, New Orleans, LA, 1986.
* Was elected president of my senior and junior class.
* Excelled academically; achieved a 3.3 GPA and was inducted into the national business honorary fraternity.
As a military officer, have excelled in some of the U.S. Army's most respected leadership and management schools, including Command & General Staff College.

COMPUTER & TELEPHONE PROFICIENCY

* Can operate, install, and maintain any computer system; was a signal officer in the Army.
* Proficient with Windows, Harvard Graphics, Multimate, and Enable programs.
* Can design computer or telephone architecture using secure and non-secure means.
* Familiar with COMSEC equipment; can install secure voice or data equipment.

EXPERIENCE

GENERAL MANAGER ("COMPANY COMMANDER"). U.S. Army, Germany (1994-95). Was handpicked as the "chief executive officer" of a 216-person company, and transformed an average organization into the one evaluated as "the best" in its parent organization because of my emphasis on training.
* Developed training programs which improved the skill of every person in the company.
* Established new cost-saving maintenance programs for equipment which included 78 vehicles, 30 generators, and 23 trailers valued at over $100 million.
* Improved the efficiency of service operations supporting my employees, and developed a top-notch dining facility providing highly efficient food service.
* Earned a reputation as a caring and compassionate leader who could motivate people to achieve their highest levels of productivity.

COMPUTER/COMMUNICATIONS CONSULTANT. U.S. Army, Ft. Ord, CA (1992-94). As the trusted advisor to a busy executive, directed the training of 38 communications professionals while purchasing computer equipment and establishing a secure data and voice line between Ft. Ord, CA and Ft. Shafter, HI.
* Developed a computer architecture that saved the parent organization over $250,000.

ASSISTANT SUPERINTENDENT OF TRAINING. U.S. Army, Ft. Bragg, NC (1990-91). Trained and certified instructors for military schools; coordinated training for a 542-person organization and maintained a budget of $2.5 million.

INSTRUCTOR. U.S. Army, Ft. Bragg, NC (1988-90). Was selected as *"Top Instructor"* while planning and teaching communications classes to more than 350 people; was personally accountable for $1.8 million in equipment.
* During the crisis in Panama which resulted in the military exercise "Just Cause," was handpicked to establish radio communication between Ft. Bragg and Panama.

BASKETBALL COACH & FIRST-LINE SUPERVISOR. U.S. Army, Korea (1986-88). Controlled $11.5 million in equipment while managing 54 personnel; led my platoon to reach the highest levels of physical fitness of any platoon in the parent organization.
* Coached a basketball team that won the championship in Korea and Japan.

HONORS STUDENT. Xavier University, New Orleans, LA (1982-86). Was commissioned as an officer upon completion of my college degree; excelled academically and as a leader.

PERSONAL

Am an extremely self-disciplined person who believes in leadership by example. Received numerous military awards for exceptional performance, including the Cross of Gallantry.

Date

Exact Name of Person
Title or Position
Name of Company
Address (no., street)
Address (city, state, zip)

Dear Exact Name of Person: (or Dear Sir or Madam if answering a blind ad.)

I would appreciate an opportunity to speak with you soon about how I could contribute to your organization through my management and supervisory skills as well as through my technical abilities, experience in program development and operation, and expertise in human and material resource management.

With degrees in Technology Management and Electrical Engineering, I offer a combination of educational areas which allows me to understand corporate operations both from the technical and the business side.

As you will see from my resume, I have risen to positions of increasing responsibility as a U.S. Air Force officer who has been handpicked for critical managerial roles due to excellent achievements and demonstrated talents. Through my management experience as an officer, I have come to believe that continuous training of human resources is often the key to an organizations' success in the marketplace. Skilled in diagnosing training requirements and conceptualizing methods needed for improvement, I have earned a reputation as a successful manager who is skilled in balancing company goals and employee needs.

I feel that, through my experience in controlling billion-dollar inventories of high-tech assets, I have reached a level where I can transfer my knowledge to benefit any size organization and quickly step into a role where I can make valuable contributions. In addition to my ability to quickly and easily grasp complex issues and systems, I am highly skilled in maximizing human resources. I have built training programs from the ground up and quickly made them cost effective and successful. My knowledge of curriculum development and experience in providing both academic and practical technical instruction would benefit an organization looking for a responsible, mature, and enthusiastic person to develop and maintain corporate training programs.

I hope you will welcome my call soon to arrange a brief meeting at your convenience to discuss your current and future needs and how I might serve them. Thank you in advance for your time.

Sincerely yours,

Gabe Wagner

Alternate last paragraph:
I hope you will call or write me soon to suggest a time convenient for us to meet and discuss your current and future needs and how I might serve them. Thank you in advance for your time.

GABE WAGNER
1110½ Hay Street, Fayetteville, NC 28305   (910) 483-6611

OBJECTIVE

To benefit an organization that can use a sharp executive who has excelled in demanding and innovative roles which required expertise in maximizing both human and material resources as well as in developing and managing highly technical training programs.

EDUCATION and EXECUTIVE TRAINING

M.S., Technology Management, South Dakota School of Mines and Technology, Rapid City, SD 1993; graduated with a **3.91 GPA**.
B.S., Electrical Engineering, University of Notre Dame, Notre Dame, IN.
Excelled in more than one year of highly technical training to qualify as a U.S. Air Force pilot as well as programs designed to prepare skilled classroom instructors and managers.
*   Received the **Outstanding Graduate Award** for leadership and practical skills and for attaining a 99% average on the academic portions of the intense, pressure-filled pilot training program which had a 30% attrition rate.

EXPERIENCE

DIRECTOR FOR TRAINING DEVELOPMENT AND OPERATIONS. USAF, Dyess AFB, TX (1993-present). Handpicked to establish a program for training professionals re-entering a highly technical field, oversaw the various aspects of smoothly operating a $9 billion program.
*   Rated in the top 10% in my career field, was evaluated as "exceptionally qualified" in providing instruction and in managerial excellence.
*   Achieved a 100% pass rate in a program where the cost of retraining each individual pilot in a sophisticated new aircraft was approximately $50,000.
*   Implemented training techniques which saved $75,000 by reducing training time 10%.
*   Taught 105 students both in academic subjects and flight instruction techniques.
*   Qualified in a $300 million flight simulator, applied my technical knowledge while providing instruction to students who had not previously been exposed to this equipment.
*   Trained and prepared long-range scheduling for 20 instructors in an entry-level flying training program.
*   Integrated up-to-date computer graphics presentations into obsolete materials.

Steadily advanced in technical and human resources management experiences, USAF, Ellsworth AFB, SD:
OPERATIONS MANAGER. (1991-93). Supervised the various aspects of training for a four-person team of qualified professionals operating a $280 million aircraft.
*   Created and implemented a unique new system of handling one highly technical phase of operations; developed training criteria for teaching the new techniques.
*   Provided expertise as one of the senior advisors and instructors for a 16-person department by conducting formal classroom and practical flight instruction.
*   Evaluated and tested a new avionics software package which was accepted for widespread use and which made a major impact on operational capabilities.

HUMAN AND MATERIAL RESOURCES MANAGER. (1986-91). Selected from a highly qualified pool of candidates, oversaw activities including safety, resource utilization, and logistical support as well as personnel management and training activities.
*   Accepted into the first group of professionals to be trained, joined in the initial phases to fly what was at that time the world's newest and most complex intercontinental bomber.
*   Applied my logistical and managerial skills to put together a project to test the capabilities of the system: successfully used $1.1 billion in assets (five aircraft) and 50 people to prove that the system was fully operational and ready for use.
*   Organized a five-day conference/demonstration utilizing 212 people and 64 aircraft.

OPERATIONS MANAGER and **PILOT**. (1982-86). Quickly became known for my superior technical knowledge, skills, and leadership abilities and performed with distinction as a leader of a six-person team operating a $50 million aircraft.
*   Developed clear and concise written materials while preparing narratives for award and honors earned by employees and maintaining operational guidelines publications.

PERSONAL

Feel that my greatest strengths lie in managing technologically advanced programs while maximizing both human and material resources through my ingenuity, intelligence, and natural leadership abilities. Received three "outstanding service" medals. Hold a Top Secret (ESI) clearance.

Date

Exact Name of Person
Title or Position
Name of Company
Address (number and street)
Address (city, state, and ZIP)

Dear Exact Name of Person: (or Dear Sir or Madam if answering a blind ad.)

I would appreciate an opportunity to talk with you soon about how I could apply my creativity and maturity as well as my track record of excellent performance in rapidly changing and fast-paced international settings.

As a U.S. Air Force officer I earned a reputation as a dynamic leader and responsible manger of human, material, and fiscal resources while developing a broad base of skills in diverse settings. With a degree in Radio, TV, and Film/Political Science, I have become an expert in the field of producing and directing informative and responsible broadcast products. Through positions as a director of audiovisual services in locations ranging from Italy, the Middle East, and Panama to Florida and Nevada to Washington, DC, I have become known as a subject matter expert.

While advancing to the rank of major, I have been on the "front line" of many historic events. For example, I produced broadcast products during the capture of General Manuel Noriega and during the Grenada rescue operation. In one job as Chief of Audio-Visual Operations at The Pentagon, I managed the still photographic and motion picture contract for Air Force activities worldwide while documenting Department of Defense events throughout the world. I have also worked on Las Vegas TV productions including Jerry Lewis telethons, Don King-produced fights, and Evel Kneivel's jump over the fountain at Caesar's Palace.

Most recently in Turkey, and earlier in Italy, I have spearheaded multimillion-dollar projects which resulted in turning dilapidated buildings and seriously poor quality facilities into lodging, dining, and recreational facilities which enjoyed unprecedented levels of customer satisfaction. These projects earned the praise of senior officials for my creativity in finding ways to keep costs down while improving quality.

I am a results-oriented professional who offers a detail orientation, proven intellectual and creative abilities, and an effective leadership style which consistently results in superior products. Through my many years as a producer and director, I have excelled in capturing important historical events which have directly impacted on global issues and national policy.

I hope you will welcome my call soon to arrange a brief meeting at your convenience to discuss your current and future needs and how I might serve them. Thank you in advance for your time.

Sincerely yours.

David Smith

DAVID SMITH

1110½ Hay Street, Fayetteville, NC 28305   (910) 483-6611

OBJECTIVE

To contribute to an organization that can use a producer and director of informative and responsible broadcast products who offers expertise in managing human and fiscal resources and multiple large-scale projects, communicating with people at all levels, developing successful programs, and negotiating contracts.

EDUCATION & TRAINING

B.S., Radio, TV, and Film/Political Science, the University of Wisconsin, Superior, WI. Studied Public Administration at the Aviano, Italy, campus of University of Maryland. Was selected to attend numerous programs emphasizing the refinement of managerial and leadership skills for military officers.

HIGHLIGHTS OF EXPERIENCE

* Have directed video, field, and still crews broadcasting/documenting global events.
* As Chief, Audio-Visual Operations at The Pentagon, managed still photographic and motion picture contract for Air Force activities worldwide while documenting Department of Defense events throughout the world.
* Produced broadcast products during the capture of General Manuel Noriega and during the Grenada rescue operation.
* Have worked on Las Vegas TV productions including Jerry Lewis telethons, Don King-produced fights, and Evel Kneivel's jump over the fountain at Caesar's Palace.

EXPERIENCE

Advanced to the rank of major in the U.S. Air Force while earning a reputation as a creative and dynamic professional with the ability to excel in rapidly changing, fast-paced environments while gaining a global perspective working and living overseas:

PROGRAM DIRECTOR/RESOURCE MANAGER. Turkey (1994-present). Totally revitalized a lodging/hotel organization known as "the worst" in the country: personally sold the importance of the project and managed $2.5 million worth of renovations for a facility which now enjoys an unprecedented customer satisfaction rate.
* Administered a $13 million annual budget in a 600-employee organization which provided food, lodging, athletic and recreational, laundry, and child development/youth services for a 10,000-person community.
* Located equipment assets from facilities which were closing or downsizing and acquired badly needed recreational and leisure items which improved the quality of life.

COMMUNITY SERVICES DIRECTOR. Italy (1992-94). Controlled a $7 million annual operating budget and managed 322 employees while providing the leadership for planning and organizing activities so that resources were optimized while ensuring essential services for a 7,000-person community.
* Planned, procured funding for, and managed more than $1.2 million in contracts for renovation projects; turned a dilapidated building into a top-notch fitness center.
* Handpicked to organize more than 20 VIP visits on the basis of my communication and diplomatic skills, flawlessly coordinated lodging, security, and transportation while ensuring Turkish, British, American, Italian, French, and Greek visitors from the fields of education, government, business, and entertainment were expertly handled.
* Ensured the highest quality of support for the Air Force's largest lodging and food service operation.

DIRECTOR OF AUDIOVISUAL PRODUCTION AND SERVICES. Italy (1989-92). As the senior official in charge of audiovisual products throughout the Mediterranean region, supervised 81 specialists in six subunits in Turkey, Greece, and Italy with a total annual operating budget of $230,000 and $400,000 worth of state-of-the-art equipment.

* Received a commendation medal for my accomplishments while documenting such activities as Joint Task Force Proven Force operations during the war in the Middle East.
* Provided the audiovisual products which gave the Joint Chiefs of Staff and White House their first-hand look at American involvement during Provide Comfort refugee relief operations in Northern Iraq and Turkey; established a field still video satellite system.
* Was officially evaluated as "the best video producer/director in the Department of Defense."

OPERATIONS MANAGER FOR AUDIOVISUAL SERVICES. Hurlburt Field, FL (1985-89). Directed the day-to-day activities of 51 employees including video, film, and still crews who provided products in response to the needs of national and Joint Chiefs of Staff as well as Special Operations requirements.
* Managed a $1 million annual operating budget and $300,000 worth of equipment.
* Established the field satellite unit which was able to give the White House a first-hand look at American involvement during the invasion of Panama and the capture of General Manuel Noriega.

CHIEF OF AUDIOVISUAL OPERATIONS. The Pentagon, Washington, DC (1982-85). As producer and director in charge of documenting significant Department of Defense (DoD) events throughout the world while managing the still photographic and motion picture contract in support of Air Force activities.
* Wrote the million-dollar contract and represented the Air Force during negotiations.
* Produced and directed the still and video products which documented the Grenada rescue operations.
* Personally oversaw the processing, printing, editing, and delivery of products from Grenada to the White House, Air Force Chief of Staff, and national-level agencies.

MANAGER OF STUDIO OPERATIONS. Nellis AFB, NV (1979-82). Wrote, produced, and directed television productions which supported Tactical Air Command and A.F. activities worldwide from a facility with three production professionals and $1.5 million worth of electronic and production equipment.
* Produced a program rated as the best of its type during a project in Cold Lake, Canada.
* Gained experience as a cameraman, gaffer, key grip, and technical director on local Las Vegas TV productions such as two Jerry Lewis telethons, Don King-produced fights at Caesar's Palace, and Evel Kneivel's jump over the fountain at Caesar's Palace.

Highlights of earlier experience: During an internship at a Duluth, MN, TV station was production specialist, cameraman, floor director, and director of an early morning news program and produced a video clip used by the university for recruiting purposes.

SKILLS

Offer familiarity with video and still cameras, post-production equipment including CMX editor and Grass Valley switcher, and night vision technology.
Am experienced in using PCs with both MS-DOS and Windows operating systems.
Hold a Top Secret security clearance with SBI/SSBI.

PERSONAL

Am an energetic and enthusiastic professional who thrives on a fast pace. Have a proven track record of producing exceptional products that capture history while working under adverse conditions in often remote locations. Am results oriented with an eye for detail.

PATRICK STEWART
1110½ Hay Street, Fayetteville, NC 28305   (910) 483-6611

OBJECTIVE   To contribute to an organization that can use a creative professional with technical expertise as a television cameraman, editor, director, and producer along with skills in preparing video and written products designed to advertise, market, and promote ideas.

EDUCATION   **Bachelor of Science (B.S.)** degree, Broadcast Communication, California State Polytechnic University, Pomona, CA, 1985; named to Dean's List and President's List (3.3 GPA).
A.A. degree *with honors*, Liberal Arts, Victor Valley Community College, 1982.

LICENSE   F.C.C. Radio Operator's License

EXPERIENCE   **SUPERVISING WRITER/EDITOR/PRODUCER**. U.S. Army, Ft. Bragg, NC (1993-present). Wrote and produced a video for a NATO Joint Task Force which was distributed to military executives and to the heads of state of NATO countries while also supervising six technical writers and analysts in the collection, analysis, and presentation of intelligence material.
* As a Psychological Operations Sergeant at the rank of E-5 ("middle manager"), was specially selected for this job which is normally held by an E-6.
* Developed written and video materials for a psychological operations package which provided an exchange of information between the U.S. and emerging former Soviet republics.
* Received the Physical Fitness Award for scoring the highest on a fitness test.
* Volunteered my time to help other soldiers who went on to earn prestigious honors including being named *Soldier of the Month* for the battalion and the group.
* Have become known for my professional style of meeting every deadline without getting flustered; always promote a cooperative team spirit.

TRAINING DIRECTOR. U.S. Army, Ft. Bragg, NC (1992-93). Was selected as an E-4 for an E-5 position, and then went on to receive Army Achievement Medals for being singled out as *Soldier of the Month* in my battalion and group and as *Soldier of the Quarter* in my group; this honor identifies one as "a leader among leaders."
* After excelling in a nine-month Serbo-Croatian Language School, was handpicked to manage technical and language training for a 150-person organization; took over a program evaluated as average and increased its rating to "outstanding."

TRAINEE. U.S. Army Airborne School, Advanced Individual Training, Basic Training (1991). Graduated in the top 20% from all leadership schools, and achieved the distinction of being named student leader throughout Basic Training.

DIRECTOR/EDITOR/CAMERAMAN/PRODUCER. Little Frog Productions, Apple Valley, CA (1989-91). For a daily show and three weekly programs aired by a local station in the High Desert of southern California, performed work on location and in the studio.
* Was responsible for pre-production, production, and post-production.
* Performed 90% of my work on a 3/4″ tape and editing system.
* Since all shoots were accomplished with minimal equipment, became very creative and resourceful in turning inexpensive gadgets into useful production equipment.
* Became skilled in interacting with community agencies and personalities through producing several shows featuring local news makers and law enforcement officials.

CAMERAMAN/EDITOR. Desert West Media, Victorville, CA (1987-89). Shot and edited commercials for local cable ad-insertion in a small market; assisted in writing commercials.

ASSISTANT PROJECT MANAGER. Illini Construction Co., Victorville, CA (1985-87). Began as a laborer and was promoted to supervise subcontractors.

PRODUCTION ASSISTANT. Desert West Media - Channel 27, Victorville, CA (1984-85). Assisted on remote and in-studio segments for local shows and commercials as a cameraman, lighting technician, and technical director; this was a college internship.

PERSONAL   Have worked with different editing systems and master new ones easily.

Date

Exact Name of Person
Title or Position
Name of Company
Address (no., street)
Address (city, state, zip)

Dear Exact Name of Person: (or Dear Sir or Madam if answering a blind ad.)

I would appreciate an opportunity to talk with you soon about how I could contribute to your organization through the outstanding human resources management abilities I have refined as a junior military officer.

As you will see from my resume, I offer a strong background of excellent results in managing human, material, and fiscal resources while advancing to the rank of Captain in the U.S. Army. One of my proudest accomplishments was being selected to manage the largest military police company in the world in Korea. In this position I oversaw the daily operations in a 7,500-square-mile area with a population of 8,000. I managed a 200-person police force where I held accountability for more than $3 million worth of equipment and eight working police dogs.

I offer outstanding leadership and motivational skills displayed in jobs where I built teams of specialists into award-winning performers. Able to handle rapidly changing requirements and situations, I have a positive attitude which translates into a strong leadership style based on outstanding motivational skills and an aggressive style.

I excel in taking concepts and ideas and finding innovative and creative methods of translating them into workable and successful programs and projects. Through my strong training management experience and planning skills I am able to find a way to accomplish organizational goals and objectives by maximizing available resources.

I hope you will welcome my call soon to arrange a brief meeting at your convenience to discuss your current and future needs and how I might serve them. Thank you in advance for your time.

Sincerely yours,

Ray McCormick

Alternate last paragraph:
I hope you will call or write me soon to suggest a time convenient for us to meet and discuss your current and future needs and how I might serve them. Thank you in advance for your time.

RAY McCORMICK

1110 ½ Hay Street, Fayetteville, NC 28305   (910) 483-6611

OBJECTIVE To offer exceptional communication and motivational skills to an organization that can use a mature professional who has excelled in law enforcement through outstanding managerial abilities refined as a military officer along with an enthusiastic, determined personality.

EXPERIENCE *Advanced to the rank of Captain while gaining a reputation as a skilled manager, U.S. Army:*
TRANSPORTATION OPERATIONS MANAGER. Ft. Bragg, NC (1994-95). Supervised, trained, and motivated 10 employees as the liaison between a headquarters and 24 subordinate transportation offices involved in arranging movements of personnel and equipment.
* Because of shortages of experienced managers, was selected to perform duties outside of my area of expertise and achieved outstanding results in all areas.
* Saw a need for and singlehandedly established a successful and comprehensive training section where none had previously existed.
* Was officially described as enthusiastic in meeting challenges and transforming concepts into realities.

TRAINING PROGRAM MANAGER. Korea (1994). Polished my public relations and interpersonal communication skills while developing and conducting programs designed to teach and expand law enforcement knowledge and skills of more than 1,400 American and Korean personnel.
* Excelled in learning to plan for complex activities at high levels in a position requiring maturity, experience, and diplomatic skills usually seen in higher ranking managers.
* Created, from scratch, the organization's training management guidelines.

GENERAL MANAGER. Korea (1993). Directed the operations of the largest military police force in the world with more than 200 employees and in excess of $3 million worth of equipment protecting 8,000 people in a 7,500-square-mile region.
* Became highly skilled in presenting concise, thorough briefings during crisis situations.
* Learned to handle and work with military police dogs.

FIRST-LINE SUPERVISOR. Ft. McClellan, AL (1992). Managed the details of moving large amounts of equipment by air, rail, and sea while also providing the leadership and supervision for the training and performance of 30 military police.
* Coordinated the complex details of relocating the company from Ft. Meade, MD, which included ensuring the safe relocation of 50 vehicles and communications equipment.
* Earned praise from high-level executives for my skill in managing a 900-mile road march with no breakdowns or accidents and for my dedication shown during Hurricane Andrew relief efforts.

ADMINISTRATIVE MANAGER. Ft. Meade, MD (1989-92). Supervised a 30-person police force; provided leadership and administrative support actions for a highly trained team of specialists who frequently were called on for international assignments.
* Led the first military police units into Cuba in support of the Guantanamo Bay Haitian refugee camps.
* Received numerous medals and awards (including the Southwest Asia, National Defense, and Army Commendation Medals) for my outstanding achievements during the war in the Middle East.
* Was awarded four Army Achievement, one Valor Unit, and two Humanitarian Service Medals in recognition of my accomplishments during actions in Panama which led to the removal of Manuel Noriega.

EDUCATION B.A. degree in Criminal Justice, Pembroke State University, Pembroke, NC, 1989.
Excelled in more than ten months of advanced training in military police procedures and management techniques as well as a course in coordinating and moving equipment.

SPECIALIZED KNOWLEDGE Offer knowledge related to the following areas:
<u>Computers:</u> Word, Prowrite, WordPerfect, Harvard Graphics, Windows, Excel, and PowerPoint software
<u>Weapons:</u> Expert with the 9mm pistol, M16 rifle, and 12-gauge shotgun
<u>Other areas of expertise:</u> VIP protection, reconnaissance, and surveillance

PERSONAL Hold a Secret security clearance. Offer excellent skills in human, material, and fiscal resource management and accountability. Am creative with a high level of initiative.

Date

Exact Name of Person
Title or Position
Name of Company
Address (no., street)
Address (city, state, zip)

Dear Exact Name of Person: (or Dear Sir or Madam if answering a blind ad.)

I would appreciate an opportunity to talk with you soon about how I could benefit your organization through my experience in overseeing passenger service operations as well as my abilities as a supervisor and motivator.

While serving my country in the U.S. Air Force, I have trained and supervised up to five passenger service agents processing 1,000 passengers on 250 aircraft monthly with an on-time departure rate of 100%. Previously as a passenger service agent, I processed up to 42,000 passengers on 1,800 aircraft monthly and maintained a space-available roster of up to 1,400 names daily.

I offer thorough knowledge of automated passenger check-in systems and a reputation for handling a variety of projects simultaneously. While tracking down and recovering lost baggage, I achieved a 97.6% success rate related to nearly 100 claims monthly.

You would find me to be a dedicated and adaptable worker who is known for attention to detail and the desire to satisfy the customer.

I hope you will welcome my call soon to arrange a brief meeting at your convenience to discuss your current and future needs and how I might serve them. Thank you in advance for your time.

Sincerely yours,

Barbara Barrett

Alternate last paragraph:
I hope you will call or write me soon to suggest a time convenient for us to meet and discuss your current and future needs and how I might serve them. Thank you in advance for your time.

BARBARA BARRETT

1110½ Hay Street, Fayetteville, NC 28305   (910) 483-6611

OBJECTIVE

To benefit an organization through my experience in overseeing passenger service operations as well as my ability to supervise and motivate personnel.

EXPERIENCE

PASSENGER SERVICE SUPERVISOR. U.S. Air Force, Pope AFB, NC (1989-90).
Supervised and trained five passenger service agents while reviewing travel authorizations and border clearances; maintained flight status boards.
* Provided information on ticketing, meals, and transportation; ensured that passenger security requirements had been met and tracked down/recovered lost baggage.
* Led my section to maintain a 100% departure efficiency rate while processing over 1,000 passengers on 250 aircraft monthly.
* Was able to process 262 passengers and five tons of baggage for a special assignment group without disrupting normal services.
* Developed and implemented a training plan for new agents.
* Am known for identifying and correcting potential problems.
* Chosen "Supervisor of the Month"; earned a respected medal.

PASSENGER SERVICE AGENT. U.S.A.F., Hickam AFB, HI (1986-89).
Processed up to 42,000 passengers and baggage on 1,800 aircraft monthly while determining military travel eligibility and coordinating with the air terminal operations center to determine available seating.
* Handled in-flight meal orders and lost baggage claims; operated an automated check-in system and aircraft servicing equipment.
* Maintained a 99% on-time departure rate while solving passenger problems.
* Achieved a lost baggage recovery rate of 97.6% while researching 90 claims monthly.
* Was commended for my knowledge of the Passenger Automated Check-In System.
* Prepared a "space available" roster with up to 1,400 names daily.
* Played a role in transporting up to 21,500 personnel on special projects; assisted with food, beverages, and bedding before flights; often handled four aircraft at once.
* Was chosen to handle aircraft transporting VIPs.

QUALITY CONTROL SUPERVISOR. Max Factor Cosmetic Co., Oxford, NC (1982-86).
Maintained a section efficiency rate of 90% overseeing the quality of components and finished cosmetics while making hourly production checks.

EDUCATION & TRAINING

Bachelor of Arts (B.A.) degree in Sociology, University of North Carolina at Greensboro, Greensboro, NC, 1982.
Associate's degree in Social Work, Louisburg College, Louisburg, NC, 1982.
Completed course work toward Associate's degree in Logistics Management, Community College of the Air Force.
Excelled in U.S.A.F. training in management/leadership and airline passenger service.

SPECIAL SKILLS

Operate airline servicing and security equipment including:

29-45 passenger bus	mobile boarding staircases
mobile baggage conveyer	X-ray machines
hand-held magnetometer	warehouse tugs/forklifts

Operate a Honeywell Passenger Automated Check-In System and 10-key calculators.

PERSONAL

Hold Secret security clearance. Go out of my way to satisfy customers.

Exact Name of Person
Title or Position
Name of Company
Address (no., street)
Address (city, state, zip)

Dear Exact Name of Person: (or Dear Sir or Madam if answering a blind ad.)

I would appreciate an opportunity to talk with you soon about how I could contribute to your organization through my experience in solving problems and managing projects in industrial environments.

As you will see from my resume, I have excelled as a military officer while serving my country in the U.S. Army. As I advanced to the rank of captain, I was handpicked for jobs which required exceptionally strong analytical and problem-solving skills as well as the ability to communicate with others. For example, in one job as a Logistics Officer, I was specially selected to oversee the delivery of two new aircraft from a Philadelphia factory to a site in Panama. During the war in the Middle East, I won a medal for leading a combat mission that recovered two Iraqi aircraft and delivered them through dangerous territory to an American general. In a recent position, I excelled as a Company Commander in charge of 105 people and a fleet of 63 wheeled vehicles and power generation equipment.

Known for my resourcefulness, I am respected for my ability to "stretch a dollar" to its maximum utility. I have applied that resourcefulness in situations ranging from managing repair parts procurement, to overseeing expenditures of a $4.2 million budget, to developing programs that improved the efficiency of logistics, supply, food service, and personnel administration. Because of my ability to figure out innovative solutions for difficult problems, I have frequently been selected as project manager for difficult assignments or as a management consultant helping top executives determine the best course of action.

You would find me in person to be a congenial individual who prides myself on my ability to motivate others and inspire a spirit of teamwork. A safety-conscious person accustomed to working in environments where there is "no room for error," I can provide outstanding personal and professional references.

I hope you will welcome my call soon to arrange a brief meeting at your convenience to discuss your current and future needs and how I might serve them. Thank you in advance for your time.

Sincerely yours,

Brian Borek

Alternate last paragraph:
I hope you will call or write me soon to suggest a time convenient for us to meet and discuss your current and future needs and how I might serve them. Thank you in advance for your time.

BRIAN BOREK

1110½ Hay Street, Fayetteville, NC 28305   (910) 483-6611

OBJECTIVE

To add value to an organization that can use an astute problem solver and leader who offers strong communication and sales skills along with proven ability to improve the efficiency of administrative functions and production operations while managing multiple projects.

EDUCATION

Bachelor of Science, Business & Political Science, Mt. St. Mary's College, MD, 1984.
While serving my country as a military officer, completed courses and schools sponsored by the U.S. Army and Department of Defense which refined my abilities related to quantitative problem-solving; personnel administration; the planning and management of cargo shipments by rail, sea, and air; Total Quality Management; and industrial safety.

EXPERIENCE

TRANSPORTATION CONSULTANT. U.S. Army, Port-au-Prince, Haiti (1994-95). Because of my proven ability to solve problems and make decisions in unique environments, was handpicked for this job which involved assigning Special Forces teams to 28 locations in Haiti, organizing aviation assets, and coordinating relocation of several thousand refugees.

GENERAL MANAGER (COMPANY COMMANDER). U.S. Army, Ft. Bragg, NC (1994). Was selected for one of the military's most prestigious line management jobs as a company commander in charge of 105 people and a fleet of 63 industrial wheeled vehicles and power generation equipment.
* Resourcefully managed the repair parts budget with the result that we improved equipment maintenance quality while decreasing maintenance costs.
* Was commended in writing as "always honest, forthright, and a loyal team player."

MANAGEMENT CONSULTANT/LOGISTICS OFFICER. U.S. Army, Ft. Bragg, NC (1993-94). Acted as the trusted advisor and consultant to a top executive on logistical matters while supervising all supply and maintenance activities for three companies with 32 helicopters and 81 wheeled vehicles; monitored expenditures of a $4.2 million budget.
* Combined my analytical and "sales" skills in persuading top executives to purchase state-of-the-art refueling equipment; supervised the fielding and integration into inventory of equipment which greatly extended the range of required refueling.
* On my own initiative, developed standard logistics packages tailored to the needs of the famed XVIII Airborne Corps.

OPERATIONS OFFICER. U.S. Army, Korea (1992-93). For an aviation regiment with 18 airships, maintained aircrew flight records while also managing flying operations including maintenance and refueling support.
* Was selected to lead the organization through a rigorous annual inspection.
* Was chosen to organize and lead a special project in a remote location, which required me to organize and manage the use of 12 aircraft and 25 vehicles.

DIRECTOR OF SERVICE OPERATIONS. U.S. Army, Ft. Hood, TX (1991-92). Directed the provision of all services, including these, supporting a company with 176 personnel along with a $225 million inventory of vehicles, helicopters, and support equipment:

supply and inventory control	vehicle and equipment maintenance
dining facilities operation	personnel training and administration

FIRST-LINE SUPERVISOR. U.S. Army, Ft. Hood, TX (1990-91). Was in charge of 27 officers and others while maintaining accountability for equipment valued at $104 million.
* Was handpicked to lead a larger organization into Iraq during the war in the Middle East.
* Won a prestigious medal for leading a combat mission that recovered two Iraqi aircraft and delivered them through dangerous territory to an American general.

Highlights of other experience:
As a **LOGISTICS OFFICER,** planned and coordinated the relocation of four companies with hundreds of people and multimillion-dollar assets from three states to southwest Asia by rail, sea, air, and truck; was specially selected to oversee the delivery of two new aircraft from a factory in Philadelphia to Panama, which involved coordinating diplomatic and country clearances.
As a **PLATOON LEADER** and **EXECUTIVE OFFICER,** refined my management skills.

PERSONAL

Offer an exceptional ability to motivate and work with people while solving stubborn problems. Hold an FAA Commercial Instrument Helicopter License. Am proficient with computer software including WordPerfect, Harvard Graphics, First Choice, and Excel.

The sample resumes and cover letters in this book were written for real military professionals by the professional writers and published authors who form the writing team of PREP Resumes, a company established in 1981 which specializes in preparing career transition materials for military professionals. The sample resumes in this book can be used as models for people who wish to write their own resumes translating military experience into "civilian" language. The resumes presented here embody many years of practical, professional experience and research in "translating" and marketing the unique background, skills, experience, and accomplishments of military professionals.

PREP'S resume writing service is worldwide by mail. A copy of the Personal Review Form used in the resume writing process is available for $3.00 by writing PREP, Box 66, Fayetteville, NC 28302, or call (910) 483-6611 for a brief free telephone consultation.